KING WILLIAM III

By the same author

The Real Francis Bacon
I was James the Second's Queen
King James the Third of England
Nell Gwyn
The Great Seamen of Elizabeth I
Charles the Second's French Mistress
James Duke of Monmouth
Marlborough the Man
Royal Westminster Abbey
Charles the Second's Minette
The Duchess Hortense
King Richard II
Edward III
Robert Louis Stevenson
Henry IV
King James VI of Scotland & I of England

KING WILLIAM III

*Prince of Orange,
the first European*

Bryan Bevan

The Rubicon Press

The Rubicon Press
57 Cornwall Gardens
London SW7 4BE

British Library Cataloguing in Publication Data

A catalogue record for this book is available from the British Library.

ISBN 0-948695-53-6 (hbk)
ISBN 0-948695-54-4 (pbk)

Designed and typeset by The Rubicon Press
Printed and bound in Great Britain by Biddles of Guildford
and King's Lynn

CONTENTS

List of Illustrations   vii

Map of The Netherlands in the second half of the
    seventeenth century   xi

PART I

I	His Forebears	1
II	William's Education	9
III	Friends and Enemies	18
IV	The Years of Crisis	29
V	Turn of the Tide	39
VI	William's Marriage	48
VII	Early Marriage	55
VIII	Exclusion	62
IX	D'Avaux at The Hague	73
X	Troubled Relationships	83
XI	Prelude to Revolution	91

PART II

XII	The Invasion	101
XIII	William and Mary	110
XIV	King William in Ireland	120
XV	A Massacre and More Battles	131
XVI	William in Adversity	140
XVII	A Lonely, Saddened King	148
XVIII	Portland and Albemarle	159
XIX	After Rijswijk	166
XX	William's Failing Health	175

Notes   185
Bibliography   195
Index   199

LIST OF ILLUSTRATIONS

Cover illustration: Prince William of Orange by unknown artist (1677). *By courtesy of the National Portrait Gallery, London.*

Frederick Henry, Prince of Orange and Amalia of Solms-Braunfeldt, grandfather and grandmother of William III by Gerard van Honthorst, 1637. *By courtesy of the Mauritshuis, The Hague.*

William II, Prince of Orange and father of William III by Gerard van Honthorst. *By courtesy of the Mauritshuis, The Hague.*

William of Orange aged sixteen, 'Child of State' by Abraham Ragneneau. *By courtesy of the Frans Hals Museum.*

Mary, Princess of Orange by A. Hanneman. *By courtesy of the Scottish National Portrait Gallery.*

Prince William of Orange by an unknown artist (1677). *By courtesy of the National Portrait Gallery, London.*

Hampton Court Palace. Façade designed by Sir Christopher Wren. *Crown Copyright. Historic Royal Palaces.*

Queen Mary II by Sir Peter Lely. *By courtesy of the National Portrait Gallery, London.*

King William III about 1690, the period of the Battle of the Boyne. *By courtesy of the National Portrait Gallery, London.*

For Gerda Craven

ACKNOWLEDGEMENTS

To the Director of the Koninklijke Bibliotheek (National Library), The Hague for enabling me to study there.

To Heer Marcus Paulusma for kindly taking me round the Binnenhof at The Hague.

To the Director of the Public Record Office for giving me permission to study State Papers in King William's Chest and the original documents concerning the massacre of Glencoe.

To Dr. Dorothy B. Johnston for giving me permission to study the Portland Collection in the Hallward Library, University of Nottingham.

To the Directors of the British Library for their helpfulness.

To the London Library as always for their generous assistance.

To the National Portrait Gallery Heinz Archive and Library for invaluable advice concerning illustrations.

To Dr. Iain Brown of the National Library, Edinburgh for bringing to my attention some original activities of the celebrated Jacobite Neville Payne in Scotland.

To my sister Win for listening so patiently when I read my typescript to her and making invaluable comments

To my publishers Anthea Page and Juanita Homan of The Rubicon Press for their close co-operation and work.

To Ann Holland for her help and encouragement.

To Sadika Tancred for her generous hospitality.

NORTH

SEA

HOLLAND

Groningen
Leeuwarden
FRIESLAND
GRONINGEN

Hoorn
Alkmaar
Kampen
Haarlem
Amsterdam
OVERIJSSEL
Leiden
Nearden
Zutphen
Scheveningen
UTRECHT *GELDERLAND*
Rijswijk
Dieren
The Hague
Utrecht
Arnhem
Den Briel
Nijmegen
Dordrecht
Grave
Cleve

ZEELAND
Breda
Middelburg
THE GENERALITY
SPANISH
Flushing
GELDER-
LAND

Ostend
Sluys
Roermond
Nieuwpoort
Bruges
Dunkirk
FLANDERS
Ghent
Antwerp
Cologne
Dixmude
Mechlin
Calais
Oudenaarde
Brussels
Louvain
St.Omer
Ypres
Courtrai
BRABANT
Maastricht
Enghien
Waterloo
Aix-la-Chapelle
Tournai
Ath
Steenkerk
Limburg
Bouvines
Soignies
Serieffe
Fleurus
Liège
Conde
Mons
Namur
Spa
Valenciennes
Binche
Charleroi
BISHOPRIC OF LIEGE
Arras
Cambrai

LUXEMBOURG
Luxembourg
Treves

0   50   100 miles

The Netherlands in the second half of the seventeenth century

xi

PART ONE

I   HIS FOREBEARS

William Prince of Orange born on November 4, 1650 at the Binnenhof, The Hague, was descended from a long line of doughty warriors and statesmen. His great-grandfather on his father's side was William the Silent of Orange-Nassau, Orange being a small principality in the south of France. He was a heroic personality, the leader of the Dutch in their revolt against the Spanish in the sixteenth century, a man indomitable both in victory and defeat. He was assassinated on July 10, 1584 at the former convent of St. Agatha, now known as the Prinsenhof, lying west of the Oude Kerk of the small city of Delft. William the Silent had just left the dining-room and was about to ascend the stairway to his study when his assassin Balthasar Geraerts, a fanatical young Catholic lawyer, fired on him. The bullet marks on its ancient walls are still visible today and are a terrible reminder of the tragic event. The patriot prince's last words, an agonizing cry, echoes down the centuries. "My God, my God have mercy on me and this poor people." He remained an inspiration for the prince born almost a century later, destined to head a desperate resistance for many years against another foreign aggressor.

William the Silent was succeeded by his second son Maurice, a very experienced soldier, but despotic and harsh. He did not shine as a statesman, for he disputed with the actions of the provincial states of Holland, antagonizing them by imprisoning several leading deputies in the Castle of Loevenstein and ordering the execution of an important Pensionary of Holland. Frederick Henry his half-brother inherited Maurice's title and offices in 1625, another Prince of Orange remarkably gifted, and not only as a soldier. His talents included diplomatic finesse in foreign affairs and his cultured tastes certainly inspired what is now known as the Golden Age, when art, architecture, learning and overseas trade flourished in Holland.

1

Unlike his half-brother, Frederick Henry was a kindly man, "so mild he would not willingly hurt a sparrow".[1] A few months before he became Stadtholder he made a love marriage with Amalia of Solms-Braunfeldt, the beautiful daughter of a minor German princeling, a woman of remarkable character and very determined. Their attractive portrait is in the Mauritshuis Art Gallery. The office of Stadtholder suggested that the holder of it was the Chief Magistrate of the Republic, serving as a member of the Council of State, and possessing the right to make military appointments. His powers were limited, however, although a stadtholder in Frederick Henry's time enjoyed vast social influence. He had no powers of life or death, of declaring war, of levying taxes or raising troops.[2] Frederick Henry and Amalia had a large family, but only one son William and four daughters reached maturity. She had originally come to Holland as a lady-in-waiting to Elizabeth, the exiled Queen of Bohemia, the daughter of James I of England, who lived in The Hague.

William of Orange, son of William II and of Princess Mary Stuart, elder daughter of Charles I and of his French-born Queen Henrietta Maria, was born in deeply troubled times. Two years before his birth in 1648 a peace treaty had been signed - the Treaty of Westphalia, thus ending the disastrous thirty years' war of religion. By it, Catholic Spain was at last forced to acknowledge the independence of the seven northern provinces of the Netherlands. These were Holland, Zeeland, Gelderland, Groningen, Friesland, Utrecht and Overijsel.

At this period (1650) France was plagued by its civil war and struggles of the *Fronde* with Mazarin and the Court of King Louis XIV, then a mere boy of twelve years. In England the bloody civil war was over, and Charles I had been tried in Westminster Hall, to be executed in Whitehall on a tragic day at the end of January (1649). In a few years Oliver Cromwell would become Lord Protector of the Kingdom. Spain at the height of its power under Philip II in the sixteenth century was now in fast decline, but she still possessed a vast empire.

The Dutch in 1650 were on the whole a happy, prosperous people, hard-working and relying on the fruits of their labour. Their religion was mainly Protestant, though a third of the population were Roman Catholic. By conviction, Calvinists, they believed in predestination. Indeed they were a fiery, passionate people, deeply engrossed in trade and maritime commerce. They possessed an increasing fleet of ships that traded as far as China, Japan and Brazil and owned, for a time, the former Portuguese colonies such as Java, Ceylon and the Cape of Good Hope where they first explored in 1652. John Maurice of Nassau-Siegen, a first cousin of Frederick Henry, had been Governor of the Dutch colonies in Brazil (1636-44); he was an able and enlightened administrator and an excellent soldier.

The Dutch freely imported from the shores of the Baltic masses of raw materials, copper, wood, wheat and iron.

Amsterdam, a beautiful city with her bank founded in 1609, was the universal centre of commerce. Her graceful canals were lined with tall, gabled houses, and her streets were paved with French cobbles. Other lovely, ancient cities were Leiden, Dordrecht, Delft, Haarlem and Utrecht. The Hague was originally a wild, marshy wood celebrated for its hunting, a favourite diversion of the Counts of Holland. A palace had been built on its site called the Hof van Hollandt and it gradually became the centre of a small Court of courtiers and servants. The buildings were divided into two parts, the Binnenhof or Inner Court, and the Buitenhof, or Outer Court. The Knights Hall (Ridderzaal) is a Gothic building, dating from 1296.

William of Orange, the subject of this study, is often mentioned in a disparaging way as "Dutch William", but he had in fact very little Dutch blood, though he was passionately Dutch by birth, education and sentiment. However, he had German blood through William the Silent and his paternal grandmother Amalia of Solms-Braunfeldt, French blood through Louise de Coligny, daughter of the celebrated Admiral de Coligny (of the Massacre of St. Bartholomew) and mother of William's grandfather Frederick Henry. His maternal grandmother was Henrietta Maria (Charles I's queen) and his grandfather Henri IV. His Italian blood was mainly derived from Marie de Medici, second queen of Henri IV. William also inherited Scottish blood through his maternal great-grandfather James I of England and Danish blood through James's Queen Anne of Denmark. He was indeed a cosmopolitan, above all a European, born with a subtle understanding of her problems.

It so happened that during 1637 the widowed Queen Maria de Medici was paying a visit to the court of her daughter Henrietta Maria in England and passed through Holland. There she found Frederick Henry Prince of Orange so attentive that she discussed with him a possible marriage between his son William and her grand-daughter Elizabeth, younger daughter of Charles I and the cleverest of the Stuart princesses. By 1640 Charles was not loath to treat with the Dutch, for he was on terms of hostility with his parliaments and embarrassed financially. Now Heenvliet the Dutch Ambassador in London suggested that it was more politic to ask for the hand of Princess Mary, her eldest sister, because Elizabeth's health was very fragile.

Mary the Princess Royal had been born on November 4, 1631 and at the age of five lived much at Richmond. A pretty child, she had large dark eyes, and the heavy curls of her hair were auburn in colour. Among her early memories at the age of ten was to attend the trial in Westminster Hall of the Earl of Strafford together with her mother and eldest brother (later Charles II).[3] Her bridegroom Prince William, five years older, was an accomplished young man, ambitious and enterprising, a clever mathematician and well read in history. An able linguist - he spoke fluently Dutch, English, French, Italian and Spanish. His portrait painted by Gerard Honthorst at the Mauritshuis in The Hague gives him a curiously Latin appearance. Unfortunately her mother Henrietta Maria and her father had done the Princess Royal ill service by prejudicing her mind against Calvinist Holland and saying that she was marrying beneath her. Her mother had opposed the marriage, wanting her to marry a Roman Catholic heir of Philip IV of Spain.

Mary's marriage to William took place in London in early 1642. England was on the brink of civil war and her parting from her father on a stormy day at Dover was very sad, for they dearly loved one another. She closely resembled him. Her mother accompanied her to The Hague. The ostensible reason was not so much to place her in the hands of her boy husband, but to obtain essential arms and money for her Charles in his inevitable war against the parliamentary forces. She stayed several months in Holland. Mary's first love was for the Stuarts, mindful of her early days at her father's urbane and elegant court. She always disliked Holland, never bothered to learn the language and showed no interest in Dutch politics. Stuart interests were all important to her. Her proud, arrogant character made her believe that she was superior to her Dutch relations. Although she learnt to love her husband, she was too possessive. She disliked her mother-in-law Amalia, pouring scorn on her and apt to remind her that she had held the humble position of lady-in-waiting to Elizabeth of Bohemia when in 1625 Amalia had married Frederick Henry. Mary's bitter feelings against Amalia were reciprocated, fostered no doubt by Frederick Henry's insistence that his daughter-in-law should be treated with royal honours not given to his own wife.[4]

However, there was much that was loving in Mary's character, for she established very friendly relations with the exiled Elizabeth her aunt and best friend in The Hague. In her correspondence the Queen of Bohemia writes to her with great affection. She was also a most loyal and caring sister to Charles II her favourite brother when he was in exile in Holland during the Commonwealth. For his part Charles tried to reconcile his sister with her mother-in-law.

Mary was jealous when William, fond of the theatre, had passing affairs with French actresses. He loved his young wife, but he told his cousin Count Dohna: "I know she loves me as her own soul, and I care for her more than for anyone in the world, but," he added wistfully, "one can't live in such constraint *all* the time." She never recovered from the shock of her father's execution in 1649. Reared in the doctrine of the divine right of kings, such a horrible deed was sacrilege. William II proved a steadfast and generous friend, giving a warm welcome to his exiled brother-in-law Charles II and James Duke of York at The Hague. In their desperate need he advanced them vast amounts of money. However, he had his own troubles as Stadtholder and Captain-General, for the Loevestein Party were hostile to the Princes of Orange.

By the Treaty of Westphalia the States had agreed to some scaling down of their armed forces, but differed as to the number. The States-General's decision was so long delayed that the province of Holland, especially the City of Amsterdam, becoming impatient, proposed to disband their quota of men without receiving permission to do so. William, who had succeeded his father Frederick Henry in 1647, was allowed to act as he deemed best. He proceeded to arrest six important deputies, including Jacob de Witt, the Pensionary of Dordrecht. They were temporarily imprisoned, to be soon released by William. Jacob de Witt's son, Johan de Witt, always a Republican, would never forget or forgive his father's imprisonment in his enigmatic relations with William II's son.

William of Orange never knew his father. He had been born in 1626 and died at the age of twenty-four. During October 1650 he had been hunting at Dieren in the Gelderland when he decided to return to the Binnenhof. It was October 31 and William, on rejoining his wife Mary, could not conceal from her that he was very unwell. He was in fact suffering from smallpox, a very common disease in the seventeenth century. Mary was about to give birth to their only offspring and loving her husband as she did, longed to be with him in his sickness, but was restrained by her attendants. William died around midnight in very early November.

The Princess Royal was grief-stricken and inconsolable, while his mother the strong-willed Amalia of Solms-Braunfeldt whose influence on her son had been powerful, felt deep sorrow. As for Elizabeth of Bohemia, she divided her time between visits to Amalia the formidable Dowager Princess of Orange and her favourite niece, the widowed Mary. She wrote to her eldest son Charles Louis, Elector Palatine on November 16, "but my poore niece is the most afflicted creature that ever I saw, and is changed as she is nothing as skin and bone."[5] Eight days after the death of his father, an infant son was born a little prematurely to Princess Mary on November 4 between eight and nine o'clock at night. The birth very probably took place in Mary's room in the Binnenhof with its fine seventeenth century ceiling. While the candles flickered feebly in their sconces in the chamber where Mary lay, deep gloom reigned in the Binnenhof. Winter that year came early, with snow even descending in the streets of The Hague. To the sounds of the muffled church bells, people rejoiced at the birth of the infant prince. "There is the greatest love in the people that can be," wrote Elizabeth to Charles Louis. "She (Princess Mary) was deliuved upon her owne birthday,"[6] she added. Prince William had made a will augmenting her jointure to £15,000. Unfortunately he had omitted to sign it. According to Elizabeth of Bohemia, Doctor Verstrate treated his patient "verie strangelie and gaue him so manie cooling things that it killed him."

The Prince even from birth was extremely delicate, for he nearly died when three days old. There is a story that one of his nurses saw three circles of light shining round the baby's head after an icy blast of wind had snuffed out the candles.[7] Another nurse named Elizabeth Boers had been promised an allowance for the upbringing of her own child. Fifteen years later she was obliged to appeal to the Prince of Orange: "On behalf of my son William Boers, in whose place I gave your Highness suck."

When hardly ten weeks old on January 21, 1651, the Prince was borne to the Grote Kerk to be baptized. It was snowing and the congregation were upset by the extreme cold in the church. From the first there were violent quarrels between Mary and her mother-in-law Amalia as to the Prince's name. Mary wanted her son to be christened Charles. On the other hand Amalia quite rightly insisted that he should be named William Henry after his heroic ancestor William the Silent and after her own husband Frederick Henry. To Mary's deep indignation her mother-in-law won the point, and to show her displeasure she ostentatiously stayed away from the ceremony.

There were further disputes about the infant prince's guardians. His mother wanted to be sole guardian, basing her claim on William II's unsigned will. At first the Courts upheld her claim. Later, however, in 1652, Amalia of Solms-Braunfeldt and the Elector of Brandenburg, the infant prince's uncle by marriage, were created co-guardians. However, when decisions had to be made, Mary's say in her son's affairs remained more important. Her influence for the first ten years of his life must not be overlooked.

The year 1653 marked the rise to power of Johan de Witt, an ambitious, able man, Jacob's elder son. He came from Dordrecht, becoming the new Grand Pensionary, the leader of the Loevestein Party opposed to the Orangists. The Grand Pensionary was a kind of Secretary of State of the Province of Holland, who presided at the meetings of the provincial state. He was a staunch Republican. De Witt was a tall, serious, scholarly man, interested in mathematics. His statue stands benignly at the Platz in the centre of The Hague, and it is easy to understand why foreign diplomats were impressed, describing him as "*un esprit prompt et hardi.*"[8]

Meanwhile Prince William's relations, particularly his mother and grandmother, were advocating that he should be recognized as his father's successor as Stadtholder and Captain-General under a regency, positions not automatically granted. Unfortunately he was not recognized.

England during the Commonwealth was engaged in the first Anglo-Dutch war, 1652-54. This war was precipitated by a series of Navigation Laws hostile to Dutch trade and commerce. Admiral Blake won a victory over the Dutch Admiral Van Tromp after a hard-fought fight and by April 1654 peace was signed between England and Holland.

Oliver Cromwell, now Lord Protector, was hostile to a nephew of the Stuarts ruling in Holland and demanded a promise from the States-General that the Prince of Orange and his descendants should for ever be excluded from office. Knowing that most of the people loved the small boy, de Witt dared not agree to this, for the States of Zeeland and Gelderland strongly favoured the Prince, as did the aristocracy and the clergy. But the Loevestein Party backed by the wealth and power of Amsterdam opposed him. Consequently the Act of Seclusion was passed, preventing the House of Orange from attaining its former offices. Riots followed in the streets of The Hague and an infuriated mob besieged de Witt's house until dispersed.

Now that the power and influence of the Princes of Orange had been weakened, it was feared that the French might be tempted to attack Orange, the strongly fortified principality of William in the south of France. It had been part of the dowry of the French-born Louise de Coligny, Frederick Henry's mother.

Elizabeth of Bohemia was an entertaining and gifted letter-writer in an age that abounded with brilliant writers of letters. She was not in the least intellectual, for her father James I had not believed in too much education for his daughter. In a letter to Sir Edward Nicholas, one of the English Secretaries of State in exile, she refers to Prince William, aged scarcely four, attending a christening on January 10, 1655: "My little nephue was at the super and satt verie still all the time: those states that were there were verie much taken with him."[9] Again she wrote to Nicholas on January 18:

My Sweet Nephue is not yett gone from Antwerp, but I hope now the weather is better, and I shall see him I hope shortlie, for as soon as he comes to Teiling I will be there.

During his years of exile in Holland and the Spanish Netherlands, Charles II became very fond of the boy Prince of Orange and was struck by his intelligence at an early age. At twenty-five Charles was very different from the later popular idea of him as a 'Merry Monarch'. Impoverished, disillusioned, cynical, he had learnt about life in a harsh school. There was always the charm, and sometimes the gaiety, which proved the attraction of this man for the female sex. The king's features were striking and his hair dark and curling. With his marked French and Italian blood he resembled rather an Italian than an Englishman.

William's earliest letter to his Uncle Charles was written under the direction of his tutors, Cornelius Trigland, a Calvinist pastor warmly attached to his pupil, and Abraham Raguineau, a Frenchman and painter, who taught the Prince of Orange to read, draw and write. "Sire," he wrote,

> I should long since have replied to your Majesty's most honourable letter, that I have not done so has been due not to any want of goodwill but to my incapacity, as until now I have been unable to handle the pen ... Pardon then, Sire, this my tardiness, and permit me to assure you that I shall endeavour in obedience to Your Majesty's good counsel, to apply myself to study, so following from afar your example and that of such other great men as have had the signal glory of happily wedding the humanities and the sciences to the arts of war, and who have both made salutary laws and performed great exploits.

Trigland or Raguineau must have given William generous help in his letter. Pastor Trigland formed a high impression of the six year old boy, finding him sometimes on his knees in his bedroom at prayer. His influence on William's religious education cannot be overestimated. For instance, the Prince developed an ardent belief in predestination, for Trigland had taught him that the life of every individual is divinely foreordained. Even in his boyhood, William gave promise that he had some exceptional destiny to fulfil.

II WILLIAM'S EDUCATION

The Princess Royal was so devoted to her eldest brother Charles that she was sometimes jealous of his fondness for her only child. He reproved her for this. In a frequently quoted letter she wrote:

> You are so partially kind to him, that I fear at last my desiring your kindness to him will turn to jealousy and he may take some from me. I must assure you, that I shall obey all your commands except of loving him (though he is my only child) above all things in the world as long as you are in it.[1]

Above all, Princess Mary longed for a Stuart Restoration. Though often away from her son, she had plenty of affection for him, taking him for daily excursions into the country during a period of convalescence, and borrowing books from the family library to show him. An emotional woman, like the daughter-in-law she was never to know, it has been too easily assumed that she neglected William, treating him coldly. That she established no intimacy with William at Breda or elsewhere is highly unlikely. We know very little concerning William's sentiments for his mother, but he later deeply grieved for her early death in England and always cherished her memory.

Of her love and zeal for the cause of her Stuart brothers there is far more evidence. When they met at Spa in the Spanish Netherlands after an interval of four years, a contemporary remarked, "Her tender love and zeal to His Majesty deserves to be written in brass with the points of a diamond."[2] Charles's youngest sister Henriette - the Minette of the tender letters - was only a child in France in those days. Mary's generosity deserves high praise, for after Cromwell's death (1658) she sold some of her jewels to finance her brother, pawning a diamond called the Little Sancy of Carats, set in a bed of silver and worth 80,000 guilders.[3]

An amusing story is related of William in his early life. One of his teachers described the British Isles as "a little world in themselves". William said, "I wish I had a little world like this." "What would you do with it, Highness?" asked the teacher. "Just give it to me," rejoined William, "and I will show you." His mother never lost her dislike of Holland. She once wrote to Charles, "The greatest punishment of the world would be to live all my life here."

When William was not yet four he was involved in a carriage incident (August 30, 1654), mentioned by Elizabeth of Bohemia in a letter to Sir Edward Nicholas:

> You will heare by Mrs. Howards letter how great a scape my little nephue escaped yesterday upon the bridge of the Princess of Orange's house, but God be thanked there was no hurte onlie the coach broken: I tooke him into my coache and brought him home.[4]

She did not care for children much, but had a fondness for William, the son of her beloved niece. He was often a visitor at the home of his grandmother, 'The House in the Hague Wood', completed in 1655. She was an excellent *hausfrau* and despite her diminished income lived extremely well. William would have enjoyed excellent food. The boy would listen to interminable stories about his father and grandfather Frederick Henry, a splendid patron of the arts and the builder of the Palace of Honselaersdijk.

In Amalia's entourage was her Secretary, Sir Constantine Huygens, a former secretary of her husband, and he was charged in 1654 to compile plans for William's education. Huygens was an eager Italian scholar, who had been knighted by James I during a diplomatic visit to England. His *Discours sur la Nourriture de Monseigneur son altesse le Prince d'Orange* is learned, and designed for the training of a Dutch prince as a patriot and strong Calvinist, a potential Stadtholder and Captain-General of the United Provinces.[5] In his *Discours* Huygens stressed that it was necessary for the Prince to be instructed in geography as well as history, for without geography, history is often obscure and difficult to understand. Latin, especially as it was the language of documents, was then a most important source of study. In early and later life the Prince was too ready to pardon the perpetrators of crimes and Huygens seemed to anticipate this when he wrote *mais c'est une peste en la société humaine quand le prince est trop facile à pardonner les crimes*.[6] Above all, William of Orange was to prefer the good of the state to all his private interests. He was admonished to be careful not to get involved in the disputes of theologians. The appointment when he was about nine of William Frederick of Nassau-Zuylestein as the boy prince's governor, favoured by his mother, was objected to by his grandmother because Zuylestein was a natural son of her husband Frederick Henry, a gay philanderer in his youth. When William was nine he was sent to Leiden, a town north of The Hague, for further education. Leiden, famous as the birthplace of Rembrandt, is an ancient town, renowned for its resistance to Spain in the later sixteenth century. Its early prosperity was largely due to the Flemish weavers, who settled here after the Black Death (1350). It was William's great-grandfather, William the Silent, who had founded the University in 1575 as a reward to its inhabitants for their heroic resistance a year earlier and for the sufferings they had endured. The Burgomaster, Pieter van der Werff had refused to surrender, and William the Silent eventually relieved the town after cutting the dykes and flooding the country between Leiden and Dordrecht. John Evelyn is among many Englishmen associated with the university.

Prince William did not study in the university, but classical scholars such as Jacob Gronovius the Elder and the Jurist Van Tienen attended on the Prince as tutor. He stayed in the ancient convent of St. Barbara, now known as the Prinsenhof, and his mother took a lively interest in making suitable arrangements for William's arrival in Leiden.

On November 14, 1659 the somewhat delicate prince, for he sometimes suffered from asthmatic attacks and a hollow cough, accompanied by his mother and grandmother arrived at the convent. Before leaving for Leiden, William had spent time with the Princess Royal at Breda. Because he was small and delicate his mother nicknamed him Piccinino. William's education was varied and besides history, geography and Latin, he studied French, Dutch (in his mother's household Dutch was never spoken), English and mathematics. Cornelius Trigland superintended the Prince's religious education, while a French tutor Samuel Chapuzeau taught him French. He was compelled to go to church twice daily, once to the French church and once to the Dutch church. It was not all work, however, for William would spend the afternoons riding, driving and walking. He would become an accomplished horseman.

On November 17 the Prince returned to The Hague to meet a lively little girl Elizabeth Charlotte, Liselotte as she was called, eldest daughter of Charles-Louis, the Elector Palatine. She was visiting her grandmother Elizabeth, the 'Winter Queen', and her youngest daughter Sophie, her aunt. To everybody's amusement she made an immediate conquest of her grandmother, who wrote to Charles-Louis:

> But for Liselotte she is very prettie and you may believe it since I am taken with her, for you know I care not much for children, but I never saw none I like so well as her. She is so good natured and wittie, all the Hagh is in love of her, both my niece and the Prince of Orange are verie fonde of her, there is already great acquaintance betwixt the little Prince and her, he is come from Leiden to take leave of his mother, who goes tomorrow to Breda.[7]

Some even thought how suitable a match between William and Liselotte would be. They often played together at the Binnenhof and on one occasion, as she recalled in later life, Liselotte asked William who was the lady "with such a fiery nose?" "Oh that is the Princess Royal, my mother," he replied jocularly. Liselotte never forgot her early friendship with the boy prince and many years later, as second wife of Philippe Duke of Orléans, she would refer to him in an affectionate way in her brilliant correspondence with her aunt Sophie, now Duchess of Hanover.

The Princess Royal's relations with Charles were occasionally clouded by quarrels and misunderstandings. When he heard that the dissolute Harry Jermyn, nephew of Lord Jermyn, was courting Mary, and that she favoured him, Charles recalled Jermyn from The Hague. "Consider," she wrote, "what consequences your severity will bring upon me."[8] It had been rumoured that his sister would marry him secretly or become his mistress. The Princess of Orange was deeply annoyed when she heard that Charles wished to marry Henriette Catherine of Orange, one of the daughters of her mother-in-law. She was a lovely girl, very much in love with Charles. The Dowager Princess at first seemed to accept the match, but eventually told him that she would not give him her daughter without the permission of the States-General. Charles never forgave the slight. Princess Henriette was hastily married to Prince William of Anhalt.[9] About this time the Duke of Ormonde's eldest son Lord Thomas Ossory was married to a Nassau cousin of the Princess, Emilia van Beverwaert. He later became an intimate friend of Prince William.

The Thurloe Papers reveal Mary's intimacy with her brother Charles and her sisterly jokes about Lucy Walter, Charles II's Welsh mistress whom he had at first loved passionately. She was of a good Pembrokeshire family, the mother of the future Duke of Monmouth, whom William of Orange came to know well. Known among the exiles as Mrs. Barlow, Princess Mary wrote to her brother on June 21, 1655:

> Your wife (she is referring to Lucy Walter) desires me to present her humble duty to you, which is all she can say. I tell her, 'tis because she thinks of another husband and dos not follow your example of being as constant a wife as you are a husband.' Tis a frailty they say is given to the sex. Therefore you will pardon her, I hope.

This is sometimes cited as evidence that Charles had married Lucy privately, but it is untrue. 'Wife' was used often as the equivalent of 'sweetheart' or loved one.[10] Her scandalous, wanton behaviour was to cause the exiled king deep embarrassment.

Among Mary's ladies-in-waiting was Anne Hyde, daughter of Charles's Chancellor Sir Edward Hyde. She was a lively, intelligent girl at seventeen (Elizabeth of Bohemia refers to her as Nane Hyde at a masked ball "as the chief of our players, she doth act very well"). She soon, however, caught the fancy of James, Charles's younger brother, who visited her at Breda, and made her pregnant. James's affair with Anne was not at first suspected.

William Prince of Orange was not yet ten years old when his uncle Charles II was restored to his kingdom in May 1660. Oliver Cromwell had died during September 1658, to be succeeded by his son Richard, a man ill-suited for such a position as Lord Protector of the Kingdom. Subject to slights and even insults whilst in exile, Charles was loaded with honours and given 600,000 guilders by the States of Holland. The States Deputies and many hundreds of Englishmen hastened to the Castle of Breda to salute Charles. Always a staunch Republican, Johan de Witt realized the necessity of acquiring his good will, although he abstained from making any promise regarding William's future position. Among lavish presents bestowed on Charles were a superb yacht and a handsome bed, once intended for the confinement of the Princess Royal, but never used.

When Charles was given two magnificent receptions in The Hague, young William was brought from Leiden to be present at some of the festivities. Charles returned in his State coach together with his sister Mary and William sitting on his Uncle James's knee. William was present at the splendid dinner given by the States in Charles II's honour in the Mauritshuis.[11] On Charles's right sat William's mother, while Elizabeth of Bohemia, 'the Winter Queen', was on her nephew's left. William was seated next to his Uncle Harry Duke of Gloucester, whom he very much resembled, as is evident in his portrait aged 16 by or after Abraham Raguineau in the Frans Hals Museum, Haarlem. During May 1660 Samuel Pepys had visited The Hague. He thought it

> a most neat place in all respects ... About ten at night the Prince (William) comes home, and we found an easy admission. His attendance very inconsiderable as for a prince, but yet handsome, and his tutor, a fine man.

He considered William a very pretty boy.[12]

When Charles triumphantly returned to his kingdom on May 23 in the *Naseby*, now rechristened the *Royal Charles*, he was acclaimed by more than 100,000 people. He sailed from Scheveningen, then a small village two miles from The Hague. On taking leave of his sister Mary and his nephew William, he invited them to England as soon as possible, having previously commended his sister and her son, "two persons peculiarly dear to us" to the benevolence of the States-General. William's guardians, taking advantage of King Charles's restoration to his throne, pressed his claims to be recognized as the future Stadtholder. De Witt, though courteous, refused to be committed, remarking to the French envoy de Thou that he was not prepared to grant great offices to a boy of nine, who might or might not prove fitted for them. Let the young prince be further well trained and educated before his guardians move their claim.

Meanwhile the Princess Royal and William made a triumphal progress through the cities of Amsterdam, Haarlem and elsewhere. Bells chimed and trumpets sounded in the summer air. It was the month of June, and on a Sunday they both attended a service at the Niewe Kerk before travelling to Haarlem. At The Hague they were also received with ovations before William returned to Leiden. He soon, however, went to the Binnenhof to say farewell to his mother, who was about to embark for England to visit her brother Charles. September 29 was the last time William was to see his mother, who had written with anxiety to the States-General imploring them to have a particular care of her boy, "the being who is dearest to us in the world, and of his training in princely virtues and exercises." The States of Holland had already repealed the Act of Seclusion, which barred him from obtaining his hereditary offices.

For eighteen long years Mary had longed to return to England, but just before embarking on her ship the *Tredagh* she was desolate to hear of the death of her younger brother Harry Duke of Gloucester from smallpox, to whom she was deeply attached. Whilst in exile his mother Henrietta Maria had tried to convert him to Roman Catholicism, but Charles II had told him to remain a staunch Protestant. So, Mary on arriving in Whitehall was a saddened woman. In many ways the Stuarts were very unfortunate.

To her consternation and anger she now heard that her brother James Duke of York had been secretly contracted in marriage to Anne Hyde, her former Lady-in-Waiting, and together with her mother Henrietta Maria, who had come over from France, she made violent protests against the marriage. Mary could not bear the thought that James had married a former 'servant' of hers. So, Henrietta Maria and Mary conspired to annul the marriage. The Queen actually persuaded a courtier Sir Charles Berkeley to admit that he had had physical relations with Anne and that he had been secretly betrothed to her, an admission he later denied after Anne had given birth to a child, who died in infancy. It was Charles II who had the good sense to insist that James should be privately married again at Worcester House, the home of Sir Edward Hyde, newly created Earl of Clarendon, in the presence of Lord Ossory and one of Anne's maids. The family were now reconciled to the marriage.

Mary's part in this affair does not show her character in a good light, but she was far from well during the autumn of 1660 at the English court. What should have been a happy time proved otherwise, for she disliked the fogs that enfolded London and sighed for the days of her childhood at the gracious court of her father Charles I. His son was enjoying an affair with the vicious Lady Castlemaine. On Christmas Eve 1660 the Princess Royal, aged only 29, died of smallpox, the disease that had killed both her husband and her brother Gloucester, and was buried in the Stuart vault in Westminster Abbey. Her will reveals her concern for her son William, for she urged Charles and Henrietta Maria

> to take upon them the care of the Prince of Orange my son, as the best parents and friends I can commend him unto ... praying God to bless and make him a happy instrument to His glory and to his country's good.[13]

In her will she bequeathed to William all the jewels given her by her husband and a financial gift of 150,000 guilders. William never received most of the jewels, any many years later he had to redeem his mother's most valuable jewel she had earlier pawned to finance her brother.[14]

Elizabeth of Bohemia, her constant friend, refers to her niece's death in a letter to her son Charles Louis, Elector Palatine (January 17, 1661):

> My poore Neece desired to be buried by her Brother (Henry Gloucester), and without anie ceremonie, all heere from the highest to the lowest are very sorie for her, all the officers are commanded by the State to mourne.[15]

In England, however, she was soon forgotten.

The first experience of death, of a mother dear to him, is very serious for a boy, and William was deeply saddened by the loss. He first heard of it from his great-aunt Elizabeth of Bohemia in Leiden, and his illness in the early months of 1661 was probably due to the sorrow and desolation that filled the mind of the reserved prince. William became really ill with asthma, severe headaches and recurrent fainting fits. When his French tutor Samuel Chapuzeau attempted to comfort him, William tearfully said, "I'm sorry for you, too. My mother was a good friend to you, and I'm too young to do very much."[16] One thinks of William when King of England thirty-four years later, even more grief-stricken at the early death of his Queen Mary II.

When the prince was convalescent during April, he visited Elizabeth of Bohemia at The Hague. She wrote Charles Louis on April 11:

> He mends strangelie and grows verie strong, you cannot imagin the witt that he has, it is not the witt of childe who is suffisant, but of a man, that doth not pretend to it, he is a very extraordinarie childe, and verie good natured.[17]

It was decided by his anxious grandmother Amalia that William should go for a while to Cleves in the Rhineland/Spanish Netherlands where he was the guest of his aunt Louise of Brandenburg and uncle the Elector of Brandenburg. In their family circle the lonely boy passed a happy few weeks in the peaceful countryside with its rock-perched castle and swiftly flowing river. William always preferred an out-of-door life, and it was there that he acquired a passion for riding and the chase that dominated his whole life. It was springtime and the prince soon recovered his health. He proudly went on a boar hunt and felt manly when he experienced, for the first time, the killing. By the beginning of June, it was time for William to return to Leiden.

On the way, he passed through Utrecht where he was very popular. He attended a concert at the Dom Kerk and services on Whit Sunday at the Cathedral. Most people were impressed by the prince, for his manner seemed to give promise of greatness in the future. Indeed there was some strange quality in William as a boy, an awareness of his destiny. It owed something to the religious training of Pastor Trigland.

William's relations with his grandmother Amalia were amicable on the whole, but not intimate. As for her, she was more concerned with his political interests than with his education. Curiously enough, this strong-willed woman may have been a little afraid of him, for Sir George Downing (after whom Downing Street is named) English Ambassador at The Hague during 1663, wrote to the Earl of Clarendon,

> She, the Princess Amalia doth really begin to fear the Prince, he seeming so apprehensive in everything and she dares scarcely herself speak anything to him that she thinks will displease him.

Downing, however, was hostile to the Dutch. And, Amalia disliked William's tutor, the gifted Frederick Zuylestein, to whom he was devoted, and set out to get rid of him.

No sooner had Charles II been restored to his throne than Amalia hastened to offer her younger daughter Mary as his queen, but Charles still smarting from her rejection of his suit in exile, when in love with her elder daughter Henriette, refused to treat with her. During 1661 he was to marry the Portuguese Princess Catherine of Braganza.

Not yet twelve, William finally left Leiden and returned to live in The Hague, moving with his suite to the Old Palace in the Noordeinde. Despite occasional violent fevers, William's health improved. His early life, though often lonely, was by no means unhappy. The winters at The Hague were enlivened by the gaieties of Carnival (the yearly Kerness), and he enjoyed skating on the lake in the wood and being driven over the snow in a *traîneau* to the sweet sound of bells. The prince was not particularly bookish or interested in music, but he early possessed a marked interest in works of art, a lifelong interest. He began to collect pictures and portraits, although his personal allowance, at first two hundred guilders, was insufficient to indulge in this taste. Later during 1666 it was raised to four hundred.

William's library boasted books on the works of art of Italian cities. Dutch cities such as Delft, Leiden, The Hague, Amsterdam and Haarlem were naturally full of the pictures of their native artists, Vermeer, Rembrandt and others.

As a boy prince of fourteen (in 1664) William was rather handsome. He was about five foot six in height, slight, and elegant in appearance. His hands were delicate and beautiful, and he resembled his late mother's Stuart family in many ways. After all he was a 'grandchild of England'. His large dark eyes remind us that he possessed Italian blood. His long curls of a dark chestnut brown almost fell on his shoulders.

As has been mentioned earlier, of his out-of-door diversions, much the favourite was hunting. He would often go to his father's hunting lodge at Dieren and he loved to pursue this sport in the Gelderland.

Elizabeth of Bohemia had departed from The Hague during May 1661 to return to England, the scene of her early life. She was to die there during the following year.

When the Prince of Orange was aged fourteen, a new page named Hans William Bentinck entered his household. Bentinck was to become his greatest friend.

III FRIENDS AND ENEMIES

William Bentinck was the third son of Count Bernard Bentinck and his wife Anna van Bloemendal, a native of Gelderland, and came of a large family. Born in 1649, he was thus one year older than his master and their relationship was one of intimate understanding and deep affection rather than master and servant. Their friendship would last over thirty years.[1] He was rather handsome with reddish blond hair. They shared mutual tastes such as the Prince's love of field sports and his fondness of works of art. Bentinck spoke and wrote French, being even more fluent in that language than the Prince, and William would later employ him in delicate diplomatic negotiations. Their many letters to one another were often written in colloquial French and they would sometimes sign their letters with the initial letter of their Christian names. No man ever served his Prince more devotedly and diligently than Bentinck, and William was very fortunate to be able to rely absolutely on him. William much preferred men to women throughout his life, but it is certainly untrue to say that he disliked females, for he liked those with minds of their own, especially if they possessed intelligence.

Cardinal Jules Mazarin, the real ruler of France, had died in early March 1661, and Louis XIV, a king of twenty-three, was at last to come into his own. He was to become a great King of France. During 1660 he married Maria Theresa, daughter of Philip IV of Spain in St. Jean-de-Luz. William Prince of Orange related to him through Queen Henrietta Maria, later became his most deadly enemy, percipient enough to see the vast danger of Louis's ambitions in Holland and in Europe. The chief bone of contention between Holland and France was the principality of Orange in the south of France. Louis was prepared to return it to Holland provided that its Governor was a Roman Catholic, which was eventually agreed to by William's grandmother Amalia, and the French troops left the town on March 25, 1665.

William, however, was exasperated by the scornful manner of Louis XIV and by way of protest refused to give way when one day in his coach in a narrow part of the Lange Voorhout he encountered the coach of the French Ambassador d'Estrades. An ugly incident was prevented when William's 'grandmother Amalia persuaded him to go on foot and leave his coach.[2] He took much interest in the lives of his pages and members of his household. To one of his former pages John Theodor Lord of Frieshan who had become a soldier, William gave priggish advice in a letter written in French during 1665: "Abstain as much as possible from drink and especially from women and all other debaucheries."[3]

About this time William became friendly with Johan de Witt the Grand Pensionary of Holland, who would often visit the Prince in his apartments in the Binnenhof, and William would go to de Witt's house in the Knenterdyck. They would sometimes play tennis together. Later de Witt would antagonize the Prince of Orange by depriving him of his friend and valued tutor Frederick Zuylestein and his other friends, with the exception of Bentinck. He replaced Zuylestein by appointing Baron van Ghent as his new governor, a man much disliked by William. He never forgave de Witt for this.

Johan de Witt as Grand Pensionary was a statesman of considerable eminence for almost twenty years (1652-72). As a republican he was on the whole unsympathetic to the supporters of William of Orange, but the violence of the popular reaction in favour of the Prince in his role as the defender of the United Provinces against the invasion of the French, was ultimately to lead to de Witt's bloody murder and that of his brother Cornelius.

The main cause for the second Anglo-Dutch war on March 4, 1665 was the deep jealousy and rivalry existing between England and Holland for commercial supremacy. For personal reasons Charles II always disliked the Dutch, bearing grudges for the many slights he had received during times of adversity, despite the generosity of William of Orange's father William II. The Dutch had mixed fortunes in the new war, for near Lowestoft in Suffolk they suffered a defeat when Opdam their Commander-in-Chief and three other Admirals lost their lives. The Lord High Admiral James Duke of York, William's uncle, distinguished himself in this battle by his remarkable courage, but his intimate friend Sir Charles Berkeley, now Lord Falmouth, while standing next to him on the quarterdeck of his ship, was killed, bespattering him with his blood. Parliament voted James the considerable sum of £120,000 for his bravery in action,[4] though they asked Charles not to permit his brother to risk his life again. He stood too near the throne, especially because Catherine of Braganza had not after several years of marriage given her husband an heir.

The war was to last at least two years, and the English felt deep humiliation when the Dutch cheekily sailed up the Medway, and carried off *The Royal Charles*, the same ship on which the King had returned to his kingdom. James had neglected to see that the land defences of Chatham were of sufficient strength. The years 1665 and 1666 were the calamitous years of the Great Plague and the Great Fire of London. On January 26, 1666 France declared war on the English in accordance with the Treaty she had signed with the Dutch four years earlier, but Louis XIV was secretly planning an attack on the Spanish Netherlands now that Philip IV was dead. The Peace of Breda finally ended the naval war. The Dutch were fortunate in Ruyter, called the greatest admiral of the seventeenth century.

During April 1666 Prince William at the age of almost sixteen was made "a child of State" in Holland, resulting in the States being made responsible for his education; but the Prince of Orange protested passionately to his German-born grandmother Amalia when she supported de Witt[5] in depriving him of the services of Zuylestein, acknowledged by her late husband Frederick Henry to be his natural son. At the same time his French Tutor Chapuzeau, Trigland and others were dismissed. The Prince never forgave his grandmother for her part in the affair. William was pained that he had been deprived of his friends, and he knew that the appointment of van Ghent was pleasing to Louis XIV, who ordered his ambassador, the Comte d'Estrades, to bribe van Ghent with an annuity of 4,000 francs. William complained to his new guardians that his grandmother was responsible for his accounts being in a muddle, and that none of his debts were paid. However, he assumed an appearance of dissimulation towards the States of Holland, acquiescing in their decisions until he gained emancipation.

Johan de Witt now took a significant interest in William's education, examining him regularly as to his work and reserving an hour every Monday to instruct him in politics. A room in the prince's palace known as the *Chamber of Education* was used for this purpose. He remarked: "My party may fall, and it is necessary that this young man should some day be qualified to govern the republic."[6] De Witt's fatal error was to omit acknowledging the Prince as Stadtholder-Elect under the guardianship of the States. If he had done so, he would have acquired the support of the Dutch nation. That he formed a high opinion of the Prince, both of his intelligence and capacity is certain. Trigland taught William an exacting sense of duty.

Though he was destined to be the foremost enemy of France, individual Frenchmen were impressed by the young prince, and William liked Jean Herault, a temporary exile in France known as de Gourville. They would meet at evening parties when they played at cards and de Gourville admired William of Orange, judging shrewdly that he had an excellent brain. Another Frenchman to praise the prince was the Marquis de Saint-Evremond, who remarked: "Never any young person of his age and quality had so excellent a turn of wit." Saint-Evremond, the celebrated philosopher and poet, was to spend long years in England, the devoted admirer of Cardinal Mazarin's favourite niece, Hortense Mancini Duchesse Mazarin. D'Estrades wrote to Louis XIV "*Ce petit promet beaucoup de luy.*" He was referring to William of Orange. The Prince of Orange lived austerely as a boy of fifteen. During the winter, a turf fire was lighted morning and evening and he was only allowed two white wax candles and a yellow nightlight in his bedroom. He was always fond of chocolate for his breakfast and he drank plenty of milk. For his main course he ate various stews, then roast dishes and green vegetables. During those days he acquired his life-long love of fresh fruit.

His horsemanship benefited much from his French instructor. Sieur d'Orivel and he liked nothing better than to gallop over the heathland of Gelderland. Old Sir Constantine Huygens, who had served the Princes of Orange with so much devotion, wrote of his pupil William on his fifteenth birthday:

> My Master, thanks be to God, is no longer a child... as he is now a most fair Prince, so assuredly he promises to be something very great and most worthy of his birth.

When the Prince was fifteen, matchmakers were busy trying to find a suitable bride for him. The Duchess Sophie of Brunswick-Lüneburg (later Electress of Hanover), youngest daughter of the thirteen children of the 'Winter Queen', favoured her niece Liselotte, who had romped with William in early childhood. Her father the Elector Palatine, Elizabeth of Bohemia's eldest son, considered that William's prospects were too uncertain and showed no eagerness for the match.

Meanwhile the Prince's friendship with Bentinck grew apace. When Bentinck's father died during August 1668, the Prince was most sympathetic, writing his friend:

> It is with much distress that I have learnt from the letter you have written of the death of your father. I can assure you with truth that there is no one who shares more nearly than myself in the sorrow that has fallen on your house, and on you especially, for I am so much your friend that I feel all that happens to you as if it had happened to myself.

While England and the Republic of Holland were at war during 1667, Louis XIV, taking advantage of the situation, had sent Marshal Turenne and 47,000 troops into the Spanish Netherlands. Philip IV had died two years earlier, to be succeeded by his feeble son Charles II of Spain.

Louis's excuse for the invasion was that he was claiming his wife Maria Theresa's dowry. Soon the fortresses of Tournai, Lille, Charleroi and Courtrai were captured by the French. De Witt was greatly agitated, because hitherto his whole policy had been based on the French Alliance. He did not heed sufficiently the constant warnings of his ambassador in France of Louis's hostile intentions.

Aged seventeen, William was fond of amateur theatricals and to celebrate the Peace of Breda he organized an entertainment in the halls of the Noordeinde. Cosimo, heir to the Duke of Tuscany, was among his most honoured guests and was delighted by the prince's courtesy and tact. It is a mistake to think of William of Orange as always a too serious, humourless person who never relaxed. Saint-Evremond mentions that French players sometimes performed at The Hague in those days. William was present on one occasion when they played *Tartuffe*, a play much appreciated by Saint-Evremond who wrote, "I shall always retain a memory of things French, this well-drawn portrait of a hypocrite made its impression." Much later the Prince of Orange, mindful of the play, called Bishop Burnet, the Scotch historian who was often at his court from 1686 onwards, '*Ein rechte Tartuffe*'. In Holland William subsidized the French players.

To counter French aggression under King Louis XIV, a diplomat of striking ability was sent to The Hague as Ambassador. He was Sir William Temple. Born in 1628 and educated at Emmanuel College, Cambridge, his early life had been frustrating because he had become deeply attached to Dorothy Osborn, a younger daughter of Sir Peter Osborn of Chicksand in Bedfordshire. Only after many obstacles was he able to marry her. She is remembered for her brilliant love letters, some of the finest, in fact, to be written in the seventeenth century. William Temple's early patron was Lord Arlington, who had succeeded the Earl of Clarendon as Charles II's chief minister when Clarendon was forced into exile (1667). Temple was well-travelled in France, Holland, Flanders and Germany, and a skilled linguist. His intimate knowledge of Latin had been useful when he was sent on a diplomatic mission to the Bishop of Munster, for the latter could only converse in that language. When Sir William Temple was appointed ambassador to the States-General he was largely responsible for the celebrated Triple Alliance between England and Holland (January 1668), with Sweden joining later. Not only did Temple establish excellent relations with Johan de Witt, but he was very soon on very friendly terms with William of Orange,[7] not yet eighteen.

In his *Observations upon the United Provinces* (1672) Temple reveals his real knowledge of the country and its people. Praised by most of his contemporaries, Sir William was criticized by Bishop Burnet. He conceded that he was a great statesman and that he possesed a true judgement in all matters, but wrote unfairly that he was a corrupter of all that came near him. He condemned him for thinking that religion was only for the mob. Admiring Confucius in China as Temple did, his followers were atheists, leaving religion to the rabble. According to Burnet, Temple was too addicted to study, ease and pleasure. Johan de Witt refutes this by writing to Arlington that "it was impossible to send a minister of greater capacity or one more proper for the temper and genius of this nation". To be incorruptible was rare enough in an age when many politicians were constantly open to bribes.

Temple observed Prince William very closely. He was astute enough to see that he might become England's future king, as Charles II, after six years of marriage, was without legitimate heirs, and the Duke of York, by his first wife Anne Hyde, had but two surviving daughters, Mary then aged six and Anne, her younger sister.

Temple thought highly of the Prince of Orange,

> I find him in earnest a most extreme hopeful Prince, and to speak more plainly something much better than I expected and a young man of more parts than ordinary, and of the better sort, that is, not lying in that kind of wit which is neither of use to one's self nor to anyone else, but in good plain sense, with show of application if he had business that deserved it, and that with extreme good agreeable humour and dispositions, and thus far of his way without any vice. Besides being sleepy always by ten o'clock at night, and loving hunting as much as he hates swearing, and preferring cock ale before any sort of wine ... His person, I think you know, is very good, and has much of the Princess (his mother) in it; and never any body raved so much after England, as well the language as all else that belongs to it.[8]

Cock ale was a sort of marinated chicken containing various spices in two quarts of sherry. After a few days eight gallons of ale were added. William liked a glass or two of Italian wine, but, perhaps, he only drank it, as a diplomatic gesture, to please Cosimo of Tuscany during his visit. The Prince of Orange and Temple had similar tastes such as gardening. It has often been said of the Prince that he did not care for music, but occasionally when he was in a melancholy mood he called for his musicians to play a quartet for him.

When William was made a Councillor of State, his authority did not much increase as its powers had been gradually declining from 1650 onwards. He was also promised the Captain-General-ship when he attained the age of twenty-two. His chief critics and enemies were the

Loevestein Party, who remained hostile to him as they had been enemies of his father William II.

The Prince of Orange was very practical and managed his household finances efficiently. On one occasion, his eighteenth birthday, he summoned his grandmother's nephew Count Frederick Dohna into his study and showed him a memorandum concerning his plans for the management of his household. Dohna was greatly impressed. It is probable that William inherited this practical trait from his grandmother.

The Prince was a staunch friend to those few Englishmen he was really attached to. He was very fond of the Earl of Ossory, eldest son of the Duke of Ormonde, who was sixteen years older than William. He liked also very much Ossory's Dutch wife Emilia of Nassau-Beverwaert, and was even fonder of her sister Charlotte, being amused by her witty sallies and impressed by her intelligence. No doubt he felt most at ease with this little group of friends, which included Bentinck. Ossory often acted as his host during William's visit to his Uncle Charles's court. Well known for his gallantry, he was a fine character, very different from most of the courtiers in Whitehall.

Charles had not seen his nephew for ten years. Making the pretext that William's journey to England would persuade parliament to pay the royal debt incurred while in exile to the House of Orange, he invited him to come over. Although England was now an ally, Johan de Witt opposed the visit, because he did not want any closer ties between the House of Orange and the Stuarts. However, William embarked on the short journey by sea and landed at Margate on the Kent coast on November 6, 1670. After passing a night at Canterbury, he drove in his coach to Rochester. From there he entered the royal barge to continue his journey by river to Whitehall Stairs. John Evelyn, the celebrated diarist, merely mentions:

> Saw the Prince of Orange newly come to see the King his uncle, he has a manly, courageous, wise countenance, resembling his mother and the Duke of Gloucester, both deceased.

The Prince was aged twenty in early November. The King made much of this nephew, who must have reminded him of his sister Mary. It is unfortunate that William did not keep a journal containing his impressions of Charles's Portuguese queen, of Anne Hyde, Duchess of York, now grown grossly fat through overeating and incessant childbearing, of his other uncle James, still handsome, but showing signs of debauchery in his face.

Charles entertained his nephew most generously, taking him on hunting expeditions near Windsor, and race-meetings at Hampton Court. There was a state ball and a visit to a theatre. In London he stayed at the

Cockpit in splendid apartments. What he thought of Whitehall with its complex buildings we do not know, but he was certainly impressed by Inigo Jones's magnificent Banqueting Hall with its marvellous ceiling.

He must have regarded Charles II's dissolute courtiers with ill-concealed disgust, especially George Villiers, second Duke of Buckingham, a mercurial character of sparkling brilliance, who succeeded in getting the Prince drunk. Buckingham invited the Prince to supper with some bibulous friends and was no doubt delighted when William attempted to break into the quarters of the maids of honour.

With his uncle Charles he held serious talks, and the King with his keen intelligence immediately perceived that William was highly endowed and able. Charles was pursuing a completely devious policy at this time, bent on deceiving the Dutch that he was their ally whilst engaged in highly secret negotiations with the French. After ten years, the first fine careless rapture of the Restoration settlement had ended. His parliaments were more niggardly with money than he had expected and since he badly needed money he had been persuaded by King Louis to change sides. Even more devoted to his youngest sister Henriette-Anne married to the Duke of Orleans in France than he had ever been to his eldest sister Mary, he had pursued negotiations with Louis for many months, culminating in the visit of Henriette, nicknamed 'Minette' by her brother, to Dover in May 1670 when the secret Treaty of Dover was signed, concealed from the Dutch and even unsuspected by some of Charles's ministers. By this treat the King was guaranteed large French subsidies for which he had promised to join in an attack on the United Provinces and agreed publicly to declare himself a Roman Catholic at a ripe moment. How sincere Charles in reality was has always been contended. Well aware of the hostility of the mass of the nation to the Roman Catholic religion, he had no desire to go on his travels again.

When Charles had last seen William he had been a boy not yet aged ten. In his cynical way, it never entered his mind that William in the intervening years had become a Dutch patriot, a zealous Protestant, with a constant love for his country of windmills, canals, sweet meadows, and woods. He himself, half-French in his sympathies, much disliked the United Provinces. His beloved sister Henriette had departed for France, only to die there shortly at the age of twenty-six. Perhaps judging from his entertaining letters to her (now among the Correspondence Angleterre, Quai D'Orsay, Paris), she was the woman he had cared for most, although he had only seen her for brief spells.

Now in his interviews with his uncle, William felt uneasy, even isolated, suspecting that the King was deceiving him. Colbert de Croissy, French ambassador at the Court of St. James, friendly with Louise de

Kerouaille formerly Minette's maid of honour and now the King's mistress, reported to his master Louis XIV:

> The King of England is much satisfied with the parts of the Prince of Orange. But he finds him so passionate a Dutchman and Protestant, that even although Your Majesty had not disapproved of his trusting him with any part of the secret, those two reasons would have hindered him.

William's suite consisted of about one hundred people, including the faithful Bentinck, old Sir Constantine Huygens and Zuylestein. Thomas Butler, Earl of Ossory was his host with whom he developed a strong friendship. It is unlikely that William shared the similar tastes of his uncle James, the Duke of York, a hardworking naval officer in his younger career. They both loved hunting. James had not yet announced openly that he had become a Roman Catholic. He was unfaithful to the Duchess of York, having many mistresses, including Arabella Churchill, his favourite John Churchill's sister.

Fearing that his nephew might get an inkling of the contents of the secret Treaty of Dover, Charles wrote to the Vice-Chancellor of Cambridge University telling him that William was about to visit that town. A resident of Cambridge, Alderman Newton, gives an account of the Prince's reception.[9]

> Saturday morning about ten of the clock came in to Cambridge, His Highnesse the Prince of Orange being then between 19 and 20 years of age (actually the Prince had attained his twentieth year on November 14), a well countenanced, a smooth and eager face, and a handsome head of hayre of his own. There were in all 3 coaches, 6 horses a peece, the Prince was in the middlemost, and sat at the head end therof on the right hand, the Lord Ossory sat at the same end with him. Mr Law then Mayor being still at London, Mr Herring was his deputy who with the Aldermen in scarlet and the Common Counsell and other gounemen in their habits being ready at the Dolphin Inn, mett and saluted the Prince at the hither end of Jesus Lane, mett against the Dolphin juste upon the turne of his coach, and Mr Herring did present himself to him, who in a courtous manner leaned over my Lord Ossory and gave audience to the Deputy Mayor who made them a short speech ... he was there to wait upon His Highnesse and to assure him of his hearty wellcome to the towne ... and wished that his stay might have bin longer amongst us ... The

coaches passed down by St. Johns to the Schools where there was a commencement for several degrees.

William was unable to stay for the completion of the ceremony. After dining with the Provost of Kings the Prince and his retinue visited Trinity College. They departed from Cambridge that night,[10] passing the night of November 26 at Audley End, that magnificent house built by Thomas Howard Earl of Suffolk. When William paid a longer visit to Oxford during the third week in December, he was dressed in a scarlet gown of a Doctor of Civil Laws. During the ceremonies at Wren's theatre, the Prince was given by the Public Orator a book belonging to his grandfather, *King Charles the First, His Works* (two volumes), today lovingly preserved in the Royal Library at The Hague.

William was much concerned when he was informed that the Dean of Christchurch had dismissed one of his students William Ellis for having attended on him in the University of Cambridge and wrote to him from London (January 9, 1671) imploring that Ellis should be restored "to his student's place". While attending the Prince he had been made Master of Arts. The incident reveals Prince William's kindness and consideration for others.

Charles II was certainly a generous host to the Prince, paying all his expenses at Newmarket races, and to entertain him cost the King about £100 a day.[11] However, he was apt to break most of his promises and seldom paid his debts. One of the main reasons for this visit was to claim the large Stuart sums owing to the Prince, and Parliament to their shame had not voted any funds for this purpose. Exactly what was owing was difficult to decide, but Charles estimated the figure as 1,800,000, 400,000 for William's mother's dowry, 500,000 for William II's loan to him, and interest of 900,000 guilders. The Prince actually claimed much more than this, the sum of 2,400,000 guilders. Sir Constantine Huygens after much argument agreed to 900,000 guilders. It is not surprising, perhaps, that over two years later only 200,000 guilders had been repaid.

William was splendidly entertained by the Lord Mayor at the Guildhall, slowly recovering from the Great Fire more than four years earlier. He made a very favourable impression, fulfilling his duties with dignity and gravity. It was certainly advantageous to become acquainted with some of the leading politicians, such as Lord Halifax, Sir Thomas Osborne (later Earl of Danby) and the Earl of Arlington.

Yet little was accomplished by the visit. True, it made him realize that friendship between England and the United Provinces was vital for the peace of Europe, but he was gradually becoming disillusioned with his uncle Charles and regarded him with a faint distrust. His first experience of the English court led him to believe that its politics were as corrupt as its morals. It is likely that William still felt a fondness for King Charles, aware of his charm, but he was wary that his uncle might deceive him. They had grown apart.

In the New Year (1671) the King and the Duke of York gave him lavish presents, twenty English horses, deer and rare birds for his parks and aviaries. During February after an absence from his country of three months the Prince felt homesick - he never throughout his life liked to be long absent. In the middle of February he endured a stormy voyage with his following and after landing at Flushing went straight to The Hague.

IV   THE YEARS OF CRISIS

William returned to Holland very uneasy that his uncle Charles II was about to desert him despite the Triple Alliance, the Treaty the English had signed with the States. The years 1672-74 when he was aged twenty-two to twenty-four were critical for him in his role as Prince of Orange, and he was to have his first experience of warfare and the responsibilities of leadership in battle. It marked the emergence of a man absolutely dedicated to his country, and one who had a clear vision of her problems and those of Europe. He emerged as one worthy to hold the position of a Prince of Orange, as a brave soldier and apprentice statesman.

When Johan de Witt had first heard rumours concerning the secret Anglo-French Treaty of Dover, he had been so bewildered that he questioned Sir William Temple during the summer (1670). The Ambassador denied any knowledge of a change in English policy. He was soon, however, recalled to England, and he realized that Arlington, the patron to whom he was attached, was bent on deceiving the Dutch. Both Arlington and the King wanted to arouse English public opinion against the Dutch. For their purpose the King appointed an ambassador Sir George Downing, a man who hated them. He was given a long list of fabricated grievances, for Minister and King wanted to provoke them into acts of hostility and then blame them for the breach.

De Witt's policy up to 1668 had been friendship with France. Then he had deep faith in the Triple Alliance, but being an honourable statesman himself, he refused to believe in the perfidy of others. He must be criticized for delaying too long in rearming his country and looking to her defences, despite the warnings of his friend and ambassador in Paris, Pieter de Groot, the son of the great jurist, who constantly told him of the massive preparations Louis XIV was making. One wonders if de Witt, who had lost his wife during 1668, had not grown weary of power, and whether he had not lost his political skill. He seemed convinced that the French conquest of the United Provinces was inimical to English interests and that their help would be forthcoming.

It was unfortunate that the Dutch army (1671-2) was below strength and most inefficiently managed. Those appointed to high places were often inexperienced, for nepotism played its part. When the Deputies of Zeeland

- always enthusiastic supporters of the House of Orange - proposed Prince William as Captain-General during November 1671, most of the Provincial Representatives favoured the proposal, but de Witt and the Loevesteiners strongly opposed it on the grounds that a law passed in 1657 provided that nobody could be appointed Captain-General before the age of 21. Actually the Prince was 21 by November 1671.

By the end of this year William was even more despondent as to the intentions of Charles II. He constantly wrote to his friend Lord Ossory that it was in England's own interests that the United Provinces should not be destroyed. "I beg you to tell me if you are going to be our friends or not. Everyone doubts it more and more." Secretly, and without the knowledge of de Witt, the Prince sent Sir Gabriel Sylvius, a former secretary of his mother's, to see his uncle. "If His Majesty would kindly tell me what he desires, I shall do my best to procure it for him ... in spite of pensionary De Witt and his Cabale." Privately William must have wondered if the King's commitments to France were already too strong. Charles made no immediate reply, and later rejected the Prince's offer.

The States-General now renewed their offer to create William Captain and Admiral-General for a single campaign, promising that the appointment would be confirmed when he reached twenty-three. The Prince was very popular. An enormous bonfire was lit before the Binnenhof and the people lustily exclaimed 'Viva Orangie'. The Prince spared no expense when the States of Holland were invited to dinner. At a magnificent banquet there were served pheasants, partridges and even much-out-of-season asparagus on a freezing winter night.

In France at the age of thirty in the year 1668, Louis XIV said emotionally, "My dominant passion is certainly a love of glory (*gloire*)." He did not realize William's mettle, for he had once scornfully offered him a daughter of an early mistress Louise de la Vallière in marriage only to be told with pride that the Princes of Orange did not marry the bastard offspring of monarchs.

Louis disliked Holland for a number of reasons. Like his cousin Charles II, he particularly resented her dominant role in world commerce and finance. He also disliked the country because she was staunchly Protestant. Holland had dared to check his complete annexation of the Spanish Netherlands by initiating the Triple Alliance. Again she was a centre of political intrigue, opposition and anti-monarchism, for many French Calvinists had taken refuge there. The free press fulminated against Louis, making personal attacks on him and his mistresses.[1]

As war became inevitable William was saddened not only that he would be at war with England, but also opposed to Ossory, his dear friend. He was distressed by the warlike preparations in London. "We are making our dispositions as best we can," he told him. "I wish with all my heart that the state of things would permit me to see you." These are not the words of a cold man. To those he loved, William could be warm indeed. He ended one letter: "Good-bye. I shall be yours all my life. I pray you love me too." He wrote in a jocular spirit to his friend: "You are the laziest man in the world," for he had not heard from him for three weeks. At least Ossory would show his real sentiments by refusing all offers of a commission with the French.

The English were the first to wage war on Holland, but they did not bother to make an open declaration, a grave breach of the accepted code of honour between two nominal allies. On March 20, 1670 the Dutch merchant fleet, homeward bound for Holland from Smyrna, were attacked off the Isle of Wight.[2] There was now a formal declaration of war on March 27. In making it on April 6, the French merely declared their ill-satisfaction at the conduct pursued for some time past by the United Provinces.

The Dutch were in a desperate situation and turned to the Prince of Orange, now Captain-General, as their only hope. In The Hague he ordered the conscription of every able-bodied man between the age of eighteen and sixty. It was vital that the defences of Gelderland and Overijssel, so neglected over the years, should be repaired. It was proposed that several districts between the Ijssel and the Rhine should be inundated to hold up the enemy, but the months of May and June (1672) were so dry that this was not possible.

Meanwhile, Louis XIV, towards the end of May, at the head of his superbly trained army of 120,000 soldiers under the command of brilliant generals such as Luxembourg, Turenne and Condé advanced rapidly through the 'Spanish Netherlands, past Charleroi, towards the fortresses in Cleves.[3] "*Jamais,*" said Voltaire in a later age, "*on n'avait vu une armée si magnifique et en même temps mieux disciplinée.*" With his love of the theatre it must have seemed to Louis a dazzling display of might. "I have decided," the King announced, "that it is more advantageous and more to my glory to attack four places on the Rhine simultaneously and to command in person at all four." "I have chosen Rheinberg, Wesel, Burik and Orsooi." Towards the end of May the forts of Orsooi and Burik fell to the French, while after being besieged, Wesel was captured in early June. The Dutch army consisted of about 25,000 men.

The only victory to relieve Dutch gloom was that of the fleet under de Ruyter, who had defeated the combined English and French fleet commanded by the Duke of York on May 7. Evelyn refers to it in his diary, for it:

shew'd the folly of hazarding so brave a fleete, and loosing so many good men, for no provocation but that ye Hollanders exceeded us in industrie, and in all things but envy.[4]

William was at Dieren, working feverishly to resist French aggression. There in happier times he had spent whole days hunting. Now he heard the dire news that the enemy had crossed the Rhine. To a deputy of the States of Holland he said, "We can't stay here and let Holland fall."[5] He was closely in touch with an able Dutch diplomat named Conrad van Beverninck. His opinion of the Prince of Orange was very sanguine. "He is very spirited," he wrote,

> but very depressed about the condition of the army, and I fear that his courage, not being well seconded, will bring him into some extremity.[6]

The Prince, however, could rely on a few senior officers such as John Maurice, Prince of Nassau-Siegen, a first cousin of his grandfather Frederick Henry, an experienced administrator and soldier, who had served as Governor of the Dutch Colonies in Brazil many years before. Others were Count Paul Wirtz and Count Hoorn.

William made desperate attempts to occupy a productive land of flourishing orchards, the Betuwe, that lay between the Old Rhine and the Waal, but he was hampered by the deputies of the States. With his small army of about 9,000 men he then moved to Utrecht, where as a boy he had been given a great reception and where he was very popular. He reached there on June 15. Because of its massive fortifications, Utrecht could have resisted the French, but the people were demoralized and its councillors fearful and divided. Despite William's arguments, Utrecht refused to admit his army. The town had a large Roman Catholic population, who favoured the French king, knowing that he was of the same religion. William was forced to retreat, therefore, and on June 23 French troops entered Utrecht.

Very different was the heroic resistance of the little town of Aardenburg in Zeeland - one so fierce that they succeeded in repulsing the enemy. Most of the seven provinces, however, had been captured that summer, and in Amsterdam the people were bewildered and demoralized. Everywhere was misery, schools, banks, shops shut down; only the churches remained open for those wanting to pray. De Witt was mostly blamed, rather unfairly, for the disastrous situation, and rioting was prevalent everywhere.

The vital decision to flood a belt of land from the Zuider Zee in the north to the borders of Dordrecht in the south was now taken. The work of inundation was hampered, however, by the drought that summer and also by the peasants who were faced not only with invasion, but with the ruin of their lands. Turenne did not at first understand the importance of water for the Dutch in the defence of their country. It was vital to hold Muiden, a little town on the Zuider Zee near Amsterdam, but the French omitted to do so. John Maurice the intrepid commander was at Muiden, but he could do little and complained that there was neither "a spade or a shovel, with never a stiver of money, and no cannon ...". It was at Muiden that the main sluices were used for flooding the countryside.[7]

To William was entrusted the work of inundation in the province of Overijssel, in an attempt to prevent the French from entering the provinces of Friesland and Groningen.[8] The chief difficulty was the drought. "The water," wrote William to van Beverninck on May 28, "is beginning to fall so terribly that between Ijsselloort and here (Dieren) there are quite ten places where one can ride through."

On June 13, the position was so desperate that the States-General resolved to send two delegations - one to Louis XIV at his headquarters near Doesburg in south Holland and the other to England. The delegation to the King of France consisted of Pieter de Groot, a former Dutch ambassador in France, Jan van Ghent, William's former much disliked Governor, and his cousin Nassau Odijk. The delegation had not been given full powers to treat for peace, so King Louis, haughty and arrogant, declined to receive them. De Groot, on his return journey, passed through Nieuwerbrug, where the Prince was roused from sleep at 2 a.m. The States-General were completely divided as to whether they should give *plein pouvoir* or not. Five provinces, Holland, Groningen, Utrecht, Overijssel and Gelderland favoured it, while Zeeland and Friesland opposed it. The French king's terms were extremely harsh, including the demand for an enormous indemnity of sixteen million guilders, the lands of Brabant and Limburg and part of the province of Gelderland, and also Maastricht. He demanded preferential trade terms and that Dutch Catholics should be freely admitted to public office and have full liberty to practise their religion. As a further insult Le Roi Soleil required the Dutch to send a yearly embassy to him to present him with a medallion as gratitude for his forbearance in returning their country to the States.

Johan de Witt and his brother Cornelius were made the scapegoats for the disastrous year of 1672. Cornelius lacked the ability to some extent of his younger brother, but he was neither corrupt nor dishonourable. He was certainly courageous as he had shown at Sole Bay. His main faults were his avariciousness and overbearing nature.[9]

Johan de Witt was accused falsely of treachery, corruption and other crimes. On June 21 he left the Binnenhof at a late hour after attending a meeting of the States of Holland, together with another man (he never walked attended by guards or armed). He was near his house in the Kneuterdyk when four youths sprang upon him, and felled him with their swords, though de Witt, a powerful man, made some show of resistance. His wounds were so serious that he lay in his bed for a month. When he recovered he resigned all his offices. On July 12 he wrote to the States asking them to clear him of corruption and treachery of which he was accused. He resented the charge that he had neglected the army, though it was obvious that this was true. He also wrote to William, who replied coldly:

> I cannot doubt that you have taken as much care of it (the army) as was possible in the circumstances; but the host of daily affairs have hindered me from examining accurately what may have been lacking and on whom lies the blame that the lack had not been properly supplied.

If de Witt had not delayed so long in making him Captain-General and actively opposed him becoming Stadtholder, William might have been more generous. On July 23 the States published a denial of the accusations against de Witt, but he and Cornelius were so unpopular by this time that it made no difference.

On June 21 - the same day as Johan de Witt had been attacked - the city of Dordrecht, where the de Witts had been born, declared the Prince of Orange, Stadtholder. He was dining in the Peacock Inn, and as the crowd acclaimed William enthusiastically, the Resolution was signed by the magistrates. Other places to accept the Resolution were Haarlem, Delft, Rotterdam and Gouda. Amsterdam did likewise on July 2.

The well-informed George Savile Lord Halifax, known later as 'the Trimmer', travelling in Bruges at the beginning of July, wrote to Lord Arlington:

> I believe it now certain that the Prince of Orange is declared Stadtholder at Amsterdam, Rotterdam, Dorft and Haarlem and the messenger I sent into Zeeland saw it done whilst he stayed for my passport. I am told that de Witt (Cornelius) who came sick from the fleet to Dorft, was forced by the people to sign to the making the Prince Stadtholder.[10]

He told the Secretary of State that "one of the men" (young Jacob van der Graeff) had been beheaded. On July 5 Halifax wrote again to Arlington from Middelburg in Holland:

What I have observed in this little time, is an extreme aversion in this people of Zeeland to the French; Your Lordship will believe they are not very fond of us at this time.[11]

Halifax was not only very observant, but deeply intelligent. He was against aggression and consequently had some sympathy for the Dutch.

William turned a deaf ear to the English peace terms, in the same way as he had rejected the French. Considering how little he had contributed to the French victories on land and that he had been defeated at sea by the Dutch, Charles II's terms were harsh. He wanted an indemnity of a million guilders, the Zeeland island of Walcheren, £10,000 to be paid annually by the Dutch for the right to fish herring in English coastal waters and various trading concessions in the East Indies. He wanted to set up his nephew as a puppet king of the United Provinces, dependent on England, thus showing how little he understood William's character.[12] Arlington and Buckingham were sent as envoys to treat with the Prince of Orange. To all Arlington's and Buckingham's demands William was obstinate and surly, telling them exactly what he thought of the English aggression. He argued that it was not in England's best interests to continue as ally of France. Buckingham was very fond of Rhenish wine and sat on talking with William while Arlington took to his bed. He even managed to persuade Buckingham to draft a treaty between England and the United Provinces, but Arlington refused to acquiesce in it the following morning. William was, above all, a patriot. He told the envoys: "We had rather die a thousand deaths than submit to them." At one stage Buckingham told William to cease thinking of his country, which was lost anyway. When William remained doggedly silent, Buckingham losing his temper, said: "It is lost. Do you not see it is lost." "It is indeed in great danger," answered William, "but there is a sure way never to see it lost, and that is to die in the last ditch." While in Holland, Buckingham paid a courtesy visit to William's grandmother Amalia at The Hague. To her he remarked: "We do not use Holland like a mistress, we love her as a wife." To which Amalia retorted, no doubt aware of the Duke's dissolute character: "*Vraiment je crois que vous nous aiméz comme vous aiméz la vôtre.*"[13] William made it plain that he had hopes that the Elector of Brandenburg, who was opposed to King Louis of France, would rise on his behalf.

It was Louis's mistake never to entirely defeat William's army by pressing on into Holland. He could have dealt with the centres of resistance such as at Groningen, Nijmegen and Doesburg. Louvois, Louis's war minister, was jealous of the French commanders Turenne and Condé, who advised him to go no further.

During that terrible summer in early July, Pastor Cornelius Trigland, William's devoted friend and former tutor, died. He bestowed his blessings on the prince, writing to him:

> I am now in a state of great pain and tribulation, longing daily for my merciful release. But though I may not again see Your Highness's face in this world, yet I remember that I have brought you up in the true faith and shown you the foundations of that blessedness in which all the saints of both the Old and the New Testaments have died ... May He cover your head in the day of battle and crown you with victory and honour.[14]

The Prince throughout his life of almost 52 years would never forget his debt to Trigland for his teaching. However, his responsibilities were such in that fateful summer for him to have little time for mourning.

While on active service with the Dutch fleet, Cornelius de Witt had behaved with remarkable bravery, and in 1672 he had been given the post of Representative of the States-General on board de Ruyter's flagship, but he returned to Holland a sick man. He was extremely unpopular in Holland and known as a vindictive enemy of the Prince of Orange, even accused by a barber-surgeon, William Tichelaar, of conspiring to murder him. On July 24 he was imprisoned in the Gevangenpoort, the medieval prison near his brother's house, in the Kneuterdyk.

No man had a stouter defender than his brother Johan, who obtained from de Ruyter glowing testimony as to Cornelius's courage. At his trial Tichelaar's evidence was disproved. Despite this, Cornelius was tortured for more than four hours[15] while he quoted Horace. The seventeenth century was an age of vile tortures. Cornelius aged fifty-seven was whipped for three hours and to the big toe of each of his feet a 25 kilogramme weight was applied and his arms were then tied behind his back. After he was laid on the torture bench he was bound with thin twine which cut into his body. Though his sufferings were almost past belief, Cornelius still maintained his innocence. Even the executioner revolted at the tortures he was compelled to administer, had a complete breakdown and on his deathbed wrote to Cornelius's widow to implore her forgiveness.

Nothing is so bestial as the unrestrained passions of ignorant men. There were people in respectable trades like silversmiths involved in the assassination of the de Witt brothers. Today one can see the little room in which Cornelius lay on a bed while the faithful Johan read to him portions of the bible. The murderers succeeded in hammering their way into the Gevangenpoort, dragging them down the stairs and heaping them with insults. Johan was wounded by a musket shot on his head. He was murdered on the actual spot where he had been attacked two months previously. Now Lieutenant van Valen fired his pistol at Cornelius, who fell dead. Within a few minutes the bodies of the de Witts were placed on gibbets in the Plaats, with their heads lying downwards.

On learning of the deed, William's first reaction was of horror as he sat down to supper in the village of Alfen, near Bodegraven. His intimate friend Bentinck, who was present, said: "I have never seen him more overwhelmed." Many years later the Prince in a discussion with Bishop Burnet expressed horror, according to the historian's *Memorials*. He believed that Johan de Witt was a great man and one who had served his country well. Gourville who had known the Prince in his early life, had an interview with him in 1681 - nine years after the assassination, and asked William whether he had had any part in the murders, and he had denied it, but had admitted that he felt somewhat relieved when it was done. Gourville was a Frenchman and consequently opposed politically to William. However, it is possible that his account represents the truth. Where the Prince must be sharply criticized is his curious inaction in not punishing the ringleaders, such as the silversmith Verhoeff and others involved in the murder. It reminds us of his inaction in not punishing later those responsible for the massacre of Glencoe (1692) when he was King of England. Not only did William fail to punish those guilty of perpetrating the crime of murdering the de Witt brothers, but he actually rewarded them. For this omission and insensitive behaviour his character is unfortunately tarnished. Hendrik Verhoeff and Tichelaar were both given annual pensions of 600 and 400 guilders respectively. A third criminal named van Banchem was promoted to be head of the local police at The Hague. Instead of reversing the appointment, William took no action, saying that "he had loved him because he had always protected his House." Six years later van Banchem was sent to the gallows.

Perhaps William's behaviour can only be explained if one accepts the notion that the Prince had never forgiven the de Witts for opposing him becoming Stadtholder. He accepted too readily whatever was done in his name and by his supporters, as services to his house and person. This had unfortunate repercussions as his contemporaries began to speak of him as the secret perpetrator of the crime. The brilliant French General Luxembourg wrote Louvois on August 22: "The people of the country are saying openly that he had caused this thing to be done."

Charles II hoped that the murder of the de Witts would lead to a renewal of the peace negotiations. He wrote at the end of August:

The last letters, having brought in the news of the people having murdered de Witt and his brother as the authors and occasion of the war, makes it plain to me they are infinitely desirous of a peace; and being very apprehensive of your person if they shall imagine you have any repugnance to it, the tender love I bear you makes me again mind you of it.

He proposed a joint peace conference at Dunkirk together with French plenipotentiaries attending it. William told his uncle that he was only willing to make peace on his own terms, although there were some like the diplomat Sir Gabriel Sylvius, who favoured peace. The chief result of the murder of the de Witts was to strengthen the Prince's personal influence in the government of Holland. What was highly beneficial for William was the appointment of Caspar Fagel as the new Grand Pensionary. He had formerly been a moderate republican, but he now gave his resolute support to the Prince. Sir William Temple in his *Memoirs* says, "his love to his country made him a lover of the prince, as believing it could not be saved by any other hand." He therefore strongly favoured giving William full powers to make any changes in the government he felt necessary.

William's intransigence angered not only Charles II, but Secretary of State Arlington, who threatened the Prince of Orange that if he pursued a policy with regard to England no longer supported by the Dutch, he might meet the same fate as de Witt. William answered him in robust manner:

Don't imagine that your threats to have me torn in pieces by the people frighten me very much; I am not in the least bit faint-hearted by nature.[16]

V   TURN OF THE TIDE

A prince of lesser calibre than William of Orange might well have accepted the King of France's humiliating conditions of peace, but William was made of sterner stuff. In early 1673 he desperately needed allies for the four free provinces to survive, but the Spanish did not relish war with France, fearing that the Dutch would abandon them. The Elector of Brandenburg proved a lukewarm ally, influenced by his second wife Dorothea Dowager Duchess of Brunswick-Luxemburg, who was pro-French. The Emperor Leopold also did not want to get involved because of the threat of Turkish armies on his borders.

Louis thought of himself as Master of Europe, making a spectacular appearance as in a theatre in the Spanish Netherlands, together with his Queen Maria Theresa and his reigning mistress, the voluptuous and beautiful Madame de Montespan. The King planned the Siege of Maastricht, a most important Dutch town, with a skilled engineer Sébastien de Vauban. He captured it after fourteen days at the end of June, another defeat for the Dutch. William, however, was successful in recapturing Naarden, an important fortress town near Amsterdam. By August 1673, William's patience and diplomatic finesse at the Council Table at last received their reward, when Spain and the Empire signed three treaties with the Prince. The Emperor pledged himself to supply 30,000 men on condition that the Dutch would raise 20,000 troops and pay him large subsidies. Spain also entered the war on the side of Holland, together with Denmark, Lorraine, Trier and Mainz. Louis and Turenne might be triumphant in the Palatinate and Alsace, but the Dutch under their great Admiral Michiel de Ruyter had won an important sea battle against the English and French off the Dutch coast at Scheveningen, near The Hague, during August 1673.

The victory owed much to William's gift for diplomacy. He never made the mistake of neglecting the Dutch navy. Knowing of the rivalry and jealousy existing between the two admirals, de Ruyter and Cornelius Tromp, William succeeded in reconciling them and making Tromp willing to serve under de Ruyter. While he created de Ruyter 'Lieutenant-Admiral-General of Holland and Westfriesland', he secretly promised Tromp this post, if he should survive de Ruyter.

William understood his fellow countrymen intuitively, but later, when he became King of England, failed to understand or to appreciate them, partly because he was unpopular there. He told de Ruyter to read aloud the Prince's inspiring letter to the Dutch seamen on May 25:

> The eyes and hearts of all our countrymen are fixed on the prowess of the fleet, and to him who should bear himself cowardly, or other than a good soldier and seaman should in face of the enemy, nowhere would be more dangerous than the harbours of the State.[1]

If the Dutch fleet were defeated, the English would land on the coast. The sea battle raged throughout a summer day, de Ruyter with his 110 ships opposed to 140 ships of the enemy, and only after sunset did the Anglo-French fleet withdraw.

James, no longer Lord High Admiral, Governor of Portsmouth, or Warden of the Cinque Ports, took no part in this battle. The Test Act passed by Parliament during 1672 had deprived him of all these offices. He had not yet become a professed Roman Catholic, but he had ceased, on grounds of conscience, to take the sacrament in the Church of England. The increasing hostility towards Papists in England and the passing of the Test Act were a bitter blow for James.

On March 31, 1671 there died Anne Hyde, Duchess of York, a saddened, disillusioned woman. Her last words were: "Duke, Duke, death is terrible, death is very terrible." She died a secret Roman Catholic, and it is more likely that her decision to become one was of her own volition rather than influenced by her husband. Bishop Burnet maintains that her chief reason was to consolidate her influence over James. Two daughters survived of their marriage, Mary their eldest daughter born on April 30, 1662, and Anne born two years later.

When they were very young Charles II, sensing that there was a danger that the two little girls might remain within their father's Catholic orbit, to be influenced by him, made them Children of the State and removed them to Richmond House. There they were given two Anglican chaplains, Dr. Lake and Dr. Doughtie, and a governess Lady Frances Villiers. They were brought up as Protestants, and much of their education consisted of Church of England dogma. They would say their prayers in the Anglican manner.[2] One Catholic remained in the household as their nurse, Mrs. Langford, and she was later with Mary in Holland. Their companions were six Villiers daughters, and various other girls, Frances Apsley, Sarah Jennings and Anne Trelawney. Sometimes Mary and Anne saw their father either at St. James's Palace or in Richmond, where he came for the hunting. James was fond of his daughters, especially Mary his favourite. Mary was more intelligent than Anne and certainly a more talented pupil.

As heir presumptive to his brother Charles II, it was highly necessary for the Duke of York to marry again, and Henry Mordaunt Earl of Peterborough was sent to scour the continent to find if possible a suitable aristocratic and royal bride for the Duke, no easy duty. Peterborough finally made a choice of Maria Beatrice, the fifteen year old daughter of Alfonso d'Este, fourth Duke of Modena, and Laura Martinozzi. This Italian girl was twenty-five years younger than her proposed husband. Peterborough sent such an enthusiastic description of her to Arlington in London that he may even have been a little in love with her himself. "She is tall and admirably shaped," he wrote,

> her hair black as jet, so were her eyebrows and her eyes, but the latter so full of light and sweetness, as they did dazzle and charm too.

Maria Beatrice had been brought up a strict Roman Catholic, having a vocation to become a nun of the Convent of the Visitation and having at first an invincible aversion to marriage. It was only after she received a letter from Pope Clement that she submitted to the wishes of her mother. Maria Beatrice was married by proxy in Modena, and later to the Duke of York after a stormy voyage to Dover (late November 1673) while the wind howled and the gulls wailed. At first the homesick girl regarded her husband with revulsion, though soon she became attached to him, making it appear that the Duke had some lovable qualities. He certainly loved his new wife tenderly, but treated her as a child, introducing her to his daughters as "their playfellow". She was in fact only four years older than Mary. The marriage was, however, very unpopular both in Parliament and amongst most people because of the Duchess of York's religion. Louis XIV encouraged the match.

The Prince of Orange continued his successes against the French. Together with his allies he besieged Bonn, which held out for eight days, only to be captured on November 12. A young secretary Constantyn Huygens had succeeded his great father as William's secretary. He gives us little glimpses in his journal of the Dutch armies besieging Bonn:

> H.H. was sitting by a fire at the edge of a little pine wood. A drummer wounded before Rheinbach died there under the pines. It was a beautiful night, he wrote.[3]

We get more descriptions of the Prince exposing himself to danger, charging to the attack, all fire and energy, as if with his strange belief in predestination he would come to no harm. His obstinacy and his refusal never to admit defeat were strikingly shown at Seneffe, a small village where he had experienced huge losses. To his grandmother Amalia he wrote:

> The combat lasted from ten in the morning until the evening at the same hour; it was very rough; we have lost many people, and the enemy, who were unable to win an inch of terrain from us, lost not less; ... their only advantage was to have taken most of our baggage train.[4]

It was now a European war, and William's successful leadership and outstanding qualities as Stadtholder of the United Provinces persuaded them to create him Generalissimo of the European coalition against France when he was aged twenty-four.

By the autumn (1673) the English Parliament and the people had grown more and more weary of the war against Holland, and more critical of the pro-French attitude of the King and Duke of York. One of the secret provisions of the Treaty of Dover was that the King should restore the Catholic religion in England and early in 1673 he had proclaimed a Declaration of Indulgence suspending the penal laws against Roman Catholics and Dissenters, but opposition was voiced in Parliament for renewed supplies of money to be voted for the Dutch war. Both Arlington and King Louis implored Charles to change his policy regarding the Declaration. Since Parliament refused to vote further supplies for the Dutch war despite Louis's bribery and presents of money and wine to important Members of Parliament, the war would have to finish. On February 19, 1674 the Treaty of Westminster was signed, although the continental war would continue for another four years and only end with the Peace of Nijmegen.

William and the Grand Pensionary Fagel were well aware that there existed a section of English public opinion - by no means negligible - which might be brought by propaganda to consider itself more endangered by Louis XIV than by Holland. Before his time William realized the importance of working on these potential allies, particularly those opposing government policies in the House of Commons by means of a kind of 'political warfare'.[5] Dutch ambassadors in London before 1672 had often failed in their despatches to explain the motives behind English foreign policy, for instance to detect the change between the Triple Alliance (1668) and the attack on Holland four years later.

The Prince's secret agent in organizing a 'fifth column' in England was a naturalized Englishman named Peter du Moulin, born of an uncompromisingly Protestant family in Dunois to the north-west of Orleans. Seeking employment, Peter, owing to the patronage of Lord Arlington, served on the staff of the Ambassador to Denmark, thus gaining useful experience. He later fell foul of influential people in the government in England, and apprehensive that he might be sent to the Tower, escaped to Holland where he acquired an invaluable new patron Caspar Fagel, who had succeeded Johan de Witt as Grand Pensionary. Du Moulin was invaluable both to the Prince of Orange and to Fagel in explaining the motives behind English foreign policy and suggesting how it could be altered.[6] He was responsible for writing and distributing pamphlets spreading distrust of the French alliance in the minds of many people. After advising William, through Fagel, for two years, the Protestant exile died during June 1676 and is buried in the Kloosterkerk at The Hague.

In December 1674 Charles II sent an embassy to Holland, consisting of Lord Ossory, together with his Dutch bride, and the Earl of Arlington, now Lord Chamberlain, also married to a Dutch woman. They had followed the return to The Hague of Sir William Temple, who had been charged by Charles to discuss terms of peace with the Stadtholder and Caspar Fagel and also to persuade the Prince to tell what he knew of the activities of the English, discontented with the government. William favoured a general conference rather than a separate peace.

He was delighted to see Ossory again, who was accompanied by his sister-in-law Charlotte Philiberta of Nassau-Beverwaert (known as Lotte), a great favourite of William's. Ossory's mission was to suggest a marriage between the Prince and Mary, the elder daughter of the Duke of York, who was then aged twelve. The Prince's opinion was, if peace was made between the two countries, he would be delighted to come to England to pay his court to Lady Mary, especially if she felt no violent objection to him. At present he felt Mary was too young and it would be hardly fair to ask her to come to Holland still in a state of war. Ossory raised Charles II's grievances, but William was forthright in discussing his own main complaint that his uncle had made wanton aggression on Holland.

Arlington was an unfortunate choice as an envoy to the Prince, for his manner was pompous and condescending, which only irritated William. He could hardly forget that Arlington had once threatened that he might be torn in pieces, like de Witt. Arlington for his part had found William "dry and sullen or at the best uneasy".

William's happiest times were with the Ossorys and with these friends he cast off his cold reserve and enjoyed the gaiety of balls, sport and the evenings playing cards. Bentinck, who was constantly with the Prince, fell deeply in love with Lotte, a girl of character, whose witty sallies delighted the Prince. She did not, however, reciprocate Bentinck's sentiments, or she was slow to respond. Bentinck was so smitten that he asked William to write a word on his behalf. William told Ossory:

> Please tell Lotte that in spite of her impudence I love her with all my heart; and reproach her from me because she has not written to me, or even answered my letter as she promised to do at parting. I hope too that she will soon declare herself on the question she promised to think over when we said good-bye, for Bentinck is getting very impatient to know how he stands, which seems to me very reasonable.[7]

Her answer when it came was negative, though he did not give up hope. Eventually he married Ann Villiers, sister of the notorious Elizabeth.

The Prince was on very friendly terms with Sir William Temple, who had returned to The Hague as Ambassador, often dining with him and his wife in the English Embassy. Untrue rumours had reached King Charles II that his nephew intended to visit London during March 1675. When Charles wrote to Temple that he must prevent this at all costs, the Ambassador replied

> that the Prince thinks no more of a journey to London at present, than to Venice; nor indeed of anything, but how to get out of this war with a little honour, and safety.[8]

William thought that the rumours were derived from those wishing him ill, to sow suspicions in his uncle's mind. He was deeply angered when he received a letter from Lord Arlington in which he referred to these supposed visits and also to Peter du Moulin, who he accused of acting as a spy in Holland. All the opposition in the English Parliament was owing to this man.[9] According to Temple, he had never seen the Prince in such a towering rage. He was not usually an emotional man.

A few days later according to the Ambassador, William fell seriously ill of a fever, soon diagnosed as smallpox, which had been very fatal in his family. He was attended by an excellent German doctor Dietrich Liebergen, and four faithful friends, including Bentinck, Odijk and Ouwerkerk, who spent long hours nursing him. William was so trustful of Temple that he would only eat food prepared by the Ambassador's cook. He was in his palace at the Noordeinde when he was taken ill.

William was now in his twenty-fifth year. For the rest of his life he never forgot Bentinck's devoted care. He tells us later,

Whether he slept or not while I was ill I don't know, but during sixteen days and nights I never once called out but he answered me.[10]

William Carstares, a Scottish clergyman William III knew well in his later life, was told by the King that at the height of his illness Bentinck slept in his bed,[11] for it was thought in the seventeenth century that if a person in good health shared the bed of somebody ill with smallpox it would lessen the attack. It was probably owing to Bentinck's devotion and care that William's life was saved. However, Bentinck also sickened with smallpox, but fortunately recovered by the end of April. It was characteristic of William that he refused to rest and by May both he and Bentinck were back with the army, always inseparable.[12]

The Prince shared all the dangers of his men, accepting their hardships and ration biscuits when necessary. He was a severe disciplinarian, but always just. It is idle to discuss in too much detail the Prince's life in Flanders during the summer (1675).

When his old grandmother Amalia died during September, Bentinck wrote of his master's grief. She bequeathed to her grandson the House in the Wood (Huis ten Bosch), a small house surrounded by beech woods. She was buried beside her late husband Frederick Henry at Delft. Temple described her "as a woman of the most wit and good sense in general that I have known."

At The Hague the Prince spent many hours being entertained by Sir William and Lady Temple ('Dorothea') at the Embassy in the Lange Voorhout. It was a happy household, Sir William cultured and urbane, a clever conversationalist, a keen gardener, and interested in art, like the Prince. The former Dorothy Osborne, a deeply sympathetic character, was an enchanting hostess. There, too, very often was Temple's widowed sister Lady Gifford. William liked an occasional glass of wine, and both Temple and the Prince had a weakness for fresh fruit.

The Ambassador liked William for his sincerity and honesty, "the sincerest man in the world, hating all tricks and those who use them."[13] He had little use for diplomatic finesse or verbiage, calling it 'whipped cream'. The Lord Chamberlain Arlington liked neither William nor Temple, and persuaded the King to send Sir Gabriel Sylvius as special envoy. The Prince did not trust Sylvius and remarked,

God! I never said anything to Sylvius that I was not content my coachmen should know.[14]

An attempt was made to begin a peace conference at Nijmegen in which Temple was much involved, but the negotiations only progressed intermittently. The war with France raged again. On his way to rejoin the army, the Prince arrived at Averonger, the home of the van Reed family, accompanied by two of his favourites, Bentinck and Ouwerkerk. As the owners were away, the housekeeper served them pork hot-pot and turnips and cold sausage. William always preferred simple food and told her that he had never tasted better sausage. He asked her to send some to Dieren.

That summer (1676) the war again favoured the French and on May 16 Bouchain was captured by Philippe Duke of Orleans, younger brother of Louis XIV. It was because of its strategic situation, good for the defence of the Spanish Netherlands and the Prince could not relieve it.

Maastricht had been in French hands for three years, a vital stronghold towering above the valley of the Meuse. It fell to William to conduct the siege of Maastricht. While launching an attack on the outworks on July 23, the Prince "exposing himself on all occasions, received a musket-shot in his arm".[15] He made light of it, telling Count von Waldeck, one of his best generals, that it was almost nothing. Then he immediately peeled off his hat with the arm that was hurt, and waved it about his head to show the wound was but in the flesh and the bone safe. Oh, the stench of war that summer with the raging heat and swarming flies breathing disease!

On August 26 William and his tired army were compelled to retreat. His experience of war was most unpleasant, and he was so far very depressed because of his fear that Flanders might eventually be lost. He was attacked by fever, but had managed to bring his troops back safely to Antwerp.

Early in 1676, the body of de Ruyter the great Dutch naval hero, who had recently died, was brought back to Amsterdam and during March buried in the Nieuwe Kerk. Constantine Huygens the younger represented the Prince at the funeral.

During June William had sent Bentinck on a mission to his uncle Charles's court to suggest peace terms or that he join the allies. Bentinck was also told to ask the King's permission for him to make a short visit later on. Meanwhile Charles sent Ossory, the Duke of Monmouth (his illegitimate son) and John Churchill, later Earl and Duke of Marlborough, on a private mission to his nephew, also giving Laurence Hyde, younger son of the Earl of Clarendon, a message allowing the Prince to come to England at the end of the campaign.

United with Ossory in August, William's spirits rapidly rose. They had many tastes in common, gardening, art, and they were both skilled in horsemanship and lovers of an out-of-door life. His only fault seems to have been an excessive love of gambling,[16] due perhaps, to his Irish blood. He would play billiards with the Prince for a wager and would later confess his gambling losses to his wife Emilie.

During April 1676, although the war still continued, William's mind had turned to thoughts of matrimony. He asked Temple to meet him at Honselaarsdijk to discuss a very private matter. There they strolled together in the gardens. Temple gives his own account.[17]

> The Prince said that he would have one that he thought likely to live well with, which he thought chiefly depended on her disposition and education, and if I knew anything particular of the Lady Mary (elder daughter of the Duke of York) in these points, he desired me to tell him freely.

The Ambassador answered His Highness that he was very glad to find he was resolved to marry, being what he owed his family and friends. "I am much more pleased," he continued:

> that his inclination led him to endeavour it in England, that it was a great step to be nearer the Crown, and in all appearance the next.

He said:

> that he had always heard his wife and his sister speak with all the advantage that could be of what they could discern in a Princess so young (she was just fourteen years of age) and from what they had been told by the governess (Lady Frances Villiers), with whom they had a particular friendship and who they were sure, took all the care that could be in so much of education as fell to her share.

Sir William Temple's advice influenced the Prince to pursue the undertaking. He would write both to the King and the Duke of York to beg them to favour the match, and permit him to go over into England at the end of the campaign. It was proposed that Sir William's wife, who was now about to visit England on her husband's private affairs, should carry and deliver both his letters. She was also to endeavour to inform herself as well as she could of all that concerned the person, humour and dispositions of the young princess. Within two or three days the Prince brought his letters to Lady Temple and returned immediately to the war front.

VI WILLIAM'S MARRIAGE

Oblivious of the interest taken in her by the Prince of Orange in Holland, the Lady Mary was in 1677 growing up a graceful girl with artistic tastes, tall with dark hair, and dark lustrous eyes. Pepys describes her as a little girl on April 2, 1669 when she was almost seven:[1]

> I did see the young Duchess, a little child in hanging sleeves, dance most finely, so as almost to ravish me.

In early life she had been chosen to appear as Calisto in a court masque written by John Crowne, and her sister Anne was cast Nyphe, her friend. Her acting talent appealed to the admiring author. "She spoke to the eyes and soul of all who saw her," wrote Crowne.[2] Mary also had a taste for music, and she certainly revealed a talent in her maturity as a miniaturist and a skilful needlewoman. Both sisters, however, received a superficial education.

In her early life Mary lived in a world of fantasy, caused by her emotional instability and lack of parental love, at least that of her mother. Her father the Duke of York was very fond of her, for she was his favourite child. There was a vein of foolishness in Mary's character when young. She fell desperately in love with Frances Apsley, beautiful daughter of Sir Allen Apsley, who had served the Duke of York for many years. Frances was nine years older than Mary, and Mary in her letters addressed her as "My dearest, dearest dear Aurelia", signing them "Mary Clorine". Romantic, naive, and longing to love and be loved, she poured out her heart to her friend.

> If you did but love me as I do you I could be content with a cottage in the contre and cow a stufe peticoat and waistcot in summer and cloth in winter a litel, garden to live upon the fruits and herbs it yields or if I could not have you so to myself I would go a beging to be pore but content but what greater hapyness is there in the world than to have the company of them as loves to make your hapyness complete.[3]

Frances Apsley later married Sir Benjamin Bathurst and these letters lay for many years in a leather box amongst papers of the Bathurst family in Cirencester. (Frances's letters to Mary were probably destroyed about 1688, before Mary came to England.) When Mary's sister Anne, in her turn, could not resist 'Aurelia's charms' and Frances gave her a valuable ring, Mary's jealousy was aroused:

> O have some pity on me and love me again or kill me quite with your unkindness for I cannot live with you in indifference, dearest loving kind charming obliging sweet dear Aurelia ...

She was still under the influence of her passion for Frances, when she heard of Prince William's imminent journey to her uncle's court. It cannot have excited any emotion in the mind of the naive girl. She was now aged fifteen, twelve years younger than the Prince of Orange. Sir William Temple wrote:

> The Prince, like a hasty lover, came post from Harwich to Newmarket. My Lord Arlington still bent on letting others think that he had the Prince's foremost confidence when the truth was otherwise.

William was very kindly received by the King and the Duke of York at Newmarket. Charles and James wanted immediately to discuss matters of business with their nephew, but the Prince insisted that he must see the Lady Mary before taking part in any peace treaty talk. When he met Mary in London, William was very impressed with her, immediately making his suit for her hand with King Charles and the Duke of York. Mary did not find William attractive; thin and austere with a marked foreign accent, he dressed unfashionably and did not wear a periwig as did most of the courtiers in Whitehall, but wore his own hair. William impressed by her prettiness and her grace, renewed his suit to his uncles. Her father the Duke of York did not much care for the match earlier on, much preferring a possible marriage between the Catholic Dauphin of France with his daughter. They both now, however, were agreeable to the marriage on condition that the terms of a peace abroad were first agreed between them. To humour his nephew Charles returned earlier than intended from Newmarket.

Thomas Osborne, then Earl of Danby, who had succeeded Lord Arlington as Lord Treasurer - he was a Yorkshire man - very much favoured the match, disliking the proposed French alliance.

According to Sir William Temple, both he and Danby were uneasy that the marriage negotiations would break up upon "the punctilio" that an agreement to sign a peace must come first. About this time he chanced to go to see the Prince after supper. "I found him in the worst humour I ever saw him," wrote Sir William Temple:

> and he told me he regretted he had ever come into England and resolved that he would stay but two days longer, and then be gone, if the King continued in his mind of treating upon the peace before he was married .... It was for the King to choose how they should live henceforth, either as the greatest friends or the greatest enemies.

Temple hastened to see the King the following morning, telling him all the Prince had said to him the night before. He stressed the ill consequences that would follow a breach between them, considering that so many of William's subjects disapproved of the late measures with France.

Much to Temple's surprise, the King changed his stance, saying:

> Well, I never yet was deceived in judging of a man's honesty by his looks ... and if I am not deceived in the Prince's face, he is the honestest man in the world, and I will trust him, and he shall have his wife, and you shall go immediately and tell my brother so, and that it is a thing I am resolved on. Odds fish, he must consent.[4]

Charles clearly admired his nephew's integrity, though he never understood his love of his native land.

James, on being informed of his brother's wishes, showed no desire for the match, saying a little stiffly that:

> he could have wished His Majesty had been pleased to acquaint him before with his mind.

However when he was summoned to the Council Chamber he was obliged to consent, saying that he always acted in the interest of the security and peace of the nation. He said:

> for whatever my opinion in religion might be, all I desired was, that men might not be molested merely for conscience sake.

He also assured the Council that he would not prevent anybody from educating his children in the Church of England.

It was King Louis who was most annoyed and upset, according to the English Ambassador Montague, by the proposed marriage. The new

French Ambassador in London, Paul Barillon, fat, sly and well informed, was not slow to tell of his master's displeasure to the Duke of York and the King. Louis's reaction to the second marriage of James to Maria Beatrice of Modena had been quite different.

When the matter of William's marriage was settled, Charles said to Prince William: "Nephew, it is not good for a man to be alone, I will give you a helpmate", adding shrewdly, "Remember, love and war do not agree very well together." He knew that the common people would rejoice at the marriage. Meanwhile William sent an express to the States General of the United Provinces informing them of these momentous events, knowing that they had expressed a wish he should be married. He asked them to despatch immediately to England his wedding present of jewels worth £40,000.

Morose and surly by temperament as he sometimes was, William was hardly an enthusiastic bridegroom. As for Mary she took refuge in floods of tears, knowing that she would have to leave Frances Apsley, her sister Anne to whom she was much attached, and her stepmother Maria Beatrice, who was about to give birth to an infant. Maria Beatrice was very fond of the Lady Mary, 'her lemon' as she called her after her wedding.

The Lord Treasurer Danby worked hard on the preparations for the marriage. There was a hectic fortnight of entertainment, including a magnificent banquet on October 29 at the Guildhall by the new Lord Mayor. The feast included roast beef pies, venison jellies, cakes and custard.

The characters of William and Mary were completely different. He was highly intelligent, engrossed in politics and military affairs, reserved, rather silent, and only relaxed and gay in a small group of friends. Mary was 5 feet 11 inches and William much shorter, 5 feet 6 inches in height. She was extremely talkative, fond of chatter around her, and very romantic. Even now she longed for the society of her "dear husband" Frances Apsley, "if you do not come to me sometime, dear husband, that I may have my bellyfull of discourse with, I shall take it very ill".

On November 4, 1677, Dr Edward Lake, chaplain and tutor to the Princesses Mary and Anne, wrote in his diary:[5]

This week hath produced four memorable things. The Lady Mary and the Prince of Orange were marryed on the Sunday, the Duchesse (Maria of Modena, Duchess of York) was brought to bed of the Duke of Cambridge on the Wednesday, the Archbishop of Canterbury (Dr. Gilbert Sheldon) dyed on the Friday, and on the same day Lady Ann appear'd to have the smallpox.

The marriage was solemnized in the Lady Mary's bedchamber on November 4 at nine o'clock at night in St. James's Palace. No royal marriage has ever taken place in such miserable circumstances, for nearly everybody in the small company felt disconsolate with the exception of the King, who was in a facetious mood. William looked solemn, Mary tried to restrain her tears, Anne was unwell and absent, and James was sad at the imminent parting from his daughter and anxious about his wife. Dr. Henry Compton, Bishop of London, officiated instead of the Archbishop of Canterbury. King Charles gave his niece away, unable to restrain a witty sally,

> desired that the Bishop would make haste, lest his sister (the Duchess of York) should bee delivered of a son, and so the marriage be disappointed.[6]

When the Prince endowed his bride with all his worldly goods, "hee willed to put all up in her pockett, for twas clear gains." At eleven o'clock they were put to bed, His Majesty drawing the curtains, and saying jovially: "Now nephew to your work! Hey! St. George for England."

In her fascinating letters to her aunt Sophia (Electress of Hanover), Liselotte (Elisabeth Charlotte of the Palatinate, Duchess of Orleans), William's flame in childhood, hastens to relate some gossip concerning the Prince of Orange. "Among other things it is said that he went to bed in woolen drawers on his wedding night."[7] When the King of England suggested that he might care to take them off, he replied that since he and his wife would have to live together for a long time she would have to get used to his habits; he was accustomed to wearing his woolens, and had no intention of changing now. The story reveals William's obstinacy. However, when she writes of the Prince supping in the town instead of eating with the English royal family and keeping the King and his bride, who had been put to bed in the bridal chamber, waiting until after midnight, it sounds highly improbable. The Prince explained that he had been gambling. Liselotte added:

> I am not surprised that the princess is struck dumb at such manners. It reminds me of the comedy of the shrewish Kate.

The Prince and his wife rose early on the following day to receive the Lord Mayor and the Aldermen. William now presented Mary with the jewels worth £40,000 and also a small ruby and diamond ring. "It was the first thing he ever gave me," she said much later. It was Guy Fawkes night and the people rejoiced at the Protestant marriage. There was the pealing of city church bells and bonfires were lit. There was sober reflection when the Catholic Duchess of York was safely delivered of an infant Prince christened Charles Duke of Cambridge. "The child is but little, but sprightly," according to Dr. Lake, "and likely to live." Dr. Crewe, Bishop of Durham, officiated at this ceremony, not Bishop Compton, who was fiercely anti-Catholic. What William thought on being asked to be godfather we do not know, for it removed his chances temporarily of succeeding to the English throne through Mary. However, the Duke of Cambridge, James's and Mary Beatrice's first son, died in infancy.

On November 10, Princess Anne having been ailing for five days, caught the smallpox. There now occurred the first row between the Prince and his young bride, for William naturally did not want Mary to be infected with smallpox, a disease she had been free of. He urged her to leave St. James's for Whitehall, but Mary refused to be persuaded.

> I perceived her eyes full of tears, herself very disconsolate, not only for her sister's illnesse, but also for some discontent occasioned by the Prince's urging her to remove her lodgings to Whitehall,[8]

wrote Dr. Lake. Six days later William's sullenness and clownishness were everywhere remarked on when he accompanied her to the theatre or balls. He seemed to neglect her and to take no notice of her. The news became even grimmer when Lady Frances Villiers, who was to accompany the Prince and Princess of Orange to Holland, sickened and died of smallpox on November 23.

To celebrate the birthday of Queen Catherine of Braganza a ball was held at court on November 15 and the Princess attired herself in all her rich jewels. The Prince was longing to return to his native Holland, but the wind had veered easterly, making it unfavourable for them to travel. His long conferences with his uncle Charles had not produced any change in Charles's relations with the King of France. There was much competition among the young ladies who should accompany Mary to Holland, and Henry Savile, Lord Halifax's brother, scornfully wrote to his intimate friend the poet Earl of Rochester:

> it were worth your while to see how the old ladies and young beggerly bitches all sueing for places.

When John Churchill enquired of the Prince how much money was needed to buy a place among those chosen, William replied that places would not be bought and sold at *his* court.

It was not until November 19 that the wind was westerly in a favourable position to make travel possible. At 9 a.m. that morning William and Mary, accompanied by the King and Queen and the Duke of York, entered a barge at Whitehall Steps. Mary was in a flood of tears, so Queen Catherine tried to comfort her, reminding her that she had never seen King Charles until she arrived in England. Mary taking leave of her said: "But, madam, you came to England, but I am going out of England."9 Charles and James, accompanied the Prince and Princess as far as Erith and returned to Whitehall after disembarking at Gravesend in the yacht *Mary*, a beautifully furnished vessel.

The Prince urged the captain to press on, but the weather had changed to a gale and the captain refused to cross the North Sea in such conditions, landing the royal travellers at Sheerness. At sea everybody except the Princess was violently sick. The King kindly sent them an urgent message for them to return to London, but the Prince wanted to continue the journey as soon as possible. The Prince was accompanied by his friends Bentinck, Odijk and Count Horn ashore, while the Princess took with her her lady-in-waiting Lady Inchiquin and one dresser. The rest of the party remained on the yacht. The following day William and Mary moved on to Canterbury. There is a story that the party ran out of money, and had to be rescued by Dean Tillotson, who offered to lend them money and his own plate, but Thomas Birch dismisses the story.10 However, Tillotson's courtesy and helpfulness stood him in good stead and William was to remember it many years later. William III seems to have been generous to Archbishop Tillotson's widow. He granted her in May 1695 an annuity of £400 during her natural life and an addition to it on August 18, 1698 of £200 per annum more. He always called for the money quarterly, and sent it to her himself.

William wrote to Lord Danby thanking him for his immense pains in forging the marriage treaty, and he also wrote to his friend Ossory.

When they resumed their journey from Margate the Prince and Princess travelled in separate ships, William in the *Mary* and Mary in the *Katherine*. A dreadful experience because the gale persisted. Everybody in the *Katherine* was sick except Mary, while William in the *Mary* is said to have remained on deck. It is probable that he felt deeply nervous that the ship on which his wife was travelling might sink. However, on November 29 the ships anchored at the small fishing port of Torheyde where the weather conditions were such that the exhausted travellers were obliged to walk about four miles to their coaches. It took a further two hours for them to drive to Honselaersdijck where they were to stay.

VII   EARLY MARRIAGE

Unlike William's mother, Mary was to become very fond of Holland, and the people in return learnt to love her for her beauty, her grace and her tact. Her favourite home was Honselaersdijck, situated seven miles from The Hague. It was a graceful manor in the Dutch Renaissance style, built of pale Leiden brick and its gardens boasted a fountain with four dolphins spouting water and an inner garden containing statues of classic beauties. William possessed many other houses, including the Binnenhof, the Oude Hof at Noordeinde in The Hague and the House in the Woods outside The Hague, known as Het Huis Ten Bosch, bequeathed in 1675 in Amalia's will to her grandson William.

In 1684 and onwards William began the building of a new palace Het Loo near Apeldoorn in a marvellous woodland setting, and it became a favourite home of both William and Mary. What attracted William was that as early as 1672 he had received the hunting rights to the region called the Veluwe in the Gelderland, described by a contemporary Englishman as "the best hunting country in ye world but good for little else."

The war with France continued and the French were besieging Saint-Ghislain. On December 12, 1677 the Prince and his young wife not yet sixteen, made their public entry into The Hague. They were seated in a golden coach drawn by six piebald horses and the people rejoiced with their beloved Prince, but his pleasure was partly spoiled by the ominous news that Saint-Ghislain had fallen. It dampened his pleasure when viewing a magnificent spectacle of fireworks that night. If he was tempted to leave Mary for the war, he refrained for the time being from doing so.

The Prince when in England was often seen at his worst, but in his own country surrounded by a few friends and married to a beautiful and sparkling girl, he was a very different character. At twenty-seven he was far from unattractive, and within a few weeks of marrying William, Mary was already very much in love with him. This was an unexpected development considering her cold relations with the morose prince in England. To explain Mary's changed sentiments is not easy, but in the early days she had many opportunities for talks with William's most intimate friends. The inexperienced, emotional girl would listen avidly while Bentinck, Odijk and Ouwerkerk and the elder Huygens would discuss the Prince's merits

55

and it would not take her long to realize that he was regarded as a hero in his own country. She was, of course, far too young to be a companion to her husband, but she could early share his tastes, including a love of gardening and flowers. The Prince revealed a certain sensitivity in ordering that her apartments should be "always profusely adorned with varied flowers".[1] The Princess of Orange was very domesticated, loving her homes, and delighting in cleanliness. The Prince also was domesticated, making the most of those rare occasions when he could relax from war. Her apartments were always hung with some of his most choice pictures. Her study in Honselaersdijck, for instance, had a copy of Van Dyck's *Madonna and Child*. Two other fine pictures were once the possession of Frederick Henry, William's grandfather: *The Burial* and the *Resurrection of Christ*, both by Rembrandt. The Prince and Princess were also deeply religious.

Less reserved among his intimates in Holland than he had been in England, William, however, was sometimes irritated by his girl wife, her endless chatter, her ignorance, and her emotional lapses. We do not know exactly what he felt for her in those early days. He undoubtedly liked her very much and admired her, but he may not have loved her. That would come later. According to the younger Huygens, William had a passing affair with an innkeeper's daughter in 1677, but we know nothing about any other possible affairs until the mysterious affair with Elizabeth Villiers.

He could not have given Mary the sexual satisfaction or spiritual comfort that she craved for, and he only partly satisfied her needs as a wife. Mary longed for a child of her own, and at first it seemed likely that her wish would be granted. Within three months of her marriage the Princess was pregnant, "grown somewhat fatt, but without very beautiful", according to Dr. Lake, who had heard from a Mr. Lee in Holland. Dr. Lake disapproved of the Princess playing cards with her ladies, especially on Sundays. It sorely troubled him also that she sometimes attended the non-conformist services at the English church at The Hague, connived at by her chaplain Dr. Lloyd.

On March 1, 1678 after William returned from a hunting expedition, he heard the ill news that King Louis was again invading Flanders with a powerful army. He now had to leave his wife, who accompanied him as far as Rotterdam, where Mary's uncle Laurence Hyde, who had come over from England, saw both William and Mary part very sorrowfully and tenderly from one another. King Louis's victorious armies swept on through Ghent and Ypres. Ghent was captured on March 18, while Ypres as a fortress was so poorly defended it was soon captured.

While William was at Antwerp, Mary was writing a melancholy letter to Frances Apsley, 'her Aurelia'. Her letter reveals that she now loved

William and hated the temporary parting from him, fearing that he might be in danger. She wrote:

> I suppose you know the Prince is gone to the army but I am sure you can guess at the trouble I am in ... but I am to be mistaken that now I find all this time I never knew sorrow for what can be more cruell in the world than parting with what one loves and nott only common parting but parting so as may be never to meet again to be perpetually in fear for God knows when I may see him or wethere he is nott now at this instant in a batell I recon him now never be safely ever in danger oh miserable live that I lead now ...

Mary had now heard that her infant half-brother the Duke of Cambridge had died of smallpox.

It was unfortunate for the Princess that she had a serious miscarriage at Breda during the spring (1678) and not at The Hague. One of William's medical advisers was a brilliant gynaecologist - a Frenchman named Drelincourt, a specialist in anatomy and diseases of the lower abdomen, who lectured at the University of Leiden.[2] It is very likely that there was no skilled doctor at Breda. William and Mary were both bitterly disappointed at her miscarriage. Drelincourt could have travelled to see his patient so easily in one of the Delft *trek* boats, a very comfortable way to travel on the waterways. James Duke of York, anxious about his daughter's condition, told her to be "more carefuller of herself" another time. He was always ready to give his advice on these matters.

Many of the Dutch sought peace by the spring, for it was increasingly difficult for them to stand on their own, particularly as the attitude of the English was most uncertain. William was unwilling to discuss peace, unless Louis was made to surrender the frontier towns he had conquered. In the middle of May, William returned from the war front to attend the important debates of the Assembly of the States of Holland. For Mary it was a happy time: the joy of her husband rejoining her at Honselaersdijck, and her first experience of a Dutch spring and summer. Sir William Temple told Henry Sidney, who was to succeed him as Ambassador, that the spring was nowhere more beautiful than at The Hague, with the gay, colourful blossom and the sweet-smelling lime trees in the Lange Voorhout. Mary liked to travel in the *trekschuyten* canal boats, gliding gently along. On land she went with her ladies in one of the Prince's coaches, drawn by dapple-grey horses.

The female members of her household, who had accompanied Mary to Holland, were mischief-makers, indulging in unworthy gossip and bent on sowing discord between husband and wife. The Prince was churlish by nature with those he disliked and made no attempt to conceal his bad temper. Mrs. Langford, the Princess's nurse, a prying woman, received an allowance of 1,000 guilders a year (£1,000), while Mary's own allowance amounted to about 4,000 guilders a year. Especially troublesome, very often acting as a spy, was Edward Villiers, and his wife Barbara (a daughter of the celebrated Thomas Chaffinch), relating scandal at The Hague to friends in England. Elizabeth, the most intelligent of the sisters, was soon to attract the Prince's attention.

Now that the Prince was a married man, William Bentinck wanted also a wife. He chose as his bride one of the Villiers sisters, Anne, a sweet-tempered, docile woman, and she was to become a warm friend of Mary as well as William. The Princess was on indifferent terms with the various chaplains sent out to her. Dr. Richard Hooper frankly disapproved of the Prince and blamed him for not coming daily to chapel with his wife, while William was surprised to discover that his sixteen-year-old wife was reading two learned works, Eusebius' *Church History* and Richard Hooker's *Laws of Ecclesiastical Polity*. "What," he exclaimed, "I suppose Dr. Hooper persuades yee to read these books."[3]

William was engaged in a very great and bloody battle according to Bentinck with the French during August 1678. Marshal Luxembourg was blockading Mons, and in order to relieve it, William attacked the French with an army of 45,000 troops, and further English troops supplied by his friend Ossory. The battle lasted from 2 p.m. for eight hours until 10 p.m. and William was in very great personal danger, for a French officer was about to shoot at him at close range when Ouwerkerk killed him. As a reward for saving his life William gave his friend a pair of gold-mounted pistols. Of the English contingent, Ossory fought with remarkable courage "expos'd to all the fire of the Enemy, as if he had been invulnerable, as well as invincible".[4] Two bullets pierced his armour, but he was unhurt. The battle of Saint-Denis was a victory for the Dutch allies, but one wonders whether it should have taken place at all. The Prince's critics maintained that he was aware of the signing of the Treaty of Nijmegen a few hours before the battle. It is possible that William had received news of the Treaty, but in the confusion of the battle had put the packet in his pocket unopened. When the Prince and Marshal Luxembourg met after the Dutch-French war had been temporarily concluded, he said sarcastically: "The Prince of Orange shed bitter tears over the Peace. He might just as well shed a few for having made war so unluckily."[5] To Fagel, William always insisted: "I swear before God, that I have only today (15 August) learned of the Conclusion of Peace."

'The Sun King' was the victor of the six years' war, retaining twelve towns in the Spanish Netherlands and Franche-Comté where William of

Orange had lost his domain. Before returning to Mary at Honselaersdijck, William, fatigued and tense from the strain of battle, turned aside to go hunting at Dieren.

It was now that Mary told William joyfully that she was again with child. She had written to her "dear husban" (Mary's spelling in her early letters was very queer) "dearest Aurelia you may be very well assured that I have played the whore a littell I love you of all things in the world."[6]

It is strange that Mary should write in such a way, for she was now very much in love with William. Her health was never strong, because she suffered from feverish ailments and from sore eyes, perhaps occasioned by having to read and write aided only by candlelight. Her father James in England worried about her, warning William that she should not be allowed to stand too much. He fretted when the letters from Holland were delayed. It is interesting that Mary informed Frances Apsley of her hopes before she confided in her stepmother Mary Beatrice "who has always charged me to do it in all her letters". The Duchess of York always said that she loved the Princess of Orange as her own daughter.

At the end of August Laurence Hyde travelled to Holland again with a message from Charles II that his nephew had been too hasty in signing the treaty without Spain's adherence and without proper guarantees for their frontiers. William, well accustomed to the King's tergiversations as he was, could not, however, conceal his irritation from Sir William Temple, saying:

> Was ever anything so hot, and so cold, as this court of yours? Will the King, that is so often at sea, never learn a word that I shall never forget since my last passage, when in a great storm, the Captain was all night crying out to the man at the helm, steady, steady, steady? If this dispatch had come twenty days ago, it had changed the face of affairs in Christendom, and the war might have been carried on, till France had yielded to the Treaty of the Pyrenees, and left the world in quiet for the rest of our lives: as it comes now, it will have no effect at all. At least, this is my opinion, though I would not say so to Mr. Hide.

The summer of 1678 in England was famous, or rather infamous, for Titus Oates - one of the most debased scoundrels in history, who launched the so-called Popish Plot, a completely false accusation that there was an attempt on Charles II's life by Roman Catholics. Such was the fear and hatred of the Roman Catholics at this period that few people doubted its truth, except the Catholics themselves. Charles II never believed in the Popish Plot, having detected Oates telling a lie.

That October Mary Beatrice, anxious to see her stepdaughter, together with Mary's sister Anne, came over to The Hague with a retinue, and hasty preparations were made to entertain them at the Noordeinde Palace. The most important persons in the entourage were the Duchesses of Monmouth (Anna Scott), Richmond and Buckingham, and the Dutch-born Lady Ossory, without her husband, because he had been obliged to go to Ireland. So Mary of Modena was delighted to see her "dear Lemon" again and to visit parts of Holland. It was a success and the Duke of York wrote in a good humour to thank William for making that possible. Ossory had no doubt heard favourable reports about it and hastened to write to William. The Prince wrote to his friend:

You will easily be persuaded how joyful I was to learn that Madame (Mary Beatrice) is pleased with her journey. For my part I was also pleased with her, which is very impertinent for me to say.

The Duchess of York returned to a London seething with party hatreds and fury at the murder of a London magistrate, Sir Edmondbury Godfrey, on Primrose Hill. Even today Sir Edmondbury's death is something of a mystery. Unfortunately incriminating papers were uncovered among the correspondence of the Duke of York's secretary, Edward Coleman, letters of a treasonable nature, in which Coleman had corresponded with the Papal Secretary of State and with Louis XIV's confessor Père Lachaise. There is no doubt that Coleman wanted to root out the pestilent heresy that had reigned so long in these kingdoms, but there is no evidence that he was involved in any plot against Charles II's life. Coleman was executed during December 1678. Many innocent victims were arrested on the word of Titus Oates and his confederate Dr. Tonge, either to languish in gaol or to be judicially murdered, and the King was powerless to prevent the injustice.

From afar the Prince watched these events, well informed as ever, and aware that a clamour was arising in the House of Commons that his uncle James, as Charles's nearest heir to the throne, should be excluded from the succession. The Country Party, led by the Earl of Shaftesbury, wanted Charles II to divorce his barren Catholic wife Catherine of Braganza, marry a Protestant, and raise up children.

The Prince of Orange had reason to regret the fall from power of the able Lord Treasurer Danby, engineered by his enemy Ralph Montagu during December 1678. Danby had earlier worked hard for William and Mary's marriage, hoping that it would be the preliminary for a military alliance between England and Holland, but Charles was secretly negotiating another agreement with King Louis during the spring (1678).

King Charles had clearly seen the political advantages of the marriage,[7] but he wanted to spite his brother by imposing a brusque and ambitious son-in-law on him.[8] The King thought his brother foolish for his open advocacy of Roman Catholicism and sometimes stupid, but did not dislike him. It is most likely that the King wished to use the marriage as a means of persuading Louis to make peace, hoping that it would diffuse parliamentary opposition to the government's pro-French foreign policy. It in fact antagonized Louis. With the connivance of the King of France, Montagu published Danby's letter in which he had expressed in deliberately ambiguous words Charles's wishes. Danby was impeached in parliament and despite the King's attempt to save him, sent to the Tower to be imprisoned for several years. Earlier William had written to Ossory showing that he was sympathetic to Danby, but thought it was impolitic to invite him to Holland. As he told Ossory:

> My friendship has never been dependent on good or evil fortune, and I so hate ingratitude that it would be very hard for me to show it towards a person to whom I feel an obligation.[9]

Danby, later the Marquis of Carmarthen, was to play an important part in the early reign of William and Mary.

There is an account in Sir William Temple's works during January 1679, of the horrible journey he had to endure to Nijmegen for the signing of the peace treaty. Winter conditions were at their worst, for heavy snowfalls made the roads almost impenetrable, and the Rhine lay frozen and desolate. Several postboys died on the road and people were moving about with long icicles at the end of their noses.

Temple was shortly to be recalled to London, and he looked forward to retirement from active diplomacy, to take his ease in his beloved garden at Moor Park.

In late February 1679 everybody in Holland was looking forward to Mary giving birth to William's infant, but during April she experienced a sharp recurrence of fever, together with a terrible pain in her hip. William's enemies now maintained that the Prince of Orange had invented the pregnancy in order to disconcert his rivals, while Sophie of Hanover declared that at a large dinner party at The Hague one of the gentlemen was of the opinion that the Prince would never have any children. Jean Antoine Comte d'Avaux, the new French ambassador, wanting to make trouble for William, was prominent in spreading rumours that the Prince was keeping his wife as a prisoner at Honselaersdijck and that she was very lonely.

King Charles was aware that many influential people were opposed to James succeeding him as king, but he was determined to uphold the hereditary principle. He was always constant as to that. James's most dangerous enemy was Anthony Ashley Cooper Earl of Shaftesbury, a man of immense ability, whom Charles II had dismissed as Lord Chancellor in 1673. He held briefly the office of President of the Council (an office taking the place of the Privy Council), but six years later he was finally dismissed from office.

Shaftesbury now became the leader of the Country Party, opposed to the Court Party. He was a very skilled propagandist, virulently hostile both to the Duke of York and to the Catholics. Shaftesbury was certainly unaware of the secret clauses of the Treaty of Dover (1670) as a member of the Cabal government, and when informed of them he was angered by the deception. He was a staunch Protestant, although apt to use unscrupulous means to effect his ends. In the Lords, Shaftesbury raised a motion that the Duke be barred from all Councils and public affairs. Five days later the Commons voted an address to King Charles demanding that James withdraw himself from His Majesty's person.

Before exiling his brother beyond the seas, Charles considered there was a chance that James might be willing to return to the Church of England. For that purpose Sancroft Archbishop of Canterbury and the Bishop of Winchester were told to wait on the Duke. James listened courteously to the prelates' arguments and then admitted that he was incapable of arguing matters of such consequence with theological experts. He had not changed his religion lightly, but for reasons of deep conviction. It would be wrong for him to change again because of political expediency.

For Charles it was a relief to get rid of him for the present. On February 28, 1679 he told him:

> I have already given you my reasons at large why I think fit that you should absent from me for some time beyond the seas, as I am truly sorry for the occasion, so you may be sure I shall never desire it longer than it will be absolutely necessary both for your good and my service.[1]

James was forced to comply with his brother's wishes. On March 4, together with Mary Beatrice, who loyally followed her husband, they left to spend a few days at The Hague with William and Mary, and then made a further journey to Brussels, then in the Spanish Netherlands, where the Governor, the Duke of Villa Hermosa, found them accommodation.

It does not say much for the contemporary medical knowledge that the doctors were mistaken as to the Princess of Orange's pregnancy. It is possible that her symptoms had been delusive from the first. The disappointment of the Prince and Princess was all the more acute because Anne and William Bentinck's first child had been born in February and named after Mary. During April Mary was again ill with an intermittent fever and given a diet of senna and asses' milk. She felt well enough, however, to look on at the May Day Kermess (Carnival) from a window of the Stadtholder's quarter in the Binnenhof. It was a gay scene with the city militia marching through the streets to the sound of drums and trumpets, and the avenues of trees, sweet with their scent of lime flowers. Together with William in the woodland setting of Dieren she gradually recovered her spirits, though not free from fever until the summer.

From Brussels James wrote often to William about his fears for the Stuart monarchy. On May 14:

> You see how violently my enemies attack me, and that Wednesday last was the day that both Houses were to take into consideration my affairs. I cannot now but look on the monarchy itself in great danger, as well as his Majesty's person, and that not from Papists, but from the Commonwealth Party, and some of those who were lately brought into the Council, that govern the Duke of Monmouth, and who make a property of him to ruin our family, and things go on so fast and so violently, and there are so very few left about his Majesty that have either will or courage to give good advice to him, that I tremble to

think what will happen; for if his Majesty and the House of Lords stick to me, then one may expect great disorders, nay a rebellion.[2]

James Duke of Monmouth, the illegitimate son of Charles II and his earlier Welsh mistress Lucy Walter, was now about thirty, very handsome, charming and attractive to women. Unfortunately he had been pampered and very much spoilt by his father in boyhood, and there were clever men in Parliament like the Earl of Shaftesbury only too ready to make use of Monmouth as a tool. His character lacked stability and he was weak by nature. Yet he was often brave in battle and generous to those he defeated. When a revolt in Scotland broke out during the summer (1679), King Charles sent him north. Monmouth acquitted himself well, succeeded in crushing a revolt of the Scottish Covenanters at Bothwell Brig, and returned more than ever the popular hero. He was the peoples' Protestant duke, and Shaftesbury's Country Party began to name him the legitimate Prince of Wales. Monmouth was ill-advised enough to act as if he was Prince of Wales. His partisans claimed that a 'black box' contained evidence of Charles's marriage to Monmouth's mother. The matter caused the King such embarrassment that he was forced to swear that he had only been married to his Queen Catherine of Braganza. To his credit, despite the suggestions of several unprincipled courtiers, including the Duke of Buckingham, he would never allow himself to be divorced from his childless Queen Catherine. In Monmouth's boyhood Charles had very likely been tempted to make him legitimate, for he loved him better than any other of his illegitimate children.

On May 17, James wrote again to William from Brussels:

Nothing will satisfy the Presbyterians but the destroying of the monarchy and the setting up of a commonwealth to which purpose they flatter the Duke of Monmouth, as the only way to pass their ends and to destroy our family.[3]

During May 1679 Shaftesbury and the Whigs, introduced the first Exclusion Bill into Parliament. It proposed that if the King died without children, the crown was to pass to the next Protestant in line of succession to the throne. That was Mary, William's wife, but Shaftesbury held out to Monmouth the dazzling prospect of being a puppet king. Among those alarmed at the development of affairs was Charles's influential mistress Louise de Kéroualle Duchess of Portsmouth. When Shaftesbury threatened to cite her as 'a common whore' in Parliament - she was very far from that - she aligned herself with the powerful Shaftesbury, offering to use her influence with Charles II in favour of Exclusion. The King would probably have agreed to limit the power of a Catholic successor - to accept restrictions - but he firmly upheld his promise that James would not be excluded. The battle waxed and waned furiously in the kingdom, and Charles was obliged to dissolve the Parliament, refusing to concede to its demands. The extremists among the Exclusionists were not prepared to compromise. Among its supporters was Robert Spencer Earl of Sunderland, one of Charles's most able ministers, but an unscrupulous career politician. Even Nell Gwyn, the 'Protestant whore', supped with King Charles's enemies.

On the anniversary of Queen Elizabeth I's accession, November 17, 1679, Shaftesbury, a master of propaganda, organized a macabre, massive anti-Catholic march through the City of London, with the burning of the effigy of the Pope, the scenes representing 'The Popish Plot'.

Of the men surrounding Charles II, Halifax was probably the most brilliant and intelligent, determined to preserve the hereditary monarchy. He disliked party allegiance, and he was called 'The Trimmer' because he was independent of it. Although he did not much like the Duke of York, and certainly did not approve of his Roman Catholicism, he disliked Shaftesbury's Exclusion policy even more. He eventually saved James in the House of Lords.

It was Sunderland and Halifax who persuaded the King to send Henry Sidney as the new ambassador to the States of Holland. The Whigs championed Monmouth, but both Halifax and Sunderland wanted to bring forward the Prince of Orange as an impeccable Protestant and one who possessed through his wife legitimate right to the throne.

Henry Sidney was on the whole an excellent appointment, a handsome man of great charm and grace, though perhaps of no remarkable ability. Sidney was born in Paris, where his father Lord Leicester was ambassador. At the age of twenty-five he was a groom of the bedchamber in the household of the Duke of York and was deeply enamoured of James's first duchess Anne Hyde. Whether his love was requited is uncertain, but according to Sir John Reresby "She was kind to him, no more." The Duke of York notoriously unfaithful to her, held a grudge against Sidney for many years, and the courtier responded by voting for exclusion in the Parliament of 1679. Burnet described him in his *History*:

> as one who had lived long in the Court, where he had some adventures that became very public. He was a man of a sweet and caressing temper, had no malice in his heart, but too great a love of pleasure.

He was very much a ladies' man. Whilst ambassador in Holland from 1679 for two years, he became an intimate friend of Prince William of Orange.[4] Sylvius, who was a member of the Princess's household in The Hague, disliked William and called him boorish, but Sidney formed his own opinion of William.

He first visited William and Mary in Dieren, where he found him in very good humour and Mary much recovered, but about to take the cure at Aix. William was thinking of acquiring Titian's *Charles V* for three million livres, but after careful thought decided he could not afford the picture. He was very worried at this time by the illness from fever of Anne Bentinck. Utterly devoted to Bentinck, William wrote to him from Dieren, thoughtful as ever in his troubles:

> It is impossible to tell you with what pain I parted from you this morning, or how distressed I was at leaving you in such a state or what anxiety I am in at the moment. I could not live without you and if ever I felt I loved you, it is today. I beg you to come here as soon as your wife is out of danger.

Anne Bentinck was not out of danger for three weeks. Henry Sidney kept the Prince well informed about the Exclusion crisis. He begged William to go to England, saying "the monarchy was absolutely lost unless he recovered it". However, William felt it was a mistake for him to take sides in this momentous crisis: to favour it was to play into the hands of the Duke of Monmouth and to oppose it an interference as a foreigner in English affairs.

In August King Charles was at Windsor, aged forty-nine and considered almost old at that age. After a hard game of tennis he caught a bad chill walking by the Thames, and he was so ill that Mary feared he would die. At this juncture the more moderate politicians such as George Savile the Earl of Halifax, realizing the great danger by which the country was beset, sent an express to James in Brussels, urging the Duke of York to come over without delay. Disguised in a black perruque and a plain stuff suit, James left Brussels and on the following morning, August 30, he arrived at 7 a.m. in the King's bedchamber in Windsor Castle, where the brothers had an affectionate reunion. Now that he was recovering, Charles was still anxious to get James out of the kingdom, but the Duke of York wrote to William that he had more friends in England than he had supposed. Now that he was back in England he could surely stay there, but the King soon made it clear that he would agree to change James's place of exile, Brussels for Scotland, but James had to depart in three weeks.

At the same time, the King decided to banish the Duke of Monmouth from England, angered by his intimate relations with the Opposition leaders in the City and by his laying the foundations for the succession to the kingdom of Scotland after his successful campaign in Scotland and others factors. Within ten days of James's arrival in England, Monmouth was deprived of his rank as Lieutenant-General and ordered abroad.

Earlier in late June, James had written to the Prince of Orange:

> There is one thing troubles me very much, and puts odd things in my head, it is that all the while his Majesty has never said a word, nor gone about to make a good understanding between me and the Duke of Monmouth. Till he spoke to me himself at Windsor, five or six years ago, of his having a mind to be general, I never took anything ill of him, nor grew jealous of him.[5]

On September 6, James wrote to the Prince of Orange that Charles was recuperating from his illness, "and now, God be thanked, he has got so much strength that he walks into the Park". James thought that by being deprived of his command of General:

> would make the Duke of Monmouth more popular amongst the ill men, and seditious people will quite dash his foolish hopes that he so vainly pursued.

The Duke of York complained later to the Prince that Monmouth had kept very ill company in London. He was still, however, wildly popular among the masses. When James was entertained at a banquet at Merchant Taylors' Hall by the Artillery Company, a large hostile crowd collected in Cheapside as he returned to St. James's shouting, "A Pope, a Pope". His journey to Scotland from Brussels with his Duchess was very tedious and bleak, but he was given a very warm reception when he entered Edinburgh on horseback.

Meanwhile, Monmouth was banished to Holland with his father's blessing, but he arrived at The Hague unexpectedly. William was kind to Monmouth, offering him hospitality and taking him hunting. He may have been affected by Monmouth's charm, but he also took the opportunity of sizing him up. He could see for himself the shallowness of his intellect, and that he did not present much threat to himself. William listened while Charles's son prattled on about his own popularity, discussing his plans. The Prince told Monmouth that if he "thought of the Crown he could not be his friend in that, but in everything else he would".[6]

James, when he visited his nephew in The Hague, spoke bitterly about the Parliament, saying that the King would be better without any Parliament at all.[7] That caused the Prince much consternation, for without it, Charles would be dependent on Louis for subsidies again and the French King's influence over King Charles's foreign office would be paramount.

The late winter and spring of 1680 was an anxious time for the healths of both Mary and William. On March 18 Henry Sidney reported that Mary was unlikely to live and William wrote anxious letters to his father-in-law. Whilst she was recovering from a bout of severe influenza, members of her household complained that her recovery was being delayed by her husband's unkindness. We do not know what was wrong. Dr. Thomas Ken, later Bishop of Bath and Wells, had succeeded Dr. Hooper as her Chaplain and disliked the Prince as much as he was himself disliked by William. On one occasion Ken visited the English Ambassador Sidney to say that he was "horribly unsatisfied" and would speak to the Prince "though he kicks him out of doors".[8] One suspects, knowing Ken's frank character, that he *did* speak to William, though he was not kicked out of doors. It is very likely that the Prince was suffering from asthma at this time and his poor health made him abrupt, and querulous with Mary. Then he was ill at Breda during July, only to hear of the extremely sad news of the death of the Earl of Ossory at the age of forty-six. John Evelyn in his *Diary*, an intimate friend of Ossory's, gives a long account of his death.[9] He had given devoted service to Charles II and to his country, to be ill rewarded in the end. Ossory had been nominated as Governor and General of the forces in Tangier by the King and the Secretary of State, Lord Sunderland, seemingly an honour, but both King and minister had already decided to abandon Tangier, part of Catherine of Braganza's dowry. His appointment was for the purpose of adding a little lustre to the English withdrawal and to make Ossory shoulder the responsibility for it.[10]

Lord Ossory, according to Evelyn:

took very ill of Lord Sunderland, and not kindly to the King, when resolving to send him with an incompetent force, seem'd as his Lordship tooke it, to be willing to cast him away, not only in hazardous adventure, but in most men's opinion an impossibility ... This touch'd my Lord deeply, that he should be so little consider'd as to put him on a business in which he should probably not only loose his reputation, but be charged with all the miscarriage and ill successe. It certainly tooke so deepe roote in his minde that he who was the most void of feare in the world (and assur'd me he would go to Tangier with 10 men if his Ma^{tr} commanded him) could not beare up against this unkindness.

Ossory accompanied the King to a dinner of a Livery Company at Fishmongers Hall, but he was taken ill with a malignant fever and died on July 30. "Unhappy England in this illustrious person's loss", added Evelyn.

William was absolutely desolate and wrote to Emilia van Beverwaert, Ossory's widow:

> The loss you have suffered is so great that only God can give you consolation ... For my part it has so deeply touched me that I can assure you that no man in the world so much shares your fitting grief. I have lost one of the greatest friends that I had in the world, whose memory will always be as dear to me as his person was.

In a restless mood to distract his mind from his grief, William decided to travel abroad to stay with the Duke of Zell, to Brandenburg to call on relations and to visit other German princes on his homeward journey. In William's train was his friend Ouwerkerk, who had once saved his life, and his secretary, the younger Huygens. At Zell during September, he was most hospitably entertained by Duke George William of Brunswick-Luxemburg, a brother of Ernest Augustus Duke of Hanover. He had travelled much in Italy and presided over a very civilized Court, being a lover of the arts, and taking great pride in his orchestra. At Brandenburg William was entertained by his uncle the Elector, now crippled by gout. Then on to Hanover where the Prince arrived on October 29, to be the guest of Duke Ernest Augustus, a very different character from George William.

William got on well enough with the Elector's wife Sophia, a witty, clever woman, but Ernest Augustus was highly immoral with his *maîtresse en titre*, the odious Countess Platen, who later was to play an ignoble part in the murder of Konigsmark, the lover of Sophie Dorothea of Zell. The latter was the wife of the Elector of Hanover's oafish son George Louis, a future King of England, George I. William had little in common with him except for their interest in warfare. Travel in the late seventeenth century was very uncomfortable and full of hazards, with appalling roads and bad conditions in the towns and villages. On November 4 William at last reached his palace of Soesdijk to rejoin his wife Mary, bearing her a gift of ortolans. His travels in Germany had hardly been a holiday, for he never knew when the couriers would arrive with official papers.

In England the bitter intrigues and wrangles over the Exclusion Bill were some of the most important episodes in our history. The Exclusionists, those who opposed the Duke of York's succession to the throne, such as the Earls of Shaftesbury, Essex, and Lord William Russell, clashed with Laurence Hyde (York's brother-in-law), Lord Halifax and others. Later the Exclusionists, much to the anger of Charles II, were joined by the Earl of Sunderland, although Sir William Temple tried hard to dissuade Sunderland from voting, for he well knew that the King "must resent it."[11] By November 8, 1680 it was evident that Charles was determined to use the full weight of his influence to defeat the Exclusion Bill.

William followed events with deep interest in Holland. Though pressed by Sidney to go over to England, he wisely refrained from doing so, thinking that any untimely intervention on his part would only do his cause harm. He agreed with Charles that James's exclusion was "an unlawful and unjust thing" only designed to weaken the monarchy. On his part Sunderland used his influence in the Commons that a clause should be passed on November 8 that the Crown should go on the King's death as if James was legally dead to his eldest daughter the Princess of Orange.[12] Meanwhile Lady Sunderland wrote vehemently to her uncle Henry Sidney in Holland:

> If the Prince will not come, he must never think of anything here ...
> If there be nothing to fix on, 'tis certain that the Duke of Monmouth
> must be the King, and if the Prince thinks it not worth coming over
> a threshold for a kingdom, I know not why he should expect anybody
> should go for him.

Let us imagine the excitement as Lord William Russell, an avid Exclusionist, on the morning of November 15 carried the bill from the House of Commons to the Upper House. It was a triumph for the Whigs. Their jubilation soon turned to mixed fury and despair. The debate in the Lords, many of whom were opposed to exclusion, lasted from 11 in the morning until after 9 at night. It was Lord Halifax, one of the most gifted speakers and debaters in the Upper House pitted against Lord Shaftesbury, who succeeded by his mighty eloquence in winning the day. The Exclusion Bill was defeated. It is unfortunate that a record of the speech does not exist. The Bill was rejected by a majority of 63 to 30 votes. When Sunderland recorded his vote for exclusion later that night, Charles murmured to his neighbours: "The kiss of Judas."

At first James Duke of York felt grateful to Halifax for preserving his position as heir to the throne, but he never understood the nobleman or really trusted him. He had spoken and voted against Exclusion on November 15, but on the following day had acted inconsistently in proposing a scheme of severe limitations designed to diminish the power of a Roman Catholic monarch. This angered James, and seemed to him even more of a threat than to actually exclude him from the throne. Politically minded, William, when apprized of these proposals wrote to Sir Leoline Jenkins:

> I hope that his Majesty will not incline to suffer such a thing ... it must not be imagined that, if they had once taken away from the Crown such considerable prerogatives as are talked of, they would ever return again.[13]

King Charles regarded as intolerable interference a so-called plea of unity drawn up by the States-General in Holland advising him to accept the Exclusion Bill. They argued that it was necessary to prevent a civil war, so bitter was the feeling in the country. It was natural for Charles to think that his prerogative was under attack. Relations with Holland became strained again. His nephew William, his ambassador Sidney in Holland, and the States were strongly criticized by the King for attempting to interfere in English domestic affairs. William always maintained that he was against the Exclusion Bill.

Although Sunderland was not dismissed until late January 1681 from his high office as Secretary of State, the King had already dissolved Parliament on January 18 and decided to summon another one to meet at royalist Oxford in March. Halifax and Laurence Hyde had been clamouring for his dismissal for some time. In his great satirical poem *Absalom and Achitophel*, John Dryden eulogizes Lord Halifax for his courage during the Exclusion crisis. He is the Jotham of his poem:

> Jotham of piercing wit, and pregnant thought,
> Endowed by nature, and by learning taught
> To move assemblies, who but only tried
> The worse awhile, then chose the better side.
> Nor chose alone, but turned the balance too,
> So much the weight of one brave man can do.

The Duke of Monmouth during the years 1680-82 reached the peak of his popularity among the people, having made a triumphal progress through the west of England in July 1680. As Dryden wrote:

> Few words he said, but easy those and fit,
> More slow than Hybla-drops,* and far more sweet.

---

*Hybla-drops - honey from Hybla in Sicily.

Charles frowned on the popularity of his wayward son, but in his heart did not cease to love him. When the irascible old peer Viscount Stafford, a Papist, at a crowded trial in Westminster Hall, largely owing to the perjured evidence of Titus Oates, was condemned to death in December 1680, the King did little to help. He expressed displeasure, however, that Sunderland was among the peers who voted for the death penalty for Stafford, impeached of high treason. Yet the King stained his memory for ever by surrendering to the vengeance of the Whig Party a helpless, innocent old man. The Duke of York wrote to the Prince of Orange, expressing his sorrow:

> that his Majesty will be so hard put to it, for I hope he will remember the continual trouble it was to the King his father, the having consented to the death of the Earl of Strafford (1641), and not have such a burthen on his conscience.[14]

William wrote to Sir Leoline Jenkins on February 11, 1681 to say that he had been on a journey to Amsterdam (to see an Italian opera with Mary) when he heard of the dissolution of the Parliament, which had much surprised him. Jenkins had mentioned some proposal in his letter, apparently that of making the Princess of Orange regent during her father's life. It is likely that Mary at this time was more preoccupied with the sudden death in a carriage accident of her Javanese dwarf than in the possibility of becoming regent.

Note: The King, his father, condemned Lord Strafford to death.

IX   D'AVAUX AT THE HAGUE

During the summer of 1679 a new French ambassador Jean-Antoine de Mesmes, Comte d'Avaux, had been sent to The Hague by Louis XIV. He was an able diplomat as he proved at the Treaty of Nijmegen, persuasive, cunning and subtle. One has only to study his own account of his activities in Holland[1] to glimpse his intelligence. He was given careful instructions to oppose the Prince of Orange and to be discourteous to the Princess, strange instructions, perhaps, considering King Louis's well-known reputation for courtesy to members of the fairer sex.

One December evening (1680) the English ambassador Sidney reported to Sir Leoline Jenkins that d'Avaux had been deliberately discourteous to Princess Mary in her dressing-room while she was with her ladies playing basset. When asked by her whether he would join in the game of chance, he was silent:

> but, looking about, he saw a chair with arms in the corner, which he drew to himself and sate down. After he had sate a little while, he rose and went to the table to play. The Prince came in shortly after, and did also seat himself to play. The next day he (d'Avaux) told some of his friends that he was not to be wondered at, for he had positive orders from his master, that, whenever the Princess sate in a great arm chair, he should do so too, and that, if there were but one in the room, he should endeavour to take it from the Princess, and sit in it himself.

D'Avaux's works contain much material concerning the Prince and Princess's cordial relations with the Duke of Monmouth while he was in exile in The Hague.

What is known as the Zuylestein Affair is of small importance, but it did succeed for a time to sow disharmony in William's domestic happiness. Zuylestein, the Prince's cousin, had been seeking the hand in marriage of Elizabeth Pompe, a very pretty woman and a considerable heiress, but her relations were making difficulties over the marriage settlement, and William was unwilling to allow the marriage until these differences had been settled. Meanwhile Zuylestein had an affair with one of Princess

Mary's maids of honour, Jane Wroth, a woman of little character, but a flirt. She told Zuylestein that she was about to bear him a child. Mary had suspicions that her maid of honour was concealing the truth, so she sent for her, imploring Jane to speak the truth. Jane lied to her mistress, saying the rumours were false. Meanwhile she confided in the garrulous nurse Mrs. Langford, who advised Jane not to conceal the birth, while Mary and William were absent in Amsterdam (February 1681). It was Ken, Mary's chaplain, who officiated at the marriage rites, having persuaded the bridegroom most reluctantly to admit his paternity.[2]

William and Mary when they returned from Amsterdam were very angry, but eventually had to accept the marriage and henceforward treated Zuylestein and his wife with indulgence. It proved a most unhappy marriage and the repercussions were to increase William's distrust of his wife's household. It would have been better if he had now ordered her entire entourage to be dismissed and sent home, but he probably refrained, knowing how pained she would be. His grandfather Charles I had no such reservation when he ordered the dismissal of those attending his young bride Henrietta Maria. Mrs. Langford, who had been censured for her part in the affair, continued her trouble-making, saying that the marriage of the Prince and Princess was one in name only.

We hear for the first time that William took his wife with him on a visit to the Duke of Zell, to a hunting lodge at Hummeling in Northern Germany during the latter part of February. Making use of the opportunity, d'Avaux advised King Louis to take advantage of Dutch quarrels and divisions. Amsterdam was prepared to ask for the French King's protection and allow him to use their fleets against England, but Louis was not impressed by this offer.

In England, Charles with political skill had succeeded in outwitting his Parliament, consisting of a majority of Whigs at Oxford. He proposed to the Houses that his brother should be banished and that while he lived, William and Mary should be Regents. The Whigs refused to accept this plan and a week later Charles dissolved Parliament. He had now a three years' guarantee of French subsidies, and could afford to be free of his Parliaments. William's relations with his uncle had deteriorated in the summer of 1681 and he favoured a visit to England if the King agreed to it. According to d'Avaux, William departed for England on July 31, telling the States-General that the King of Great Britain wished to discuss with him affairs of significant importance.[3] William arrived at Margate on August 2 and left immediately for Windsor to see King Charles. When his uncle asked him his views on exclusion and limiting the powers of a king, William answered that he was opposed to both. He urged the King to recall his parliament, but Charles replied that a new parliament would be as impossible as the last one. The several interviews with the King were very unsatisfactory. What is interesting is that at one of the interviews the King confided to his nephew that his main resolve was to keep matters quiet while he lived. Then he made an astute prediction. If his brother was ever to reign, he would be thrown out of his kingdom within four years. He showed the Prince a special seal, telling him that any document sealed with it must be regarded as his real wishes.[4]

William was tactless to accept an invitation from the Lord Mayor and City of London as guest of honour when he knew that they were very much in sympathy with the Whigs and supporters of Monmouth. Much to the Prince's annoyance, the King insisted on him coming to Windsor. There, William tactlessly complained of the food and the wine, although an opponent Dr. Edward Seymour retaliated by pointing out that the wine served by the Prince on another occasion had been equally bad. His visit was hardly a success. He had talks with Halifax, also with Arthur Capel Earl of Essex and Lord William Russell, members of the Opposition. Most of those opposed to the Court were plotting in favour of the Duke of Monmouth. Otherwise the Prince found time for gambling, losing £3,000 at basset.

On his return to Holland, according to the Comte d'Avaux, William suggested the formation and association of European powers as laid down in the Treaties of Westphalia and Nijmegen.[5] William's ultimate greatness lay in his skill in diplomacy in uniting an association of powers to resist the might of France and to promote the balance of power in Europe. He was before his time in urging that all disputes between nations be referred to arbitration. If any states, whether members of the association or not, refused, the rest were to enforce obedience. These proposals were favourably received by most countries, with the exception of France. William's proposals remained an ideal, but he was passionately opposed to domination by a single power. D'Avaux did his best to disrupt the Prince's plans, dissuading the deputies of Groningen and at first those of Amsterdam, from entering the League.[6] D'Avaux continued to work unscrupulously against William's interests, having spies in the Prince's household and intriguing with his enemies, the Loevestein Party. There was a plot to persuade Louis to invade the Spanish Netherlands and justify the invasion by declaring that he had done so to restore the liberties of the Republic. An insurrection was planned to overthrow the Stadtholder (William of Orange), so that Louis could use the Dutch navy for an attack on England.[7] Louis did not succumb to the plan.

Among the Huguenot refugees in Holland was a Frenchman named Sardan, an enemy of King Louis. D'Avaux sought his extradition to France without success. In England the Dutch diplomats, van Citters (Dutch ambassador for fourteen years from 1680) and van Beuningen, were inquiring whether there was any hope My Lord the Duke of York would become Protestant. King Charles "raising his eyes to heaven said that he desired it from his heart, that he had tried and would try again."

By March 1682 Emperor Leopold, all the United Provinces and Sweden had signed William's Treaty of Association, while the Turks launched a massive attack on Hungary, and Count George Frederick Waldeck, the Prince's friend, fought on the Emperor's side against Turkey.

William did not favour a marriage between George Louis, the uncouth son of the Elector of Hanover, and the ill-fated Sophie Dorothea, his cousin, daughter of the Duke of Zell, but by September it was to come about. The Prince was much upset by King Louis's occupation of his province of Orange during the summer 1682, and told Waldeck he would avenge it:

> Here are acts of violence hitherto unheard of in times past and all because I do my duty and try to keep this country true to its real interests.

The inhabitants of Orange took refuge in Holland where William provided them with money and acted as their protector, well knowing that the occupation was a breach of the Treaty of Nijmegen. He wanted his Uncle Charles to make a strong protest to France, but the King made only a show of it, doing nothing effectual.

In the autumn, the appearance of Edmund Halley's comet caused much wonderment. The superstitious regarded it as a portent for good or evil, while the more sceptical, like the Prince, were amused by it. However van Citters his ambassador in London thought that important repercussions were expected from the comet because it appeared when all the constellations were together.

Henry Sidney had been relieved of his post as British ambassador at The Hague, much to the sorrow of the Prince of Orange. He was on bad terms with his brother Algernon, a Republican, who was later to be involved in the Rye House plot (1683). From England Sidney had written to the Prince (June 28, 1681), warning him that his enemies had done their best to sow suspicions in King Charles II's mind, making him "believe that Your Highness is of the party that is most against him." For almost twenty years Sidney had a mistress, Grace Worthley, but he eventually left her destitute. Sidney was succeeded as ambassador by Thomas Chudleigh, a man much disliked by William of Orange.

Among the delegates sent to Paris to argue with King Louis about the seizure of Orange was Antony Heinsius, Pensionary of Delft, a Dutchman reluctant to undertake the mission, because as a learned member of the Loevestein Party he was opposed to William's policies. Before leaving, Heinsius visited d'Avaux, who regarded him as a Francophile and "also honnête homme" charged with a disagreeable mission. D'Avaux relates, however, that Heinsius returned to Holland the enemy of France and "the friend of the Prince, and so we lost a man who is now Pensionary of Holland."[8]

By early 1683 Charles had triumphed over the Whigs, and their sinister leader the Earl of Shaftesbury, having heard of fresh warrants being prepared for his arrest, during November 1682 fled to Harwich where, with two companions, Robert Ferguson and Colonel Walcot, he found a ship ready to take him to exile in Amsterdam. Tormented thereafter by excruciating pain caused by stomach gout, Shaftesbury died on January 21, 1683 in Amsterdam.[9]

There remained the other great Whig lords, Lord William Russell, the Earl of Essex, the Republican Algernon Sidney, and the Duke of Monmouth himself, bent on insurrection. Opportunity loomed during March 1683. The most dangerous of the conspirators, including Colonel Rumbold, an old Cromwellian soldier, favoured the assassination of Charles II and the Duke of York. Colonel Rumbold lived much at Rye House, a secluded farmhouse near Hoddesdon in Hertfordshire. Charles was at Newmarket where:

> he went a-hawking in the mornings, to cock matches or foot races in the afternoons (if there were no horse races), and to plays in the evening acted by very ordinary Bartholomew Fair comedians.[10]

Charles and his brother (back from exile) planned to return to London in the spring. The route in their coach lay near the Rye House where the royal brothers were to be assassinated and Monmouth proclaimed King.

Owing to a great fire, which devastated Newmarket on March 23, the King and York returned to London prematurely four days later and the machinations of the conspirators were thwarted, though they tried to turn informers. Lord William Russell, a nobleman deeply respected and loved by his friends, was tried for treason at the Old Bailey on July 13, 1683, and condemned to death; Arthur Capel Earl of Essex committed suicide in the Tower by cutting his throat with a razor. Algernon Sidney, possessing a kind of rugged independence of character, was sentenced to death on November 26 and executed on Tower Hill on December 7. The Duke of York described him "as dying very resolutely, and like a true rebel and republican" in a letter to his nephew William. Many of the lesser conspirators fled to the United Provinces, settling in Friesland and

Groningen, or in Amsterdam where William was accused of aiding and abetting them.

On November 27, the Duke of York wrote a long account from London of Monmouth's involvement in the Rye House Plot to the Prince of Orange:

> The Duke of Monmouth on Saturday last came and delivered himself up to the secretary, and desired he might speak with the King and myself alone, ... he went down to the secretary, taking me along with him, where the Duke of Monmouth after begging his Majesty's pardon in the humblest manner imaginable and owned his knowledge of the whole conspiracy, except that part of the assassination, asked pardon of me also, ... with all the promises of his good behaviour for the future, a man could say. His Majesty ordered the secretary to put him into the custody of a serjeant at arms, till further pleasure; the next day his Majesty ordered his release, and has ordered his pardon to be prepared ... and permits him to be at Court again.

By December 7 King Charles had hardened himself against his favourite son. The Duke of York wrote to William:

> I believe you will be as much surprized with the news of the Duke of Monmouth's being ordered to go out of Whitehall, and not to appear in his Majesty's presence as you were at his coming in, and being permitted to stay at Court ... being very much displeased with his not owning by a letter or paper under his hand, his knowledge of the conspiracy, as he had done it by word of mouth to his Majesty and myself.

One summer day as King Charles was setting his watch by the sundial in the Privy Garden in Whitehall, he ordered his favourite in his last years, Lord Thomas Bruce (later the Earl of Ailesbury), to go to Toddington in Bedfordshire where Monmouth lay in hiding and arrest him. Toddington Manor belonged to Lady Philadelphia, mother of Monmouth's beautiful mistress Lady Henrietta Wentworth. Lord Thomas Bruce, aware of the King's love for his son, excused himself on various grounds and Charles was always grateful to him for his forbearance and understanding.[11] On October 13 Monmouth came secretly to London where the Marquis of Halifax, perhaps now the most powerful politician at Court, acted as Monmouth's intermediary in his correspondence with his father. In one letter he protested his horror of being suspected of the notion that he was a party to the conspiracy of assassinating the King or the Duke of York. Although Halifax considered King Charles's love for his son 'extravagant', he played a vital part in negotiations. If Monmouth had accepted the wise advice of Lord Halifax and acted more prudently, he might yet have saved himself from being implicated in further insurrections.

About the beginning of 1684 he embarked at Greenwich in a fisher-boat and travelled to Antwerp and Brussels. In Brussels he was joined by Lady Henrietta Wentworth and they lived together as if they were married. The Governor of the Spanish Netherlands, the Marquis de Castanaga, had a hot temper and when informed by Sir Richard Bulstrode, Charles II's resident in Brussels, that Henrietta was Monmouth's mistress and not his wife, he reproached him bitterly for deceiving him. The Duke soon moved on to Holland.

Both the Prince and Princess of Orange received many angry letters from the King and the Duke of York, complaining that they were seeing the Duke of Monmouth. From Windsor her father wrote to the Princess of Orange on June 6 (1684):

> I wrote to you upon the subject of Lord Brandon (he had escaped to Holland after being implicated in the Rye House plot), and I easily believe that you might have forgotten for what he had been in the Tower, yet others could not be ignorant of it, nor have so short memories; and I must need tell you, it scandalises all loyal and monarchical people hereto know how well the Prince lives with, and how civil he is to the Duke of Monmouth, and Lord Brandon, and it heartens exceedingly the factious party here, which are a sort of people that one would think the Prince should not show any countenance to, and in this affair methinks you might talk with the Prince (though you meddle in no others), the Duke of Monmouth, Lord Brandon and the rest of that party, being declared my mortal enemies. And let the Prince flatter himself as he pleases, the Duke of Monmouth will do his part, to have a push with him for the crown, if he, the Duke of Monmouth, outlive the King and me.[12]

According to a contemporary, Sir John Reresby, writing after Charles II's death, the King had shown great clemency in pardoning and reprieving Charles Gerard Viscount Brandon after being condemned for breaking a boy's neck when he was drunk.

None of King Charles's letters were signed with the special seal that he had instructed William represented his real wishes. That surely explains William's friendly relations with Monmouth during 1684, and he was well aware of his uncle's love of his illegitimate son. According to d'Avaux, Monmouth was often the Prince's guest on hunting expeditions at Dieren. Officially Charles's letters were furious, and van Citters, Dutch ambassador in London, implored the Prince to pacify him. William wrote to his uncle:

> Also I owe it to him (Monmouth) to testify that, during all the time I have been with him, he has always spoken of Your Majesty with respect and veneration, and has appeared as zealous for your service as any of your servants can be.[13]

In his discussions with van Citters, King Charles asked:

> how His Highness (William) could believe that he had acted only with the best intentions, when it is evident that without communicating with me, and despite his prohibition, he had acted entirely according to his own whims.[14]

William's relations with Thomas Chudleigh, the English ambassador, were very bad. D'Avaux related that on one occasion the Prince struck Chudleigh with his stick on the nose,[15] but he does not mention that William had been provoked to behave in such a fashion. Another most disagreeable encounter occurred between the Prince and Chudleigh. William together with Mary was driving his traineau along the Lange Voorhout one day, when snow was falling, during the first week in January (1685). Driving furiously, Chudleigh confronted the irate Prince of Orange with his horsewhip in his hand. He was tempted to strike the insolent ambassador, but just refrained from doing so. Instead, he used harsh language on telling Chudleigh exactly what he thought of him. William had already complained of Chudleigh to King Charles, and he was soon recalled to England.

On the evening of January 9, 1685 Monmouth returned to The Hague. He had paid a secret visit to England, and while there he saw his father, who had assured him of his good will. D'Avaux relates that the nobleman was given the same freedom as was given Bentinck (Benting) of entering the chamber of the Prince of Orange at any time. Monmouth told his story to Bentinck, who took him immediately to the apartments of the Prince. After listening to him attentively, William escorted him to the apartments of the Princess, who was about to go to bed, the hour being late. William, however, insisted on his wife dressing again and coming to talk with Monmouth and treat him as an honoured guest. He invited

Monmouth to stay at the Mauritshuis Palace, supplied him with plenty of servants and made much of him.

That winter at The Hague was especially gay, with many balls and a profusion of parties. The Prince and Princess set the tone for fashionable society to compete in their entertainment of the fascinating nobleman. For Mary, Monmouth always held romantic interest. Every day after dinner William encouraged Monmouth to visit Mary to teach her country dances. Often they would walk together along the frozen avenues of the Lange Voorhout, although she usually never walked in public. What surprised d'Avaux was the attitude of the Prince of Orange. How could he stomach the gallantry of the Duke and the open flirting with his wife, "for he was the most jealous of men" (*le plus jaloux du monde*), hardly permitting any man or woman to visit his princess. This was untrue. William encouraged Monmouth's gallantries because he was well aware of his liaison with the Lady Henrietta Wentworth, the love of his life, whom he regarded as his real wife in the eyes of God, despite his legal marriage to Anne Scott.

D'Avaux, censorious and mocking, wrote:

> They even made her behave in a manner unbecoming in a princess and which I should call ridiculous in an ordinary woman, for in the great frosts (*gelées*) of this year the Prince of Orange obliged her, through the great complaisance she has for him, to learn to skate on the ice (*aller en patins*) since M. de Monmouth also wished to learn. It was a most extraordinary thing to see the Princess with very short skirts (*avec des jupes fort courtes*) and those tucked half-way to her waist, and wore skates on her feet, learning to skate now on one foot and now on the other.[16]

Thus she clung to Monmouth. Though she was evidently attracted to the Duke, there was only one man she ever loved in her life, William of Orange.

To disparage the Princess, d'Avaux would resort to any device. Each year Mary, like the mother-in-law whom she had never known, would celebrate January 30, the martyrdom of her grandfather Charles I.[17] She was seated in her apartments wearing black when William entered, and after making Mary change her clothes, insisted on her accompanying him to the theatre where he went, perhaps, four times a year. No doubt Mary could not resist bursting into tears, but she would always obey her husband.

The marriage of a Protestant Prince, the tall, blond George of Denmark, younger brother of the King of Denmark, to the Princess Anne, William's sister-in-law, was popular in England because of his protestantism. They married on July 28, 1683. William, however, was opposed to the union and would have preferred the German Prince George, son of the Electress Sophie Louisa of Hanover. Anne never forgave George, for on his visit to England he had behaved churlishly, seeming to neglect her. Henceforward she showed a marked distaste for Hanover.

X   TROUBLED RELATIONSHIPS

During February 1685 there arrived in The Hague the momentous and sad news that Charles II had died in Whitehall, not yet aged fifty-five, though considered old in the late seventeenth century. On his deathbed the King, who had by temperament never been religious, was converted to the Roman Catholic religion by Father John Huddlestone. Considering the drama and unrest of the previous years, James II ascended his brother's throne very peaceably. Making the excuse that he had little time, he sent a terse note to William apprizing him of his uncle's death. On hearing the news, William asked Mary to come to his apartments. She had not seen her uncle Charles since becoming her husband's child wife in November 1677, but her emotional nature made her desolate. The Prince saw Monmouth for two hours from 10 till midnight. While the King lived there was a chance of returning to Court and again being received in favour, but with his uncle's succession to the throne Monmouth realized that James II continued to bear him rancour and indeed hated him. Nor could he remain at The Hague. In his talk with the Prince, William gave him wise advice. He suggested that the fugitive should go to Vienna and offer his services to the Emperor. Meanwhile William offered him financial help for his immediate needs. If only Monmouth had heeded William's counsel.

At first King James pursued a conciliatory policy towards Holland, telling the Dutch ambassadors who came over in March to congratulate him that he favoured a continuance of all the existing alliances. He was much relieved that he had succeeded peaceably to his kingdom. With France, James wanted to take a more independent line, thinking that his brother had been too subservient to Louis. James wrote to William in his autocratic way asking him to keep the English exiles in check. He suspected that William was in touch with Monmouth and was aware of his movements. William, however, wrote to Lawrence Hyde, James's brother-in-law:

I can assure you as a man of honour that I have not known and still do not know whether the Duke of Monmouth is in Holland. It is true that there are rumours that he has been wandering between

Rotterdam and Amsterdam and even that he had been at The Hague.[1]

For a time Monmouth resided in Brussels, half tempted to live a life of retirement in Sweden with his beloved mistress Lady Henrietta Wentworth. Both William and Mary had warned Monmouth above all not to engage in further acts of rebellion, but he was weak-minded, constantly under the influence of the Whig exiles, Lord Grey of Werke, Ferguson and Rumsey. There was Lady Henrietta with her deep affinity with the Duke, a much stronger character, continually urging him to action with her belief in predestination, and that her man was the chosen Protestant champion, whose duty was to deliver England from what was likely to be the arbitrary rule of King James. How could he resist her pleas and those of the rebels?

It was the fiery, impetuous little Scotsman Archibald Campbell Earl of Argyle, who was the first to act. His expedition to Scotland ended in failure, for he was defeated and executed. England's ambassador in Holland was now an unfortunate choice, Sir Bevil Skelton, formerly an army man as much disliked by Prince William as Chudleigh and even more stupid. If he had taken the trouble to acquire the correct procedure for preventing both Argyle's and Monmouth's expeditions, he would have served a useful purpose.

There is no possible reason to believe that William encouraged Monmouth as a rebel to embark on his disastrous expedition to England. The last thing the Prince wanted was Monmouth's success, for he required King James as an ally and wanted to prevent any breach with his uncle. He hastened when requested by the King to send the Scottish regiments in the service of the States, although the deputies of Amsterdam did their best to prevent their departure. William's enemies, the Loevesteiners, backed the rebels, reluctant as they were to accept an agreement between William and James.

The Duke of Monmouth's expedition consisting of eight-three men in three ships, landed at Lyme on the borders of Dorset and Devon on Tuesday, June 11. His treasonable declaration read by Robert Ferguson at the market-place described King James as a usurper who had poisoned his brother, a murderer who had caused the death of the Earl of Essex and Sir Edmondbury Godfrey, and other accusations such as depriving Protestants of their freedom. As the Protestant Duke's army advanced through parts of Somerset, Taunton, Bridgewater and Chedzoy, it swelled to several thousands, but hardly any men of gentle birth joined his ranks. At Taunton Monmouth had himself proclaimed King.

On hearing of Monmouth's landing, William felt deeply uneasy. He immediately sent Bentinck to England, where he offered King James the

Frederick Henry, Prince of Orange and Amalia of Solms-Braunfeldt, grandfather and grandmother of William III by Gerard van Honthorst, 1637

William II, Prince of Orange and father of William III by Gerard van Honthorst

William of Orange aged sixteen, 'Child of State' by Abraham Ragneneau

Mary, Princess of Orange by A. Hanneman

Prince William of Orange aged twenty-seven by unknown artist

Hampton Court Palace. Façade designed by Sir Christopher Wren

Queen Mary II by Sir Peter Lely

King William III about 1690, the period of the Battle of the Boyne

services of the English regiments in Holland. If his presence was required, William would himself come over. King James believed that Monmouth's and Argyle's rebellions had been encouraged by France. William followed events in England with keen anxiety and was greatly relieved when Monmouth's forces, outnumbering those of Lord Feversham and Lord Churchill, were defeated at Sedgemoor (July 1685).

He was brought to Whitehall, a desperate fugitive, having been discovered lying in a ditch of brambles on the estate of Lord Shaftesbury. During his interview with the King, his nephew pleaded that he would spare his life, saying: "I am your brother's son, and if you take my life, it is your blood that you shed." Far wiser, though Monmouth had committed grave treasonable offences, if James had ordered his nephew to be imprisoned for life in the Tower rather than have him executed. With the removal of Monmouth, William of Orange presented a far more formidable danger for James, as candidate to succeed him, being fully acceptable to the Whigs.[2] William's object as Prince of Orange, however, was to detach Britain from France, and to be able to have her resources at his disposal in his war with Louis XIV. Nor did his Princess, though she remained heiress presumptive, ever want to be Queen of England. She was on the whole happy in Holland.

Bishop Gilbert Burnet was for a long time *persona grata* at Charles's Court, so intimate with both King and Duke that he was able to show his disapproval of their private lives.[3] His estimate of the Duke of York in the earlier years is fair enough:

> The Duke would pass for an extraordinary civil and sweet tempered man if the King were not much above him in it, who is more naturally and universally civil than the Duke. He has not the King's quickness, but that is made up by great application and industry, insomuch that he keeps a journal of all that passes of which he showed me a great deal... He has naturally a candour and justice in his temper very great and is a firm friend but a heavy enemy and will keep things long in his mind and wait for a fitting opportunity. He has a strange notion of government, that everything is to be carried in a high way and that no regard is to be had to the pleasing the people, and he has an ill opinion of any that proposes soft methods and thinks that is popularity; but at the same time he always talks of law and justice.

Though certainly anti-Catholic at the time of the Popish plot, Burnet courageously protested at their persecution. During 1684 he incurred the hostility of King Charles and the Duke of York, and yet was permitted to go abroad. He travelled widely, visiting Rome, Geneva, Paris, Strasbourg, Heidelberg, Frankfurt and Utrecht. In 1686 Burnet was invited by William of Orange to visit his Court at The Hague and there he remained for some time. As a historian his two most celebrated works are *History of the Reformation* and *History of His Own Time*. At The Hague he became Princess Mary's greatest admirer. For him she was perfect and could do no wrong. In his own writings Gilbert Burnet is sometimes prejudiced, criticizing Archbishop Sancroft adversely and also Sir William Temple, as already related. He later knew Prince William intimately, finding him cold and aloof at first, but gradually warming to him. He soon learnt that "the depression of France was his ruling passion".

Some time during the summer of 1685 when Monmouth had departed on his ill-fated rebellion to England, William bought an ancient and dilapidated castle in a wonderful woodland district of Apeldoorn in Gelderland. The Princess laid the foundation of the Palace that was to take nine years to build. Het Loo was to become a favourite home for both William and Mary, not far from Dieren, a countryside teeming with deer, wild boar, woodcock and pheasants and even a few wolves.[4] There William could entertain important visitors. The gardens with their exquisite fountains where jets of water spouted, contained walks where Mary and her ladies wandered. Het Loo's architect was a Dutchman Jacob Roman, while Daniel Marot, a French Huguenot designer and architect, had a strong influence in its building, providing various decorative touches.

Princess Mary always maintained that the eleven years she passed in Holland were happy. She liked the Dutch people and they in their turn admired her immensely, loving her for her charitable nature. She was happier in Holland than she would have been in the feverish gaiety of Whitehall during her uncle Charles's reign, for she had simple tastes, walking every day, taking eager interest in the gardens of her palaces, interested in pictures like the Prince and skilled in embroidery and needlework. Far from being deprived of her freedom, Mary was more free than she ever was in England.

Naturally there was friction in her married life, periods when she found William difficult, wont as he was to leave her on his business affairs or when fighting the French. Sometimes when desperately worried or ill, he was impossible to live with. Yet he had learnt to love her. Burnet relates in *History of His Own Time* that William "had only one vice in which he was very careful and secret". He was a very discreet man. The Bishop is referring to the Prince's mistress Elizabeth Villiers. Some historians have assumed that the Bishop was alluding to William's alleged homosexuality, but there was little evidence of it. He certainly liked the society of handsome young men, including a page who accompanied him to

England, Arnold Joost Van Keppel, a great favourite in England in his later age. He came from Laag Keppel near Doesburg. Nearby lay the battlefield where Sir Philip Sidney received his fatal wound near Zutphen, an ancient town. All we can say with certainty is that William had homosexual tendencies.

According to the moral standards of his own age, William was far from licentious. Elizabeth Villiers, the elder sister of Anne Bentinck, is a somewhat mysterious personality, never a grand passion for William. He liked women of character and clever conversation, admiring her brain rather than her body. What most appealed to him was her wit, for she was one of the wittiest women of her time. George Villiers First Duke of Buckingham was her great-uncle, James I's most important favourite, "his Steenie". Elizabeth was about seven years older than Mary, though we do not know the date of her birth, and she died in 1733 over thirty years after William II. Lely and Kneller both painted her. Lely reveals in his portrait that her only beautiful features were her white and well-shaped neck and shoulders. Jonathan Swift, who knew her well in her later life, relates that "she squinted like a dragon". She had a muddy complexion and crooked figure. Writing of Elizabeth in her later life as the wife of another man, Swift remarked: "She is perfectly kind, like a mother."[5] This quality may well have appealed to William, who needed an older woman to confide in. The affair was conducted in secrecy and neither Henry Sidney nor d'Avaux make any mention of it in their Diaries. Exactly when Elizabeth Villiers became William's mistress is unknown, though probably within three years of his marriage. Elizabeth had another lover named Wanchope, but the Prince managed to get rid of him abroad. It is not known whether Elizabeth cared for William or not. She was certainly no Madame de Pompadour or Lady Castlemaine.

Princess Mary, very jealous of her husband's secret relationship with the lady, first learnt of it by means of the malicious gossip of Mrs. Langford, Anne Trelawny and Dr. Covell, who had succeeded Dr. Ken as her Chaplain. They acted as agents at the Prince's Court, seeking to stir up trouble, much desired by Mary's father in England, now King, bent on making strife between her and William. James was now openly hostile to his son-in-law, having different opinions on political matters.

Matters were brought to a head when Mary one night during the autumn of 1685, when she and her husband were at the Binnenhof, after pretending to go to bed, rose again. Much agitated she went to the back staircase leading to the apartments of the maids of honour.[6] After what seemed an interminable time William appeared - it was 2 a.m. Mary tearfully reproached him for his infidelity, and there was a heated scene. It was customary for William to come to Mary's bed every night, but for several nights William let her sleep alone.

For some time he had been convinced that Dr. Covell, whom he had at first trusted, had been a secret spy in his household, reporting to the English ambassador Sir Bevil Skelton all sorts of harmful stories of what was occurring at Court. And it transpired that these accounts of William's intrigue with Elizabeth Villiers were at once sent to King James in London.

William Bentinck took Princess Mary's side in the affair, and always frank in his dealings with his master, told him of his disapproval. Bentinck wrote to Henry Sidney on October 22 from Dieren:

> You will be extremely surprised to learn of the changes that have taken place in our Court. His Highness accidentally had a letter, which showed that Dr. Covell had for a long time been a malicious spy in the household, injuriously reporting many concocted stories; thereupon her Royal Highness had him dismissed, without giving him any other punishment because of his cloth.

Mary had discovered that Mrs. Langford and Miss Trelawney were in league with Covell, so the Princess also dismissed them. Bentinck added:

> It is a horrid thing that people can be wicked enough to injure those to whom they owe their bread, but much worse that ministers should be capable of it.

The Prince of Orange wrote to Lawrence Hyde, now Earl of Rochester and a man of power in Whitehall, telling of his disillusion concerning Covell:

> You will doubtless be surprised that a man of this profession can be so great a knave. I own that I have been greatly deceived in this man ... and have always treated him very civilly, about which he publicly boasted in order the better to deceive me.

William now pressed that Sir Bevil Skelton should be removed from his post by King James, but for the present the King obstinately allowed him to remain at The Hague. Charles II would have probably dismissed him.

The Princess insisted that Elizabeth Villiers should be sent home, but she soon returned to Holland and her association with the Prince continued intermittently. It is evident that William was entirely reconciled with Mary. He swore to her in his solemn way that the affair had been "only an amusement". It made no difference to his love for her. It is very much to William's and Elizabeth's credit that they behaved with such discretion. William, by this time, realized his wife's worth, but he was too reserved in his expressions of love to her.

Dr. Burnet in his writings almost seems to be in love with Princess Mary. "There was," he wrote, "a sweetness in her deportment that charmed and an exactness in piety that made her a pattern to all that saw her." She was "the best wife that ever was and the most wonderful person that I ever knew."[7] He clearly saw William's faults, "his disobliging manners", and that he was unfaithful to his wife. To Burnet, William was "the closest man in the world"and liable to dry silences where Mary was garrulous.[8] William was slow to warm to Burnet, but in England he became almost intimate with this large florid man.

The Bishop was of a calculating nature. He thought that since no male children had survived of James's marriage with his Italian-born Queen Mary of Modena it was likely that Mary as his eldest daughter might succeed him on the throne. James in 1686 was about fifty-four. Knowing William as Burnet did, he was certain that he, with his ripe military reputation and mature experience as a Dutch statesman, would never be content that his wife would wield the real authority as Queen, while he remained a mere Prince Consort. One day, late in that year, Burnet took the opportunity of a long talk with the Princess while the Prince was on a hunting expedition. If she was to become Queen, it was possible for her to surrender the real authority to her husband. Philip II of Spain, when he married Mary Tudor I in 1554, had merely been King Consort. It was an interesting precedent.[9] She was inexperienced in politics, though she now took more interest in the duties of a queen if that was to come about.

"I did not know," she told Burnet:

the laws of England were so contrary to the laws of God. I don't think that the husband should ever be obedient to the wife.

When William had returned from hunting, Mary assured him that he would always bear rule. She only required of him one thing that he would be willing to obey, the command of "Husbands, love your Wives." Burnet had told her:

that such an attitude would please the Prince and mend their marriage, laying the foundation of a perfect union between them, which of late had been a little embroiled.

William was delighted by Mary's submissive attitude, saying to various people about the Court, that although he had been married to the Princess for nine years, he had never discussed the matter with her. In relinquishing her royal prerogative, Mary hoped to wean her husband from his adulterous relationship with Elizabeth Villiers by offering him the crown.[10]

XI   PRELUDE TO REVOLUTION

One of James II's main defects was that he was a very poor politician, and an even worse judge of character. He failed altogether to understand the views of those with whom he disagreed. Unable to grasp the strength of feeling of most of his contemporaries to anti-Catholicism, he committed many blunders, making it impossible for his plans to succeed. Yet James had been misunderstood both in his own age and subsequently. He was not the villain described by Macaulay and later Whig historians.[1] He did not aim to establish Catholicism as the sole religion of the country, nor to get rid of Protestantism by force. His main aim was to establish the rights of English Catholics to worship without persecution and to take full part in the political life of the country. For this purpose he wanted the repealing of the Corporation Act (1661) and the Test Acts of 1673 and later. The main purpose of the Test Acts was to make it illegal for anybody to hold a post, civil or military, or vote in Parliament, unless he took Communion as a member of the Church of England and swore an oath denying 'transubstantiation'. He tried to persuade his nephew the Prince of Orange to agree to the repeal of the Test Acts, but William objected to it not from reasons of intolerance, but because most Englishmen were strongly opposed to it. Without the consent of Parliament such a repeal was clearly illegal.

Whether or not James sought to become an absolutist monarch will always remain controversial, but the important thing is that most of his subjects believed that was his intention. Two reasons for James II's failure were his gross lack of tact and that he wanted to proceed too hastily.[2]

James wanted to raise the standing army from 5,000 to 15,000, but the Whigs and his other enemies feared that the King's purpose was to use this army to persecute English Protestants. Renewed fears were raised when Louis XIV decided to repeal the Edict of Nantes in October 1685 and to persecute French Huguenots. Numerous refugees fled to England and Holland.

In Ireland the Catholic Richard Talbot Earl of Tyrconnell replaced the Protestant Earl of Clarendon (the King's brother-in-law) as Lord-Deputy of Ireland in 1687, and pursued a policy of ridding the army of Protestants with some success.[3] Similarly he favoured a policy of Roman

Catholicism in the Irish administration. James's plans and hopes for Ireland were no doubt misunderstood in England, for the English feared that his plans represented a policy of Catholic-inspired regression. Where southern Ireland differed from England was that the majority of people were Catholics. One terrible blunder of the King was to bring Irish troops into England, lending a pretext to his enemies in claiming that he intended to terrorize England with them.

Mass conversions of Englishmen to Catholicism were a total failure, though Sunderland, now back in power, gained favour late in James's short reign by becoming a Roman Catholic. It certainly pleased the Queen, but Sunderland's conversion was not genuine.

The King thought that there existed a chance that his daughter Mary might become a Catholic. He wrote to her on November 4, 1687 telling her that he himself had been educated in the Anglican Church according to his father's instructions, but further study had convinced him that the Catholics had been much maligned by the Protestants. He had studied their arguments for the infallibility of their church and to deny them was to destroy the whole foundations of Christianity.

Mary was very religious and refuted her father's arguments with deep logic. She had read widely books about the Reformation. She believed that the infallibility of the Catholic Church had never been proved. "One does not need to read much history," she wrote, "to find out that not all the Popes have been guided by the Holy Spirit. Must they still be considered successors of St. Peter, when their lives contrasted so blatantly with his doctrine?" His younger daughter Anne with her belief in the Anglican faith and natural stubbornness was no easier to convert.

In England James enjoyed a strange friendship with William Penn the Quaker, son of Admiral Penn, James's shipmate during the naval campaign of 1665. Liberty of conscience was Penn's passion. When the King claimed a tolerant spirit, Penn was immediately attracted to him though most of his subjects thought him bigoted. In November 1686 James sent to The Hague on a special mission, his Quaker friend Penn. He was instructed to endeavour to induce William and Mary to declare publicly in favour of the repeal of the penal laws and the Test Act. He had long conversations both with the Prince of Orange and with Bishop Burnet, who described Penn as "a talking vain man", much in James's favour.[4] He had such a high opinion of his powers of persuasion that none could withstand them. Burnet refers to his tedious, loquacious way of speaking to tempt William to acquiesce in this policy. James agreed to join in the coalition against France. The mission failed because despite William's tolerance for religious beliefs, he was deterred from accepting such an alliance because he knew well such a declaration would prevent him claiming the leadership of the English

Protestants. He was very much opposed to giving the Test Acts up, arguing that it would betray the security of the Protestant religion. Mary suspected that Penn was a concealed Papist (there was no justification for this), certain that he was much with Father Petre (James's sinister Jesuit adviser) and with the Earl of Sunderland. What probably weighed most with the Prince was that the repealing of the Test Acts needed the consent of Parliament and that was not forthcoming.

In September 1686, Bevil Skelton had been succeeded as English ambassador by Sir Ignatius White, Marquis d'Albeville (in the Roman Empire), who came of a family of Irish adventurers.[5] A Roman Catholic, d'Albeville was among James's harmful appointments, said to be acting in the interests of the Jesuits in Whitehall. D'Albeville was instructed to seek a personal interview with the Prince. He was to argue that the Test Act was a restraint on the royal prerogative, but once repealed it would be to the advantage of William and Mary. He said that his master had been influenced to repeal the penal laws from the knowledge he had acquired of the benefits gained by the United Provinces by their policy of religious toleration. D'Albeville failed, like Penn, to convince William and he wrote an uncompromising reply to his father-in-law. James became deeply incensed with William and their relations worsened. On April 4, 1687 after proroguing Parliament, James issued his first Declaration of Indulgence, granting freedom of worship to all Dissenters, Roman Catholics and Protestants.

During February 1687 William sent his trusted friend Dijkvelt on a special mission to England. It was to last four months. William intended to argue decently but firmly with the King about the methods he was pursuing both at home and abroad. He was afraid that James might tamper with the succession and wanted to ensure in due course that Princess Mary should come to the throne. The Prince had no thought of usurpation at this time. As might be expected Dijkvelt made no impression on the King who was convinced of the justice and expediency of his policy. He *did*, however, assure Dijkvelt that he had no intention to tamper with the succession. There were many rumours, but such an intention was contrary to justice and to the affection be bore his children, especially the Princess of Orange. Dijkvelt stressed that the repeal of the Test Acts would put too much power in the hands of the Catholics. The King could create Catholic peers and swamp the House of Lords. The succession of a Protestant would be threatened.

Whilst in England the Dutch envoy had many interviews with members of the opposition, and he told James that he had had conversations with prominent men of all political parties. When he returned to The Hague during June, Dijkvelt bore letters from many prominent men to William. There were letters from Danby, Nottingham a moderate Tory, Bishop Compton opposed to the King, Halifax, Admiral Herbert, and John Churchill. They were of a personal nature, all protesting regard and even devotion to the Prince. They also implied that he was their leader in their opposition to James.

King James's interference and arbitrary behaviour in the affairs of Oxford University provided him with further opposition. When Dr. Henry Clarke, President of Magdalen, died on March 24, 1687, it was necessary for another President to be elected. The Bishop of Winchester, visitor of the College, advised the Fellows to choose a suitable candidate, such as Baptist Levinz, Bishop of Man, but Sunderland signed a royal mandate insisting that Anthony Farmer, a totally unsuitable candidate and not even a Fellow of the College, should be selected.[6] Meanwhile by the statutes the Fellows had every right to elect Dr. John Hough and did so, much to James's anger at their wilful disobedience. The Fellows behaved with tact and loyalty, but James in his interference made an appalling mistake. His action further antagonized those opposed to him.

One of the first demands of d'Albeville on becoming Ambassador at The Hague was the dismissal of Bishop Burnet from William's household. The Prince agreed to it rather surprisingly, and did not see Burnet again until a few days before sailing for England. James was less successful when he also demanded the Bishop's extradition, for the States-General refused, claiming that he was a political refugee and had assumed Dutch nationality. The King wanted him extradited either to England or Scotland to stand trial for high treason. The States-General were willing that Burnet should face a trial in Holland, but it did not suit James's plans. It is probable that Burnet continued to correspond with Bentinck, who was in daily communication with William.

It was a period of intense pressure, but occasionally William found leisure at Het Loo with Mary. There her weak eyesight improved. The place held happy memories for her, as she wrote Lady Mary Forester, an old friend:

I have bin but once in the little wood where we played at hide-and-seek; since I came hither, the ill weather will not suffer much walking, but I never go there without remembering how you ventured your great belly, big enough for you to brag about as long as you live.[7]

At Het Loo Princess Mary received a letter from her sister Anne written in the Cockpit, warning Mary against the Earl and Countess of Sunderland. In a further letter written on March 13, 1687 she wrote:

Everybody knows how often this man turned backwards and forwards in the late King's time, and now to complete all his virtues, he is working with all his might to bring in Popery. He is perpetually with the priests, and stirs up the King to do things faster than I believe he would of himself.

At the same time he was in close touch with Prince William, though Anne did not know this. Lady Sunderland she called "a great jade, though John Evelyn's opinion of her is quite different".

James's Queen, Maria Beatrice was aged twenty-nine. For many years she had not conceived a child, but after a visit to Bath during that autumn she made such a favourable impression on the inhabitants of that city that it became a stronghold of Jacobitism for almost a century. At the Shrine of St. Winifred at Holywell both King and Queen prayed fervently for a son. Their prayers were granted, for on November 29 James informed Princess Mary in Holland that the Queen was with child, and on Christmas Eve it was made official. For the most part the Protestant community greeted the news with consternation and scepticism, while the Catholics rejoiced.

Princess Anne was no longer on good terms with her stepmother, James's Italian-born Queen. Now aged twenty-four, Anne's vulgar, spiteful and narrow-minded character can be perceived at its worst. It is fair, however, to remember that the Princess was suffering from a miscarriage at the time. Count Terriesi, the Florentine envoy at the Court of St. James's, relates her bitterness. "Words cannot express the fury of the Princess of Denmark at the Queen's condition," he wrote, "she can conceal it from nobody." If an infant prince were to be born to her stepmother and if he were to survive, a series of Roman Catholic princes would supersede her sister Mary's and her own right to the succession. Her father had always treated her kindly and was devoted to her. She ought to have taken into account that owing to their upright characters neither her father or her stepmother were capable of such deception as to foist a pretended infant on the kingdom.

Yet she bears the odious responsibility of writing constantly to Mary in Holland to prejudice her against the Queen, to fill her mind with suspicions that Maria Beatrice was not pregnant and that it was "a false belly". Mary, too, deserves some censure for allowing herself to become too credulous. Anne's letters written in the Cockpit[8] reveal her vindictive nature. It is fair to add that the anti-Papist sentiment in England was so strong that few people were prepared to accept that there were not suspicious circumstances surrounding the birth. On March 27, 1688 Danby wrote to Prince William of Orange:

Because it is fit her Majesty should always have the greatest persons near her in this condition, I hope that the Princess Anne will always be within call ... to see (when the time is near) that the midwife discharges her duty with that care which ought to be had in a case of so great concern.[9]

It did not help that the Catholics were so positive that the infant would be a baby prince.

The Queen was hypersensitive by nature and for her the birth was miraculous. She was a strict Roman Catholic, but never really bigoted. She revolted from the slanderous stories sweeping London, and sensing the jealousy and hostility in her stepdaughter's mind, she shrank from allowing Anne to approach her too closely. It would have been wiser, however, for the Queen to offer proof of her condition to all the ladies of the Court. As it was, she could not bear Anne's prying eyes, and once in a passionate temper flung objects at her. Anne wrote to her sister:

Whenever one talks of her being with child, she looks as if she was afraid one should touch her. And whenever I have happened to be in the same room as she has been undressing, she has always gone into the next room to put on her smock.

She thought that nobody would be convinced that it was the Queen's child unless it proved a daughter. She continued in the same vein:

The great bustle that was made about her lying in at Windsor and then resolving all of a sudden to go to St. James's which is much the properest place to act such a cheat in; and Mrs. Turini's (Pellegrina) lying in the bedchamber that night she fell in labour, and none of the family besides being removed from Whitehall are things that give one great cause to be suspicious.[10]

It was natural enough for Maria Beatrice to want to give birth to her infant in St. James's Palace, her first London home. Also for Pellegrina Turini - a devoted peasant servant from Modena all her life - to be near her. She did not mind Mrs. Turini touching her or the Italian-born Hortense Mazarin (Mancini), who was in any case related to her. St. James's Palace was full of secret hiding-places, "much the properest place to act such a cheat in".

Shortly before the birth, King James issued a Second Declaration of Indulgence and commanded it to be read in all the churches on Sunday, May 20. Seven bishops, Sancroft Archbishop of Canterbury, Ken of Bath and Wells (Mary's former Chaplain), White of Peterborough, Turner of

Ely, Lake of Chichester, Lloyd of St. Asaph and Trelawney of Bristol refused to sign the petition on the grounds that it was illegal. Their number would have included Compton, Bishop of London, but James had already suspended him. The King, angered by their opposition, ordered them to be imprisoned in the Tower, where several thousand people collected at Whitehall Steps to show their sympathies and to be blessed by the bishops.

On June 10, Trinity Sunday, the Queen gave birth to an infant prince. The room in St. James's Palace was crowded with witnesses, both Protestant and Catholic, almost to suffocation. Two important people not present were Princess Anne absent in Bath - taken aback because the birth was premature and expected a month later - and Archbishop Sancroft imprisoned in the Tower of London. Others not present were van Citters, the Dutch ambassador, who had not been summoned, and the Hyde brothers, Lord Clarendon and Lord Rochester. The birth was greeted with incredulity by many people. An absurd story almost immediately arose that a substitute baby had been introduced into the Queen's bed in a warming-pan. People believe what they want to believe.

One reliable Protestant witness present in the crammed room where the Queen lay was Lady Isobella Wentworth and she verified the birth four months later before the Privy Council. Another Protestant Dr. Hugh Chamberlain unable to be present was a Whig of French Huguenot extraction and a skilled obstetrician. He, however, wrote to Sophie the Electress of Hanover eleven years later that Dr. Burnet's account of the birth was partly false and that the widowed Duchess of Monmouth had satisfied him, a few days prior to the birth, of the reality of the pregnancy.[11]

What William thought we do not know. Mary must have made him privy to Anne's suspicions, but the Prince had a poor opinion of his sister-in-law. He probably had an open mind at first, and after studying the evidence opined that the infant Prince of Wales was authentic. Mary believed that he was not her brother, a view she clung to. Both husband and wife were aghast that the birth of the Prince might mean the succession of countless Catholic heirs. Anne wrote her sister: "Tis possible it may be her child, but where one believes it, a thousand do not." Almost certainly an exaggeration of the popular feeling. William sent over Zuylestein to congratulate the King and he reported the prevailing scepticism. It was necessary that prayers for the Prince should be read in Mary's chapel, while she sent a long questionnaire to Anne trying to ascertain the truth. When Prince James Francis Edward was a month old he was very ill and Anne in July gleefully wrote her sister, "if he has been as bad as some people say, I believe it will not be long before he is an angel in Heaven."[12] However, the Prince of Wales survived. Barillon the French ambassador reported from London that there were some thanksgiving bonfires in the vicinity of Whitehall, but few elsewhere.

In the history of the dramatic events leading up to the Revolution, the Trial of the Seven Bishops in Westminster Hall on July 8 for seditious libel is pre-eminent. If only James in his blind folly had abandoned the prosecution, advised to do so as he was by even Sunderland and Jeffreys. Chief Justice Wright was the presiding judge, but it was owing to the courage of a Welshman Mr. Justice Powell, that the dispensing power used by the King was revealed as illegal.[13] He refuted the words of Lord Chief Justice Herbert reported two years previously. During the trial Justice Powell often intervened as if he was the bishops' counsel.

> The Kings of England are absolute sovereigns; the laws of England are the King's laws; the King has power to dispense with any of his laws as he sees necessity for it; and the King is sole judge of that necessity.

That was the King's case.

The jury returned a verdict of non-guilty for the bishops, and their acquittal was greeted with delirious rejoicing. On that very day the invitation for William to invade the kingdom was ready. It was signed by seven important politicians, Danby, Sidney, Bishop Compton, the Earl of Shrewsbury, a prominent Whig, Edward Russell (cousin of Lord William Russell, executed for his part in the Rye House plot), the Earl of Devonshire and Lord Lumley. Lumley, afterwards Earl of Scarborough, had formerly taken part against the Western rebels, but had been alienated by King James's conduct.

No offer of the crown was made in the document, rather was it an invitation for William to come to England with sufficient arms to protect the people till they could rise in force themselves. Though there were many people discontented and fearful of King James's rule, the revolution was never the work of a great popular movement, but rather that of a minority of powerful Whig magnates. It was Admiral Herbert, a professional sailor, who had opposed the repeal of the Test Acts under James II and resigned his commission, who was appointed as the agent to carry over the invitation to William at The Hague. According to d'Avaux (July 20), Arthur Herbert travelled disguised as a seaman. He arrived on Friday, July 16 and had an immediate conference with the Prince, Bentinck, Dijkvelt, and van Citters, recalled from his London embassy. In their declaration the seven deplored that William had appeared to acknowledge James's son, born of the Queen. He must raise this point in his manifesto.

The Prince may have held doubts about this, as after long discussions with his Dutch advisers, he agreed on July 17 that prayers for the infant Prince of Wales should no longer be read in the royal chapels at The Hague.

William now pushed on with his preparations for invasion with alacrity. It was a huge undertaking requiring all his immense ability. He appointed Count Frederick Schomberg as second-in-command for the expedition, a soldier now aged almost seventy, very experienced in the wars in Europe, and a fluent linguist. Bentinck was responsible with the Dutch admirals Evertsen, Almonde and Bastiaenz, together with Arthur Herbert, in organizing the invasion army. It consisted not only of Dutch troops and other nationalities, but about twenty-five per cent were British. Bentinck was undergoing immense strain because his wife Anne was desperately ill.

Never was William a more devoted European than before the revolution. During 1686 he had organized the German states into the League of Augsburg, an anti-French coalition.[14] His major aim surely was to gain control of England's foreign policy, and make her abandon her isolation and take part in the impending war against France. He was fearful of French expansion in Europe after the Treaty of Nijmegen in 1678. By the Truce of Ratisbon (August 1684) the conquest of Strasbourg and Luxembourg, cities that lay beyond the northern and eastern frontiers of France, had been ratified. The Prince saw the vital necessity of the balance of power in Europe, but there were many people in the United Provinces opposed to his policies, including the Republican Peace Party favouring low taxes and trade with France. In 1684, his clear vision had made him say: "It is from England that the salvation of Europe must come, without her it must fall under the yoke of the King of France."[15] After the Edict of Nantes the atrocities of France against the Huguenots harmed the business interests of many Amsterdam merchants, so those opposed to him in the past were now ready to give him their support. There were, of course, other reasons for William's invasion, not least his desire to protect his wife's succession to the throne, now threatened by the birth of James's son. He also wished to pose as the Protestant champion against the illegal actions of a Catholic king. Yet the revolution is usually referred to as 'glorious', whereas the motives of those betraying their king were for the most part shameful and opportunist.

William was very fortunate in one thing, his superb intelligence agents in England, especially James Johnston,[16] informing him of the state of opinion in England and Scotland. He saw the importance of political propaganda, corresponding with Bentinck. He was original in his belief, reporting on one occasion:

The spirit of a people is like that of particular persons, often to be entertained by trifles; particularly that of the English, who like all islanders, seems to ebb and flow like the neighbouring sea. In the late fermentation about the Exclusion, the Excluders never lost ground till they lost the press.

King James's intelligence service on the other hand served him badly. D'Albeville, however, informed him constantly of the Dutch preparations for invasion and made a special journey to England to warn him, yet James despite his ambassador's warnings and those of Paul Barillon, French ambassador, and Louis XIV, did not take them seriously until late September 1688. William hesitated for some time and calculated very carefully before embarking on his invasion. There were so many risks: that of exposing the United Provinces to a French attack while he was absent, his uncertainty about the kind of reception he would meet in England and the magnitude of the task in launching a successful invasion. All these considerations daunted William. When France invaded the Palatinate, the danger of a French attack receded. Convinced of his son-in-law's intention to invade England, there was an acceleration in naval and English preparations, but James was loath to accept the offer of French help. According to Burnet, Louis XIV offered 12,000 or 15,000 men to hold Portsmouth. No doubt James was aware of English public feeling against France. Louis made a bad miscalculation in failing to grasp James's estrangement from his subjects.

Before invading England, William may not have had any clear plan to depose James II or ambition to become King of England.

PART TWO

XII   THE INVASION

There is no doubt that Princess Mary, before her husband embarked for England, was in an agonizing frame of mind, torn between her deep love for William and her father with whom she had been close in the early years. Although now she felt estranged from him, she could not but remember that he was still her father. Her stepmother Maria Beatrice had written that she did not believe that she was to come over with William:

> for I know you to be too good. I do not believe you could have such a thought against the worst of fathers, much less to perform it against the best, who has always been so kind to you, and I do believe, has loved you better than any of his children.[1]

It was all the more painful for both William and Mary, for they could not possibly know whether they would ever see each other again. The dangers of the voyage daily pressed on her mind, overwhelming her with fears.

When the Prince came to say goodbye to the States, he spoke simply and movingly, that he had always kept their welfare in mind. He added:

> What God intends for me, I do not know, but if I should fall, have a care for my beloved wife who has always loved this country as her own.

He had an emotional meeting with Mary, finding it difficult to say the things he had in mind. Tears mounted to his eyes as William told her that if he never returned, she must marry again - it was unnecessary to say, not to a Papist. For such a reticent man he was tender and loving. The Princess was so confused by what he said that she hesitated to reply. Then she reassured William that she had never loved anybody but him, and could never love another. She confided to her diary: "Oh my God, if I have sinned in this passion ... forgive me, I beseech thee." She admitted that she had thought too much about herself, and it was this selfishness, which made her want not to survive her husband, he was so good and so dear to her. "For assuredly," she wrote, "I should never be able to find his equal." In this crisis she did not remember William in his many moods, his apparent neglect of her when overwhelmed by work. He had been very ill that autumn, and for a week incapable of active work. The Prince had told her that if faced with difficulties she should confide in Count Waldeck, or seek help from Dijkvelt or Fagel. However, Fagel, who had been such a steadfast friend since the murder of the de Witts, was thought to be dying. In late October the Prince dined with his wife at Honselaersdijck, and she accompanied him when he went to the borders of the river where he took a boat for Hellevoetsluys.

Banners streamed from the masthead of the *Den Briel*, the ship in which William of Orange sailed. It bore his motto: *Pro Religione et Libertate - Je Maintiendrai*. Armand von Schomberg, an experienced soldier with a European reputation, commanded William's land forces. He was aged 70, a man half-German and half-English, his father a diplomat. The fleet consisted of two or three hundred transports, protected by over fifty fighting ships. His army was rather less than King James's land forces of 40,117.[2] These included 4,000 English and Scots troops, two regiments of mainly English refugees, four regiments of federal Dutch troops paid by the States General, some French Huguenots, Brandenburgers commanded by the old warrior Count Schomberg and a body of Scandinavian mercenaries. Strangely enough there were probably more Catholics in William's army than in James's. Their morale was high. One of the Prince's Catholic soldiers is alleged to have said: "My soul is God's, but my sword is for the Prince of Orange."

King James's fleet was commanded by his old friend George Legge, Earl of Dartmouth, a staunch friend during the Duke of York's adversity overseas and loyal during his downfall in 1688.

The morale in James's fleet was bad as Samuel Pepys, working hard at the Admiralty, was aware. Even up to the end of October, it was difficult to get men to serve in the crews. The officers, too, were laggard. They complained that their ships were not ready, "when nothing is wanting towards making them ready, but their own attendance on board."[3] The fleet under Dartmouth's command consisted of about fifty ships, and as the crisis grew more acute the spirit of the men improved.

On October 30, William's fleet sailed with a favourable wind, but on the following day a violent storm erupted and some of the battered ships were forced to return to Hellevoetsluys. It was considered an evil omen, but only one ship was lost and the material damage much less than feared. For

William, the greatest blow was the death of several hundred horses, suffocated in their hatches. Bishop Burnet, who accompanied the Prince, wrote in *History of His Own Time* that the vessel (*Den Briel*) which carried the Prince and his retinue narrowly escaped shipwreck. He was heard by the Prince to remark that it seemed predestined that they should not set foot on English soil.

After a few days the fleet was able to resume its course. At a Council of War in the *Den Briel*, Zuylestein wisely advised that the armada should make for south-west England, Dorset or Devon instead of the Yorkshire coast, as originally decided. It was a clever stroke on William's part to change the course his fleet was pursuing from north to south-west, aided by a strong favourable wind. In the faint sunshine of an autumn day the six hundred sail presented a magnificent sight. Meanwhile Dartmouth's fleet, hampered by bad weather, lay frustrated in the Thames. On Sunday November 4, the Prince's birthday and wedding anniversary, he attended Divine Service. It was essential to deceive the English as to where William intended to land. Even now a grave risk occurred, for the pilot of *Den Briel* mistook the sea marks in a heavy mist and the ships might have continued their voyage to Plymouth, where a powerful English squadron was stationed. Fortunately the mist cleared, and the ships landed safely in Torbay.

The first to step ashore was Count Solms, commander of William's footguards. There followed the English and Scottish troops, and then the cavalry. A few hours later William disembarked at the grey, austere, little village of Brixham with the gulls shrieking overhead. His statue still commemorates his landing. The weather was temporarily propitious, for a lovely russet sunset was reflected in the waters lapping the coast.

Burnet in his account says:

As soon as I landed I made what haste I could to the place where the Prince was; who took me heartily by the hand and asked me, 'Well, Doctor, what do you think of predestination now?'[4]

It was the Prince's Scottish chaplain, William Carstares, however, who was chosen to conduct a service on the beach. He read the 118th Psalm:

They came about me like bees, and are extinct even as the fire and the thorns, for in the name of the Lord I will destroy them.

That night William slept on a mattress on the floor of a fisherman's hut.

The Prince was disappointed at first with the rather frigid reception he received in Torbay. Few people joined his banners, probably deterred by memories of the unfortunate Monmouth Rebellion three years before. He even thought of returning to Holland, and simultaneously publishing the names of those who had invited him to England. It poured with rain as his army, in high spirits, marched from Newton Abbot to Exeter, where Bishop Burnet took it upon himself to read the Prince's Declaration in the cathedral. If King James with his army had made an immediate advance to the West and attacked Prince William, he would have had his best chance of success. Instead, he procrastinated and missed the opportunity. The royalist army consisted of 2,085 officers, 4,172 non-commissioned officers and 33,860 men,[5] but the King could not count on the loyalty of some of his officers. Between November and 24, two regiments commanded by an officer named Wharton had joined William and some senior officers of the Portsmouth garrison. The two most important people to desert the King were Lord Cornbury, eldest son of the Earl of Clarendon, and Bertie Earl of Abingdon. Clarendon wrote in his diary: "O God that my son should be a rebel! The Lord in his mercy look upon me and enable me to support myself under this most grievous calamity."[6] Cornbury was Master of the Horse to Princess Anne's husband, George of Denmark, and a cat's-paw of Sarah and John Churchill, who dominated the Princess.

Prince William wanted to avoid any pitched battle on land with his father-in-law's army as he had previously been successful at sea with Dartmouth's naval forces. When the Prince heard that George Booth, Lord Delamere had risen in Cheshire, he was much encouraged because the Delameres were one of the most powerful families in Cheshire. The clergy and magistrates in Exeter were fearful of seeming to favour Prince William, for Bishop Lamplugh and the Dean fled to London, according to Burnet, where King James created Lamplugh Archbishop of York.[7]

At this juncture James's wisest course would have been to summon a parliament, a course urged on him by his brothers-in-law Clarendon and Rochester (Laurence Hyde) and by his bishops. If a parliament had materialized, William would have been obliged to negotiate with his father-in-law. James admitted that he much desired to call a parliament:

> but how can you have a free parliament now that a foreign prince at the head of a foreign force has it in his power to return a hundred members?[8]

William neither wanted to negotiate with the King, nor to fight him or to have any confrontation or meeting with him.

Hearing of Cornbury's desertion, James summoned all the available general officers and colonels to Whitehall, saying that if there were any among them who were not free or willing to serve him, he gave them permission to surrender their commissions and go where they pleased. However, he regarded them as men of too much honour to follow My Lord Cornbury's example. In James's memoirs he says that Lord Churchill and the Duke of Grafton (an illegitimate son of Charles II) were the first to make their attestation of loyalty, followed by Colonel Kirke and others.

The King delayed too long before starting for Salisbury on November 16 to join his army in the field. He arrived there on November 19. Among those at Salisbury was James's illegitimate son (by Arabella Churchill) the Duke of Berwick, who states in his *Memoirs* that the rank and file were loyal to his father, although there was some disaffection in the higher command. If James had engaged William's army at once, appealing to the national dislike of foreigners, to induce them to fight their old enemies the Dutch, matters might have turned out differently, but the King was a very different character from the brave and impetuous Lord High Admiral of the earlier years. To procrastinate further was fatal to his cause.

Then during November 20 and the following day, the King suffered a severe nasal haemorrhage - the Duke of Berwick, who was present, wrote that it was "a prodigious bleeding", making his father extremely lethargic and incapable of action.

What were the motives of Lord Churchill in then deserting the King, a brilliant soldier who in James's own words "he had raised from nothing"? They were mixed ones. Churchill was resentful that the King had listened to the advice of the Jesuit Father Petre and other extreme Catholics, although he was not a particularly religious man. In the letter explaining his desertion of his master he:

> protested that his desertion from His Majesty proceeded from no other reason than the inviolable duty of conscience, and a high and necessary concern for his religion with which nothing could come in competition.[9]

Churchill also wanted to be on the winning side. He stole away in the night together with the Duke of Grafton, making for Axminster, William's headquarters. When Churchill rode into the enemy camp he was greeted by Marshal Schomberg, who said sarcastically that "he was the first Lieutenant General he had ever heard of who had deserted from the colours". A few days later James's son-in-law went over to William, too. He had remarked when this fresh desertion occurred: "So! Est-il possible he has gone too! A good trooper would have been a greater loss." Another to join William was the Second Duke of Ormonde, son of the brave Lord Ossory. Louis de Duras Earl of Feversham, French by birth, was among those who remained loyal. He now counselled the King to retreat to London.

William entered Salisbury with his army, nine days after James had left it. Whilst there, he was not too busy to ride to Wilton to see the exquisite van Dycks, although suffering from a bad cough and cold, all the worse in the bitter weather of December. On his return he told his secretary Huygens that he must see them.[10]

James, on reaching London on November 26, was aghast at receiving the news that his daughter Anne had deserted him. She was one of the few people he was devoted to and he had always treated her kindly. In his agony he cried out: "God help me. My own children have deserted me." Accompanied by Sarah Churchill, she had escaped from Whitehall through the door emptying her lavatory, and escorted by Bishop Compton, the Earl of Dorset and a regiment of Dragoons, by way of Epping to Nottingham, the headquarters for the insurrection in the north. "Whom then could I trust, if my own daughters have deserted me," he was heard to say. "If only my enemies had cursed me, I could have borne it."

James now thought mainly of the safety of his Queen Maria Beatrice, who had always given him magnificent loyalty, and of his son James Francis Edward (Prince of Wales). On November 29 he sent the infant in the care of two pious Roman Catholics, Lord and Lady Powis, to Lord Dartmouth, who was now at Portsmouth with the fleet, commanding him to bear the Prince when possible to France. Dartmouth rightly demurred at this distasteful duty, probably thinking it treasonable to transport the heir to the throne out of the realm. Much better if James had left the infant prince to be brought up in England, but he feared that there was a plot to capture him. However, the Prince of Wales's mother was soon to fly to France together with her infant son, now aged six months. James dreaded the prospect of another civil war with possible imprisonment in the Tower, or even his execution on Tower Hill. He had no fear of death, but the dignity of kings was sacrosanct in his mind.

For three days William stayed at Sherborne and then moved to Hungerford in Berkshire. He had no further need of his transport fleet and it now embarked for Holland. On December 9 he received a short, loving letter from Mary, but his own letters to her were much delayed. Soon afterwards he was saddened by the news from Dijkvelt that Fagel the Grand Pensionary was on his deathbed. The Prince wrote from Hungerford: "It is a heavy blow to me and to the whole country and touches me to the heart." When Bentinck, constantly at his side, heard of the death of his wife, he was grief-stricken and was comforted by the Prince. Whilst at Hungerford three commissioners arrived, nominally sent by James, but in reality representing themselves. These were 'Trimmer'

Halifax, Godolphin and Daniel Finch Second Earl of Nottingham, sent to treat with William. Nottingham was nicknamed 'Dismal' because of his often lugubrious expression.

At this stage the King was prepared to make various concessions. He would agree to the summoning of a parliament on January 25 (1689). He would also concur in a free pardon to all William's supporters, and consider the removal of all Catholics from office. It is extremely doubtful whether James was sincere in making these promises.

On the night of December 10 the King had secretly allowed his Queen Maria Beatrice to escape to France, together with her baby prince and wet-nurse, Madame de Labadie. It was a very dangerous journey, dramatic, too, as the Queen tried to shelter with the Prince in the lee of Lambeth Church, while the rain fell piteously down in torrents and the resourceful, devoted Comte de Lauzun and the loyal Italian Riva attended the Queen with other escorts to Gravesend, where they embarked for Calais. The King intended to follow her into exile as soon as possible. Lord Halifax knew of this and told Bishop Burnet, who was with Prince William.

Meanwhile the Prince of Orange had made a further Declaration in the London streets, denouncing the Catholics and announcing that Catholics captured in arms by William's forces would receive no quarter. He immediately repudiated this, but it probably came from his printing press.

To the many English lords and gentlemen who had joined him, William was taciturn and morose, never seeking popularity. For hours he would maintain deep silence. So marked was this that a lord asked Arnold Joost van Keppel, a Dutch gentleman-in-waiting, whether the Prince ever spoke at all. "He talks enough at night over his bottle, when he is got with his friends," replied the youth.[11]

Soon after midnight in the early hours of December 11, James made an unsuccessful attempt to escape from England, accompanied by Sir Edward Hales, an unpopular Papist. James had reached Faversham in Kent, having already dropped the Great Seal overboard near Horseferry on the Thames. In Whitehall all the writs for the Parliament to be called in January had been burnt. James was captured, but rescued by his loyal friend, the French-born Lord Feversham, whom he sent with a message to William. The King's instructions to his army commander were couched in such a vague way that Feversham decided to disband his forces. This angered William so much since he was counting on their service in his wars in Europe that he ordered Feversham's arrest and had him confined in Windsor Castle. The mood of a nation is always unpredictable and as James reached Blackheath and crossed London Bridge through the City to Whitehall in his coach, the King was widely acclaimed. Church bells rang, bonfires were lit in the streets, and excited people crammed the balconies. It was but a temporary burst of popularity.

On the night of December 11, there were riots in the City of London. Mobs composed of apprentices swarmed in the streets, attacking and destroying the Roman Catholic embassies of foreign powers and anybody suspected of being a Catholic. The Spanish Ambassador had to be rescued and lodged in Whitehall, free of expense. Night was made hideous by delirious mobs and the crackling of the flames in the lurid light. The hated Lord Chancellor, better known as the notorious Judge Jeffreys, was found skulking in a house in Wapping and taken to prison. All was chaos.

It very much suited the Prince of Orange's purpose for the King to escape abroad. For James it was one of his worst mistakes, for had he remained in London William would have been compelled to negotiate with him. If he had remained in England, he might possibly have retained his crown, though his power would have been severely restricted. William now had his uncle completely in his power. He wanted him to leave Whitehall and stay in Ham House, owned by the Duchess of Lauderdale, near Richmond, but James declined on the grounds that Ham House was too damp in winter. He preferred to go to Rochester, as he was determined on flight to France, where he would rejoin his Queen and infant son. James's loyal friends, such as the Earl of Ailesbury and John Graham of Claverhouse, Viscount Dundee, implored him on their knees to stay. To no avail. He was haunted by his father's fate.

It is evident that Lord Clarendon did his best for King James.[12] He asked a few of the lords why the King must leave Whitehall. "I then asked," he wrote in his Diary, "Why must he go to Ham House?" Lord Halifax answered, "the Lords are agreed, and have sent to desire the Prince (William) to come to them." Lord Clarendon asked why James might be not at liberty to go where he pleased. To go to one of his own houses, Hampton Court or Windsor. This caused Lord Delamere - "a little thing puts him in a temper", wrote Clarendon - to remark angrily: "I do not look upon him as my King and will never more pay him obedience."[13]

To the disgust of the gallant old Lord Craven, Dutch troops had taken over sentry duty at the Palace to replace English troops and James had made not the slightest resistance.

William was greatly relieved when he received the agreeable intelligence of the King's flight from Rochester on December 22, and departure by boat for France accompanied by the Duke of Berwick. At Rochester the King stayed in the house of Sir Richard Head in the High Street, a house which still bears a plaque stating that fact. Clarendon wrote:

The treatment that the King had met from the Prince of Orange and the manner of his being driven, as it were, from Whitehall ... moved compassion even in those who were not very fond of him.

The Prince lay at Syon House while his uncle was in Rochester. Dusk fell early on the Tuesday afternoon, December 18, as the Dutch troops marched through Westminster. The church bells rang and many people among the excited crowd waved oranges impaled on sticks. William felt little sense of triumph, only a growing sadness. He made his way through St. James's Park to St. James's Palace. To Count Waldeck he wrote: "I am more distressed than you can imagine. I hope God will guide me as he has done hitherto." Everything was predestined.

Lord Clarendon found the crowds so dense that he could not see the Prince. Lord Mulgrave, a rejected former suitor for the hand of Princess Anne, was at the bedchamber door, an eager opportunist. Bentinck accosted him thus, according to Clarendon: *"Comment! Milord, vous avez quitté votre bâton."* Mulgrave replied cynically, *"Il est bien temps."*[14]

The Prince acted decisively when he heard of King James's flight. He immediately signed an order for the departure of Barillon the French Ambassador from the country within twenty-four hours. In his last letter to Louis XIV, Barillon had written that the Prince commanded in London as if in a camp, and that his troops mounted guard everywhere, not without some murmurs on the part of the English at seeing the Tower and other important places in the hands of the Dutch. To Louis, the ease with which William had conquered the kingdom gave him grave concern. He had certainly misjudged the situation.

It had been a bloodless revolution.

XIII WILLIAM AND MARY

Louis XIV treated James and Maria Beatrice with exquisite courtesy, installing them in the Palace of Saint Germain, and behaving to them in the days of their adversity with the utmost generosity. It naturally suited his own plans, for James was now the tool of France. If he was restored, he would owe it to Louis as the faithful satellite of France. Maria Beatrice made a much more favourable impression than her husband, who was considered slow and foolish, while Le Roi Soleil said of the Queen after her first visit to Versailles, "This is what a Queen should be like."

Meanwhile in England there was no king for seven weeks, so legally there could be no parliament. At the end of 1688 the Lords asked William to take over the administration and the Prince almost immediately summoned a Convention Parliament to meet in January 1689. He was extremely anxious lest the French should seize the opportunity to invade Holland now that he was absent. He was determined that Mary should remain there until their positions were established. When his friend Dijkvelt and Nicholas Witsen, a former opponent and now burgomaster of Amsterdam and a loyal supporter, arrived in England to congratulate the Prince, he was eager to hear the opinion in Holland. "Are they pleased that you counselled me to do this?" he asked.[1] They told him that they were. They were mistaken, however, when they congratulated him on his popularity in England, for William was never popular there, nor did he seek it. He now denied it, saying "Hosanna today, and perhaps tomorrow crucify."

When John Evelyn visited the Archbishop of Canterbury, William Sancroft, the Bishop of Bath and Wells, Ken, the Bishops of St. Asaph, Ely and others on January 15, he found much disagreement as to what course to pursue. The Lords and Commons were equally divided. Some favoured the Princess being made queen "without any more dispute, others favoured a Regency",[2] a small extreme group of Tories wanted King James to return on conditions, and the Republicans wanted the Prince of Orange, who would be like a Stadtholder. A majority of the Whigs in Parliament wanted the Prince as King. As for the Bishops, they were all for a Regency.

The Prince was very much opposed to a Regency, but declared to the Convention Parliament, when it met on January 22, that if they were to offer him the Crown for life, he would accept it. Meanwhile Lord Danby wanted very much to place Princess Mary alone on the throne and wrote her accordingly, but her answer was delayed by contrary winds. She would never accept such a project, she wrote. Later when they reigned jointly as King and Queen she was to say:

> My heart is not made for a kingdom and my inclination leads me to a retired life, so that I have need of all the resignation and self-denial in the world, to bear with such a condition as I am now in. Indeed the Prince's being made King has lessened the pain, but none of the trouble I am like to endure.

One thing is clear. William would never have agreed to become his wife's gentleman usher or to be tied to her apron strings. Nor would he accept the position of a Regent. He told members of the Convention Parliament that he esteemed Princess Mary as much as any man esteemed a woman. If the Crown was offered to him for life, however, he would accept it. If the English did not want him he was prepared to go home, otherwise they must accept him on his own terms. The Prince remained firm and the Convention Parliament consented to William and Mary reigning jointly during their joint and separate lives, though the administration would remain in his hands. There was nothing now to prevent Princess Mary coming to England.

She had been on the whole happy in Holland, had taken the trouble to study the Dutch language, and had a sincere love for its people. So, although her sentiments were mixed, she was saddened at having to leave Holland to return to her native country, which she had not seen since the age of fifteen. Her strong premonition that she would never return to Holland proved to be true. However, there was the longing to see William again and increased anxiety about his health.

The Princess sailed in a yacht on the Maas with a favourable wind. As the shores of England became visible, she felt "a secret joy", her melancholy at her father's misfortune soon stifled by her pleasure at the thought of seeing the Prince again.

She was met by William and her sister Anne, several months pregnant, at Greenwich and they travelled immediately to Whitehall. Mary was deeply troubled by William's appearance, for he was a sick man, suffering from an incessant cough. In Whitehall Palace when they could at last be alone together, they both wept tears of joy, but wished the reunion could have been in Holland. "We both bewailed the loss of the liberty we had left behind and were sensible we should never enjoy here."[3] William took the opportunity to tell his wife that whatever her real sentiments, she must appear jolly and happy in public. Mary, whose early days had been passed in England, should have shown a more sensitive awareness of the situation.

That evening Mary overplayed her part, and was much criticized by her contemporaries. Evelyn in his *Diary* wrote:

> It was believed that both, especially the Princess should have shew'd some seeming reluctance at least, of assuming her father's Crown and made some apology, testifying by her regret that he should by his mismanagement, necessitate the nation to so extraordinary a proceeding; ... but nothing of all this appear'd; she came into Whitehall laughing and jolly as to a wedding, so as to seem quite transported. She rose early the next morning, and in her undresse, as it was reported, before her women were up, went about from roome to roome to see the convenience of Whitehall, lay in the same bed and apartment where the late Queene lay, and within a night or two sate downe to play at basset, as the Queene her predecessor used to do .... This carriage was censur'd by many."[4]

She certainly gave a false impression.

Sarah Churchill describes her conduct as "strange and unbecoming".

> For, whatever necessity there was of deposing King James, he was still her father, who had been so lately driven from that chamber, and that bed and, if she felt no tenderness, I thought she should at least have looked grave, or even pensively sad, at so melancholy a reverse of his fortune.

She did not understand, this disapproving woman, that Mary was concealing her real feelings to please her husband. Sarah considered that Mary *wanted bowels*. Even Burnet, who idolized the Princess, was a little critical.

The following day, February 13, 1689, in the Banqueting House at Whitehall, the Crown was offered to William and Mary by both Houses of Parliament. They were then proclaimed King and Queen. William was now a care-worn man of thirty-eight and Mary almost twelve years younger.

As the late Sir Charles Petrie states in his fine work *The Jacobite Movement*, as many as four hundred beneficed clergymen refused to take the oaths to William and Mary because they would be breaking the oaths they had previously made to James II. Foremost among them were the Archbishop of Canterbury, William Sancroft, the Bishop of Bath and Wells,

Thomas Ken, and four other Bishops, those of Peterborough, Gloucester, Ely and Norwich. Their conduct was all the more admirable since they had defied James by refusing to read the Second Declaration of Indulgence and suffered imprisonment. Many of these non-juring clergymen made great sacrifices, being deprived of their livings, and in many cases facing poverty. A few calculated, however, that James would be restored and that they would receive preferment. There was a schism in the Church of England. When Princess Mary asked for the Archbishop's blessing, Sancroft told her she must first seek her father's blessing, for he otherwise would not be heard in heaven. He refused to crown her.

One Bishop, talkative and vain, who benefited by the Revolution, was Gilbert Burnet, created Bishop of Sarum (Salisbury) March 11, 1689. According to Lord Clarendon, the Bishop of Bristol was in "great discontent" because he maintained that he had been promised the see.

In Ireland, Richard Talbot, later Duke of Tyrconnel, had been nominated Lord Deputy by James II, an intimate friend. According to the Duke of Berwick "Tyrconnel was a man of very good sense, very obliging, but immoderately vain, and full of cunning."[5] He was at Cork when James landed at Kinsale in Southern Ireland in an attempt to regain his kingdom on March 12, 1689, with a supply of French arms and a host of French officers sent to train the Irish troops.

For the Jacobites the situation seemed very promising. It was Tyrconnel who had begged James to come to Ireland to lead the Irish in their resistance against William III and the new government. He met James in Cork and was able to report that the whole of Leinster, Munster and Connaught were in Jacobite hands. Only in Ulster, Londonderry* (a small town then largely composed of Protestants) and Enniskillen held out for William. James's Irish army had one fatal weakness. The men did not lack courage, but were ill-disciplined. There were too many inexperienced officers. D'Avaux, who was accompanying James, said that the army was composed of tailors, butchers and shoemakers.

William had attempted to negotiate with Tyrconnel. His Secretary for War in April 1689 was John Temple, the only surviving son of Sir William, the King's friend. On John Temple's advice, he sent a distinguished soldier and a Roman Catholic, Lieutenant-General Richard Hamilton to Ireland bearing generous terms, but he betrayed his trust and, influenced by Tyrconnel, joined the Jacobites. Blaming himself for the defection, "Temple took a pair of oars at Temple Stairs and bid the men row to Greenwich where he committed suicide by drowning", a drastic act in the circumstances.

---

* Today it has a large number of Roman Catholics.

The English love tradition, and William as King should have adapted himself to their way of life. He was half Stuart, but he had no feeling for tradition or ceremony. He disliked his coronation intensely and asked Nicholas Witsen of Amsterdam, who was present in London, if he had seen the comedy of the coronation and what he thought "of those foolish old ceremonies".[6] They smacked of Rome. The coronation of William and Mary had taken place on April 11, 1689. Archbishop Sancroft, who refused to take the oaths, was absent, so Compton, Bishop of London, officiated, though he was military-minded and would have been more at home leading a troop of horse.

William was feeling very ill and coughed incessantly, even spitting blood. He failed to respond when he had to offer up a roll and thirty pieces of gold. In the ensuing, embarrassing silence, Danby fulfilled this duty. When Mary was being presented to the peers, Princess Anne whispered to her sister, "I pity your fatigue, Madame," to be promptly snubbed by the new Queen replying, "A crown, sister, is not so heavy as it seems." Evelyn wrote: "I saw the Procession to and from the Abbey Church of Westminster, with the greate feast in Westm' Hall." What was different from former coronations was some alteration in the Coronation oath. Dr. Burnet, now made Bishop of Sarum, "preach'd with greate applause". The Parliament men were feasted in the Exchequer Chamber, and had each of them a gold medal given worth five and forty shillings.

One thing William was adamant about. He refused to touch for the King's evil, although he lay his hand on one person, saying, "God give you better health and more sense." The man recovered.[7] Mary was far more gracious than her husband, so more popular. One reason given by Burnet for the King's unpopularity in England was that people complained that he was too inaccessible. His continued ill health was partly due to the enforced long hours in St. James's without the exercise or hunting he was accustomed to. He became peevish, morose and bad tempered, spending long hours working feverishly in his closet.

Disliking Whitehall and certain that it was inimical to his health, William, encouraged by Mary, decided to live mostly in Hampton Court Palace, where he found the air agreed much better with him. Consequently William and his Queen decided that new buildings should be erected for their apartments. From Hampton Court William only came into Whitehall on council days, leading to "an early and general disgust"[8] because people missed the gaiety and diversions of a Court.

The King chose two Secretaries of State, the Earls of Shrewsbury and Nottingham. Shrewsbury was a moderate Whig, one of the signatories to the invitation to William to come to England before the Revolution. William was sincerely attached to Charles Talbot, the Earl of Shrewsbury, one of the few Englishmen he really liked. His childhood and youth had been utterly ruined by the nymphomaniac behaviour of his mother Anne Maria Brudenell, sometime mistress of the Second Duke of Buckingham. She had stood by while Buckingham had mortally wounded his father in a duel. The experiences in his early life made him reserved and slightly neurotic.[9] Both his parents were Roman Catholics, but he succeeded to the title when only aged eight, and later became a convert to the Church of England. William had a high opinion of this handsome nobleman, and according to Burnet he had the greatest share of the King's confidence. Because of his tact, William considered him the only person capable of conciliating the Whigs and the Tories and gave him the nickname of 'King of hearts'. From the first William loathed party politics in England.

The Whigs had helped him to the throne, but he became alienated from them, suspecting that they intended to diminish his prerogative. Shrewsbury had a guilty conscience because, like others of William's ministers, he had flirted with the Jacobites.

Daniel Finch, Second Earl of Nottingham, had voted for a Regency prior to William becoming King. Burnet wrote that:

> Nottingham had always said that although he would not make a king, yet upon his principles, he could obey him better than those who were so much set on making one.[10]

He was a man of integrity, a High Churchman and High Tory, and served both the King and later the Queen, when she was temporarily Regent, with loyalty.

Bentinck continued to serve the King with distinction for some years and was created Earl of Portland and Groom of the Stole in 1689. Probably from motives of jealousy and because he was a foreigner, the English disliked him. Churchill, created Earl of Marlborough, was continually at loggerheads with Bentinck and was soon to complain that his services were not appreciated. William did not much like Churchill, but respected his ability as a soldier, though he did not trust him. Henry Sidney, who had enjoyed the King's favour as Prince of Orange, continued to benefit from his friendship in England. He was created Lord Sidney and later Earl of Romney, but he was so partial to pleasure, preferring it to business, that he later failed as Lord Lieutenant of Ireland and had to be recalled. The Earl of Danby was created Marquis of Carmarthen and President of the Council, and Lord Halifax, who was highly regarded by the King, was given the Privy Seal. Carmarthen could not tolerate the favour given to Halifax and from jealous motives intrigued against him. William, though impressed with Halifax's ability, did not relish his mercurial wit. The Whigs had never forgiven him for opposing the Exclusion Bill. Lord Mordaught, 'a violent Whig', was created Earl of Monmouth, while Lord Delamere, who had led an insurrection for the Prince of Orange in Cheshire, was made Earl of Warrington. The Earl of Devonshire, a Whig, became Lord Steward, and Lord Dorset, Lord Chamberlain. Arthur Herbert was created Earl of Torrington and Whig Commissioner of the Admiralty. He was a man of bad reputation, being extremely licentious and drinking to excess. Born in 1647 he had entered the navy at the age of seventeen and gained much experience during the Dutch wars. Pepys hated him, saying that he did not possess one virtue to compound for all his vices, for he was immoral, cruel, lazy, vain and bellicose. Yet he seems to have been supported by some of his captains and sailors in the fleet at the time of his downfall after the Battle of Beachy Head.

Both William and Mary were often homesick for Holland during May 1689. On May 10 when his secretary Huygens was with him, William could no longer restrain himself. He exclaimed:

> The weather is warm, now, at the Hague, The Kermesse (Carnival) is on. Oh, if only one could fly over there now, just once, like a bird through the air! I would give a hundred thousand gelders, yes, two hundred thousand, just to be there.

Mary was homesick for the Lange Voorhout in The Hague where the tender green of the trees would be coming into leaf and for Het Loo, where the building work was continuing. She longed for a private life, to escape there to walk in the gardens and the woods.

In his early days of kingship William could not endure his sister-in-law Princess Anne. Whilst in Holland he had once told Bishop Burnet that if he had married her, he would have been the most miserable of men. Anne reciprocated in her dislike of William, calling him 'The Dutch monster' or 'Caliban', or even, occasionally, 'The Dutch abortion'. Unfortunately Lady Fitzharding, a sister of Elizabeth Villiers, Anne's Lady of the Bedchamber, repeated all she heard to Elizabeth, so that the King disliked the Princess of Denmark even more. Mary, too, found Anne irritating, on account of her lack of small talk, while she loved conversation, enjoying the society of her Flemish-speaking Lady-in-Waiting, the Countess of Derby - the widow of Lord Ossory.

Kensington was, at that period, a quiet country village near London, and it was in 1689 that William and Mary bought the lease, for eighteen thousand guineas, of Kensington House from the Earl of Nottingham and began to transform it into a royal residence, aided by Sir Christopher

Wren. Sarah Marlborough, who disliked William, tells an amusing story about him and Princess Anne. One evening Anne was dining with William and Mary when a dish of green peas - the first of the season - was placed before her. According to Sarah, instead of handing any to Anne he snatched the plate and ate them all himself. They were both rather greedy. Sarah wrote:

> Whether he offered any to the Queen I cannot say, but he might do that safely enough, for he knew that she durst not touch them.

Now heiress presumptive to the throne, Anne was prompted by Sarah to persuade Parliament to grant her a permanent and independent allowance, instead of being financially dependent on William. Her father had given her an annuity of as much as £30,000. William and Mary were angry when they heard of Anne's attempt to influence Parliament. One evening at Kensington, Mary charged her with trying to obtain a large life grant. Anne answered the Queen that her friends had a mind to make her some settlement, to be rebuffed by her sister, saying, "Pray what friends have you but the King and me?" Finally a settlement of £50,000 a year was proposed by Parliament and agreed to by William, but animosity had been stirred up between the two sisters, lasting until the Queen's death.

On July 24, 1689, Anne gave birth to an infant son at Hampton Court, christened William Henry, after the King. William created Anne's son Duke of Gloucester and took considerable interest in the prince from infancy. He had little in common with Prince George of Denmark, despising his brain and for the most part neglecting him altogether, much to Anne's resentment.

William understood foreign affairs better than any of his ministers and had an intimate knowledge of foreign countries. Antony Heinsius, now the Grand Pensionary in Holland, was a dedicated politician, hard-working, prudent, and of great integrity. In some ways he strongly resembled William, for they were both delicate, solitary men, utterly dedicated to their work. William spent many hours in correspondence with Heinsius concerning European politics, discussing relations with Spain and the Empire, the Papacy, the Northern powers, Germany, the Italian princes, Russia and Poland,[11] and with France. By May 1689 William was again at war with France, having withdrawn from the Palatinate. Philip William of Neuburg, a Roman Catholic, had succeeded on his death in 1680 the Protestant Elector Charles Louis (father of Liselotte Duchess of Orleans). France was now free for the ensuing fighting in Flanders.

The Lowlands of Scotland had acknowledged William and Mary, but in the Highlands William's most dangerous enemy was John Graham of

Claverhouse, Viscount Dundee, a devoted Jacobite, who had implored James II not to leave England. William's army in Scotland was commanded by General Hugh MacKay, who had earlier served in Holland. MacKay was no match for Dundee, but at the Battle of Killiecrankie (some miles from Dunkeld) fought on July 27, 1689, Dundee was leading a charge of the clansmen down the hillside when he was killed, so his victory was only a pyrrhic one. The Whigs in Scotland were alarmed, sending desperate appeals to William for troops, but he knew the danger was over, remarking with insight, "Armies are needless: the war is over with Dundee's life." If Dundee had survived the battle, James might have been able to go to Scotland with a Franco-Irish army and been restored as King.

Many beneficial matters were translated in Parliament in 1689. The Bill of Rights abolished the dispensing power, so frequently resorted to by James. A vast prerogative was still vested in the King, and he may have at times been tempted to abuse it.

William has been criticized for caring nothing for his kingdom, regarding it only as a source of supply for his foreign wars, but it is hardly true. He was a successful King, having a marked sense of his responsibilities, and he understood the necessity of guiding the country through the transition from the old arbitrary government to the new. In his relations with Parliament he was often obstinate, but he knew instinctively when to give way. Though he talked of abandoning everything and returning to Holland both early and late during his reign of thirteen years, he remained King and succeeded in preserving the Crown, during periods of great difficulty, when his life was threatened by the Jacobites or the wars in Europe were going badly.

The King was tolerant by nature, believing deeply in religious liberty, where his father-in-law's opinion was more controversial. He considered that the Jews should not be compelled to keep the Christian Sunday, nor the Quakers penalized for refusing to swear an oath. Neither Irish Roman Catholics or Scottish Episcopalians were savagely persecuted. He had known freedom of the press in Holland, and after it was granted in England in 1695 he never favoured censorship being imposed again. His views were enlightened regarding the Judiciary as well, and he would never tolerate corrupt judges or the intimidation of juries. The commissions granted by him allowed them to serve '*quam diu si bene gesserint*' (as long as they behave properly), instead of '*durante bene placito*' (during the King's pleasure). The principle of the independence of the Judiciary was slow to get established. The Toleration Act, passed by Parliament, gave liberty of conscience to the Dissenters, but they were not admitted to civil office.

There was opposition also to any reconciliation between the Church of England and Dissenters.

The King did nothing, however, to alter the vile abuse of torture, prevalent at the time. There is no record that he ever protested at the torture of the Jacobite agent Neville Payne in 1690 in Scotland. He merely accepted it.

One is revolted, too, that Titus Oates, an evil, depraved man, who had by his lies sent many innocent Roman Catholics to their deaths, was actually received by William early in 1689 after he was freed from prison. True, he had been mercilessly flogged and punished during the reign of James II, but he richly deserved such treatment. William was requested by the Lower House to grant Oates a pension of £5 a week. Instead of complying, William should have indignantly refused to see him. Sarotti, the Venetian ambassador wrote to the Signory that misguided people defended Oates when he stood in the pillory and would not allow others to inflict the slightest hurt on him.

XIV KING WILLIAM IN IRELAND

No historical event evokes more wonder and admiration than that of the brave men who resisted the Irish and French forces under James II and refused to surrender Londonderry in Ulster. It is a story of heroism, of sacrifice, of unparalleled suffering, of starvation, and also treachery by Robert Lundy to the cause of William III. One of the best historical accounts is by Cecil Devis Milligan.[1]

How many people know anything about Londonderry's history? The island of Derry (founded in 545 B.C. by St. Columba) had been declared escheat to the English Crown by the Earl of Salisbury, James I's chief minister and Lord High Treasurer of England. He established in Derry a Protestant colony of English and Scottish settlers. There is a close association between Derry and the City of London, and Derry's nomenclature was later changed to Londonderry.

Londonderry in 1689 was only a small town, protected by a wall but certainly not a fortress. It is situated on the left bank of the River Foyle, some five miles above the junction of the River Lough Foyle. It was vital for the Jacobite army to capture Londonderry, but the Protestants in that town were determined on resistance. In December 1688 thirteen apprentice boys led by Henry Campsie closed the gates of Londonderry on the Redshanks, the troops of Alexander Macdonell, Earl of Antrim, sent to occupy the town. Tyrconnel was so annoyed by this act of defiance that he burnt his wig.

From the first King William took great interest in the resistance of the inhabitants to the occupation of the Jacobite army. He saw Counsellor Cairnes of the Old Londonderry Corporation in London in early January 1689 and ordered that measures should be immediately taken for the forwarding of military supplies to the garrison. The motives that dominated the minds of the Ulstermen were not really any unbridled enthusiasm for the cause of William III, but the instinct of self-preservation. King James and his Jacobite advisers in Ulster were mistaken in their belief of an early conquest of Londonderry. They did not take into account the heroic spirit of the people. Within the scope of this work it is impossible to discuss the siege in too much detail.

Foremost among those who successfully resisted the Jacobite army, were a clergyman, the Reverend George Walker, Governor of Londonderry during the siege, and Colonel Henry Baker, a co-Governor, a man of invincible spirit who died bravely during the siege. Walker was later killed during the Battle of the Boyne (July 1690). The siege lasted one hundred and five days. John Hunter of Maghera, who served as a soldier throughout the siege, kept a diary in which he wrote:

> I could not get a drink of clear water, and suffered heavily from thirst, and was so distressed by hunger that I could have eaten any vermin, but could not get it.

Indeed the hardships and sufferings endured by the inhabitants could hardly be borne.

Thomas Babington Macaulay was to write: "A very small quantity of grain remained, and was doled out by mouthfuls."[2] And again, "Such was the extremity of distress that the rats who came to feast in these hideous dens were eagerly hunted and greedily devoured." One mighty thing sustained people to the end, their invincible belief in God. Eight thousand people perished.

Relief was slow to come, but King William told the Earl of Shrewsbury that he was anxious that Major-General Percy Kirke should sail with his forces to Londonderry and they finally embarked on May 31, 1689. Prominent among those intrepid men concerned in the relief was Captain Michael Browning, commanding *The Mountjoy*. As his little ship gained the shores of Londonderry laden with provisions, Browning was struck in the head by a bullet as he stood upon the deck with his sword drawn. In Macaulay's well-known words:

> But her brave master was no more, a shot from one of the batteries had struck him; and he died by the most enviable of all deaths in sight of the city which was his birthplace, which was his home, and which had just been saved by his courage and self-devotion from the most frightful form of destruction.[3]

King William honoured his widow by tying a diamond chain round her neck and giving her a pension.

Later during August the Reverend George Walker visited Hampton Court, where he was received by the King and Queen. William listened to the tale of suffering with close attention and, as a token of goodwill, both William and Mary gave Walker £5,000.

A strange incident happened that summer, mentioned by Burnet. A fisherman 'drawing a net' between Lambeth and Vauxhall, found a great weight, which with some difficulty he landed on the shore. It was the Great Seal, thrown into the Thames the night of King James's escape. The fisherman brought it to the King and was handsomely rewarded.[4]

It might be thought that William was indifferent to what happened to his father-in-law, but according to Burnet he would never have had a hand in treachery if it was possible to get him in his power. He certainly wished him no harm and had a certain tenderness for King James's person.

Mary, too, often thought of her father tenderly, though she was criticized for assuming his throne. She was deeply saddened by the thought of the imminent parting from William, who was about to campaign in Ireland.

While he was absent overseas he had decided to leave his wife in control as Regent, though as she was completely inexperienced, her powers were restricted. The Regency Bill granted her the exercise of the administration with the power to deal with matters that needed immediate attention, but matters that could be postponed would be left to the King's return. In a crisis, she was given powers to summon a Parliament. A Council of nine persons was formed to assist her, consisting of the Whig, Thomas Danby, now Marquis of Carmarthen, the Tory, Lord Nottingham as Secretary of State, Lord Stewart as Lord Chamberlain, the Earl of Marlborough as first commissioner of the Treasury, and the Earl of Devonshire as Lord Steward. Other members were Charles Mordaunt, Earl of Monmouth - Mary privately thought him mad - the Earl of Dorset, Edward Russell and Lord Pembroke. Unfortunately Lord Shrewsbury, always trusted by William III, was no longer Secretary of State, having resigned much against the King's will. He was a creature of impulse, possessed a nervous sensibility, having quarrelled with Carmarthen. Jealousy and intrigue were rife among these Counsellors. To become Regent was utterly alien to Mary, but she was to reveal for the post a capacity hitherto unsuspected in a woman barely twenty-eight. The mature Queen Mary was very different from the gauche and over-emotional girl who had married William at fifteen. Four members of the Cabinet Council were Tories and four Whigs. Lord Shrewsbury told Bishop Burnet that the King had often confided in him that, though he could not hit on the right way of pleasing England, he was confident he would in time.

The night before the King embarked on his journey, overburdened with affairs, he called Burnet into his closet, repeating with tenderness that he pitied the poor Queen. For himself he trusted in God, and would either go through with his business or perish in it. To fight against King James was hard because it would be a vast trouble both to himself and to the Queen if he should be either killed or taken prisoner. As for Mary, she was deprived of all that was dear to her:

> my sister of a humour so reserved I could have little comfort from her; the great Council of a strange composition, the Cabinet Council not much better.

She dreaded lest she might not see William ever again.

Irish history has viewed the struggle between James and William as a battle over possession of Ireland, but William, always a European, invaded Ireland for reasons that were European, not English, and that country became a theatre of war 1689-90.[5]

William embarked on the yacht *Mary* on June 11, 1690 at Hoylake and three days later, on a Saturday, arrived in Belfast Lough and dropped anchor in the Bay of Carrickfergus. Marshal Schomberg, who was to be killed at the Battle of the Boyne, met the King by the loughside and accompanied him by coach to Belfast. William immediately liked the Irish, and the rolling hills of County Down particularly took his fancy.

We get little glimpses of the King in the diary of Colonel Thomas Bellingham, an Anglo-Irish officer.[6] For instance on June 16, "Ye K. road out in ye evening, I went to see the King and drank of his wine." Bellingham had been quartered with his regiment for some time at Preston in Lancashire. He later acted as a guide or A.D.C. when William's army marched from Dundalk to the Boyne, and both the King and the Duke of Schomberg consulted him before the Battle of the Boyne. Bellingham states that Schomberg's forces were encamped about a mile from Dundalk and they suffered from disease. Whilst in Ulster, William seems to have been happy campaigning. When a Huguenot blacksmith asked the King to embrace him as French generals did when conferring an honour, William complied, saying, *"Mais oui, mon vieux, je te saluerais volontiers, et ta femme aussi."*[7]

At the Battle of the Boyne the armies of William III and those of the Jacobites under King James were largely composed of cosmopolitan troops. William's army was much stronger and better trained than that of his father-in-law. It was largely composed of professional soldiers from the Continent and its *corps d'élite*[8] was the brigade of Dutch Blue Guards under Solms, while other excellent soldiers were Dutch under the Prince of Nassau. There were two French Huguenot regiments, a brigade of English soldiers commanded by Sir Thomas Hanmer, and the remaining forces consisted of Finns, Danes, Swiss and Brandenburgers. William's army has been estimated at 33,000, and the Jacobites at 21,000. His army was superior in morale and in artillery. The Jacobite army had some splendid Irish officers, especially Patrick Sarsfield and the deserter Richard Hamilton. It contained some polished Irish cavalry and good French professional troops, but the Irish foot were absolutely undisciplined.

The strategy of the great soldier Marshal Schomberg to turn the left wing of the Jacobites was masterly, but he was overruled by William, when a large contingent under Bentinck and Schomberg's son advanced westward in the early hours of July 1 to the bridge of Slane, which they succeeded in crossing. Their advance presented no surprise for the enemy, for Sarsfield's horse and some French regulars awaited them. There was fierce fighting and brave action by the Jacobite cavalry before William's army succeeded in storming the breastworks. King William, though never a great soldier, fought bravely at the Battle of the Boyne, taking no measures for his own safety. Eventually the Jacobite army was defeated and King James fled to Dublin and from there to France.

Colonel Bellingham relates in his diary[9] on June 30 how the King was slightly wounded:

> On ye s. side of Boyn lay ye enemys camp, which, ye King going to view, he was hit by a cannon shot on his shoulder, wch putt us into the greatest consternation imaginable; but, blessed be God, it proved but a slight hurte. He went round his own camp and was received with ye greatest joy and acclamations imaginable.

Bellingham also relates that the brave old Marshal Schomberg was killed during the course of the battle, and Dr. Walker and Col. Callincott mortally wounded.

In the *Letters of Liselotte* written to her aunt, the Duchess of Orleans alludes to the wound sustained by the Prince of Orange (he was not recognized as King in France until some years later). It was first reported incorrectly in France that William had died of his wounds. Liselotte commented:

> The more I see of this King (James), the more excuses I find for the Prince and the more admirable I think he is. Perhaps you will think that 'old love never grows stale',* but I certainly prefer an intelligence such as his to the other's handsome face.

---

*Liselotte is referring to the days when she visited her grandmother at The Hague.

Bellingham relates that on a very hot day, July 4:

I waited on ye King with an account of ye stores and provisions yt here in Dublin and 20 miles around. I presented him with a baskett of cherryes ye first he eat since he came to the kingdom.

On Sunday, July 6, William rode into Dublin, to be acclaimed at least by the Protestants of that city, and attended a thanksgiving service in Christchurch Cathedral. It is curious that William, while his army lay at Bennettsbridge on July 19, took the opportunity of visiting Kilkenny Castle, the ancestral home of the Duke of Ormonde, where his early friend Lord Ossory had been born. He never forgot him. His successes in Ireland, however, were somewhat dampened by bad news from England of the shameful defeat of the English fleet off Beachy Head and the disgrace of Lord Torrington. A Jacobite rebellion was expected to follow. At first he thought of going home, but he wanted to achieve the surrender of Waterford, which occurred on July 25. After their victory at Beachy Head, the French had attacked Teignmouth, but the English had rallied to the Queen, who was performing well as Regent, so William decided to lead his army for the purpose of besieging Limerick. He was no longer anxious about an invasion, since the important Jacobites were in prison. On August 2 his army lay before Limerick.

Mary's letters to her William whilst overseas are those of a wife who loves her husband William with an enduring love, rather than those of a woman who had been married to a husband twelve and a half years. Many of them are in Dalrymple.[10] After telling him that the only comfort in this world she had was to write to him, besides that of trust of God, she wrote on June 29:

Though I trust every post to hear some good news or other from you, I only tell you I have got a swell'd face, though not quite so bad yet, as it was in Holland five years ago. I believe it came by standing too much at the window when I took the waters. I cannot enough thank God for you being so well past the dangers of the sea. I beseech Him in his mercy still to preserve you so, and send us once more a happy meeting upon earth. I long to hear again from you how the aire of Ireland agrees with you, for I must own I am not without my fear for that, loving you so entirely as I do, and shall until death.

While William was absent overseas, Mary had ordered a prayer for her husband's success in arms against her father to be said in all the churches throughout England. Unfortunately she had heard by some person's tittle-tattle that prayers were omitted to be read in the Savoy Chapel attached to Somerset House, where the Queen-Dowager Catherine of Braganza resided. In her widowhood Catherine's Lord Chamberlain was Lord Feversham, nicknamed 'the King-Dowager', although there was nothing improper in their relations. Mary wrote William on July 1:

> I desire Lord Nott. to send for Lord Feversham and to speak as angrily as it was possible, which he promised. He came yesterday in my bedchamber ... He seemed extreamly concerned, lookt as pale as death, and spoke in great disorder; he said, he must own it a very great fault, since I took it so; But he begged me to believe 'twas not done out of any ill intention, nor by agreement with anybody. He assured me that the Queen herself knew nothing of it; he said 'twas a fault, and a folly, an indiscretion, or anything I would call it ... But though I pity the poor man for being obliged to take the Queen Dowager's faults upon him, yet I could not bring myself to forgive him.[11]

It is possible that Mary vented her spite against her aunt by marriage. She mentions her health again in this letter. "Yesterday I had leeches set behind my ears for my swelled face, which has done little good ... and one of my eyes being again sore." One of the most important letters in this series concerns the defeat of the English in the action off Beachy Head and her criticism of Lord Torrington's part in the affair.

England lay in great danger from a French attack during the summer (1690), for under their Admiral Tourville, a brilliant naval officer, they had put to sea on June 13 with a total strength of 77 men of war, six frigates and 20 fireships.[12] At the end of January, Edward Russell had written to Lord Nottingham, a former Commissioner (from 1679-1684), who fancied he was an expert on naval matters.

> For God's sake, my Lord, cast your eye sometimes towards the next summer's fleet. I dread the French being out before us. If they are we shall run hazard of being undone ... I see all matters relating to the navy go on so slowly that I am in amaze.

Admiral Herbert Lord Torrington also feared the worst. As the weeks advanced and the fleet was not ready for sea, Torrington vigorously protested. By early May he threatened to resign his commission as Admiral of the Fleet. When he finally received his sailing orders, Torrington commanded fifty English ships and twenty Dutch. He was very pessimistic, harbouring gloomy forebodings - some said he was secretly in touch with the Jacobites. "The odds are great", he wrote Nottingham, the Secretary of State, "and you know that it is not my fault ... let them tremble at the consequence whose fault it was the fleet is no stronger." Nottingham, who personally disliked Torrington, was far more optimistic, writing to King William on June 17, four days after Tourville had sailed: "Our fleet here is stronger than any the French can sett out from Brest." However, Torrington wrote to Nottingham on June 26th:

> I do acknowledge my first intention of attacking them a rashness that will admit of no better excuse than that I thought I did beleeve them stronger than wee are.

Some questioned his courage and imputed this to fear, but this may be unfair. What is evident is that the Dutch were not supported by Torrington in their fight with the French and they bitterly complained of his inaction. Many Dutch ships were sunk or lost. It was generally agreed that if the whole fleet had joined in a close fight, we must have beaten the French.

When Torrington received imperative orders from the Queen to engage the enemy at all costs, he was stung into action, but he was much criticized for leaving the brunt of the action to the Dutch. The Queen wrote an apologetic letter in Dutch to the Admiral Evertzen, and saw him. Evertzen's attitude was not so much to blame Torrington, but to affirm that though the fleets were unequal in strength, had the English fought like the Dutch, they should at least have so shattered many of the French ships as to make them useless for further fighting. She wrote to William that Torrington would never be forgiven here. Lord Torrington resigned his command and was sent to the Tower.

As Regent, Queen Mary was daily in touch with Lord Nottingham. She wrote William: "I confess I incline to have a good opinion of him; it may be his formal, grave look deceives me." On July 6, hearing that an express had come from Ireland, Mary began to tremble as Nottingham entered with a letter. He wore his customary grave expression, but he was able to reassure her that the King was well, although wounded at the Battle of the Boyne.

She wrote him later:

> My poor heart is ready to break every time I think in what perpetual danger you are ... and yet I must see company upon my sett days, I must play twice a week, nay, I must laugh and talk tho' never so much against my will ... all my motions are so watch'd and all I do observed, that if I eat less or speak less, or look more grave, all is lost in the

opinion of the world, so that I have this misery added to that of your absence and my fears for your dear person that I must grin when my heart is ready to break, and talk when my heart is so oppres'd I can scarce breathe.

William had given orders to Lord Marlborough to leave for Kinsale to take part in the Irish war, and Mary writes of Sarah:

As little reason as I have to care for his wife, yet I must pity her condition, having lain in but eight days; and I have great compassion for wives when their husbands go to fight.

The Queen longed for her husband's return, but she had seen a copy of the *Utrecht Courant* in which was printed a letter of William's to the States, promising he would be with them soon.

Most of that summer a French invasion was feared, for France had 20,000 trained troops in readiness, but they failed to follow up the advantage they had gained in the Battle of Beachy Head.

When Mary wanted peace and quiet she occasionally went to Kensington House. Her eyes suffered from the demanding work by candlelight:

That place made me think how happy I was there when I had your dear company; but now I will say no more, for I shall hurt my own eyes, which I want more than ever. Adieu; think of me, and love me as much as I shall you, who I love more than my own life.

Work was going on in both Kensington and Hampton Court. At Kensington the Clock Court, its gateway surmounted by a cupola, was now complete, but William's closets needed more work.

In Europe there were serious reverses for William, for on July 10 he feared that Waldeck had been defeated at Fleurus. At the Siege of Limerick he encountered much trouble, failing to take the city by storm, and heavy falls of rain in late August frustrated his plans for further attacks. Limerick was heroically defended by Patrick Sarsfield and other excellent Irish officers. It was Godart van Ginckel, one of William's best generals, who eventually captured Limerick and he was created Earl of Athlone during 1692. During late September 1690, Marlborough captured Cork and Kinsale. At Cork, Charles II's illegitimate son, the Duke of Grafton, was mortally wounded, dying bravely a few days later.

William returned to England about 3 p.m. on September 5 at Duncannon Fort, after a rough passage. Stopping for the night of

September 6 at the house of Sir Robert Southwell, near Bristol (spelt Bristow in the seventeenth century), he moved on to Badminton, the Duke of Beaufort's place in Gloucestershire. William's fortieth birthday was celebrated on November 4. Luttrell relates that:

> it was observed here very strictly, by shutting up the shops, firing the great guns at the Tower, ringing of bells and bonfires at night, their Majesties dined publickly at Whitehall, where was a great resort of nobility and gentry, and at night was a consort of musick, and a play afterwards and the next day, being the anniversary of the gunpowder plott (being likewise the day of His Majesties landing in England (1688), was observed with great solemnity and general rejoicing.[13]

It is not known whether 'the consort of music' included any works of Henry Purcell, the foremost musical genius of his day and a prolific composer, but William had little taste for music, though Mary cared for it.

The King was busy during the last months of 1690 in the organization of a great conference, scheduled to take place at The Hague during February 1691. William's greatness lies far more in his patient diplomacy and ability to form and unite a coalition against the all-absorbing ambitions of Louis XIV than it does as a none-too-successful soldier.

William was incensed with Lord Torrington, who had been censured for his inactivity at Beachy Head. His enemies wanted to impeach him before the House of Lords, but it was rightly decided that a court martial would be more appropriate. It was eventually held on December 10 at Sheerness under the presidency of Sir Ralph Delavell, probably ill-disposed towards Torrington. The accusation was a capital one. The prosecution case was that he had not engaged the enemy whom it was his duty to fight, that he had kept back from the conflict. Torrington made a spirited defence, emphasizing the inferior strength of the English fleet and the probability of a major disaster if it had imitated the recklessness of the Dutch. He said that he had served at sea for twenty-seven years, and had been in more battles and lost more blood than any gentleman in England. If these facts did not prove his courage, if his sacrifices on behalf of the revolution did not prove his integrity, no man's reputation could be safe.[14] He was fully acquitted. Though previously deprived of his command, he never received another. William's motive for not employing Torrington again at sea was probably owing to Dutch hostility and Torrington's quarrels with Admiral Russell, who succeeded him. Whatever his private character, his alleged licentious, haughty and dictatorial nature, according to Burnet, Pepys and others, Torrington's views on naval strategy were in advance of his age. The King is reputed to have been friendly with him until his death. Burnet's opinion of Torrington was probably prejudiced.

For the remainder of 1690 William and Mary were much at Hampton Court. It would seem that William intended this historic place to be a rival to Louis's magnificent palace at Versailles or intended his new home to be a less grandiose Versailles. When, however, Sir Christopher Wren had presented his ambitious estimates for the cost of rebuilding the Palace in early May 1689, with a fine garden and a network of canals, the Treasury considered the cost too excessive. Wren had originally suggested pulling down almost all Tudor Hampton Court, but during the year 1689 the Tudor Base Court, the Great Hall, and Clock Court were left much as they were. Wren planned a new wing along the south and east fronts of Hampton Court, the King's apartments looking out over the Privy Garden. William's writing room and the Queen's closet had easy access to the back stairs.[15] What Sir Christopher had originally proposed and wanted was a spacious new palace in the seventeenth century Renaissance taste as appreciated in France. He found both William and Mary discriminating and intelligent patrons, but was somewhat hampered by his bad relations with William Talman, his colleague as Comptroller of the Royal Works. Work on the lovely gardens at Hampton Court would continue for several years. Jean Tijou, for instance, received £360 for his magnificent Baroque iron work in the gardens. For three years 1691-1694, the year of Queen Mary's death, £80,000 was spent at Hampton Court.

The Palace had one significant attraction for William, for nearby was Bushey Park, where he could indulge in the joys of the chase. Mary's days were clouded at the end of 1690 by thoughts of the imminent departure of her husband for Holland. She wanted to accompany the King there, where she had so many friends, sorely missed.

XV   A MASSACRE AND MORE BATTLES

So William came home to his country, the first time he had been able to return there since the invasion, on January 16, 1691. William embarked on his yacht *Mary* at Gravesend, attended by Portland, Ouwerkerk, Devonshire and other noblemen. The voyage was a nightmare, taking two weeks, for the travellers had to contend with violent storms and freezing fog and ice in the estuary. On February 5 he made a triumphant entry into The Hague while the bells of the Groete Kerk chimed merrily. There was the deafening roar of cannon, and the sound of trumpets. William, wanting to stage an impressive entry, had arranged that a large number of musicians should attend him in The Hague. They had sailed separately from the main party on January 1. It is not certain that Henry Purcell was among them, but among the papers of Charles, 6th Earl of Dorset "Hene Pursell: Harpsicall" is included,[1] so is "John Blow Composer".

There were representatives from nearly every state in Europe at the Congress, the Governor of the Spanish Netherlands, the flamboyant Marquis de Castanaga, the two Electors of Brandenburg and Bavaria, the Prince Regent of Würtemburg, the Prince of Brunswick, and the Landgrave of Hesse-Cassel.

William made a very effective speech in Dutch, emphasizing the necessity for unity, and above all, for action. He told the Congress that if he had accepted the English Crown, his motives were not personal ambition or greed. He wanted to maintain their religion and peace. He fully realized as their King, he was in a more powerful position to assist his allies against the enterprise of France. His allies agreed that an army of 200,000 could be assembled ready for fighting.

However, on March 15 William had a serious setback, harming his prestige. Louis XIV appeared in all his splendour before the town of Mons with an enormous army of 130,000 troops, and Mons soon fell to France. William had gone to Het Loo for a few days hunting, but hastened there too late to save the town.

In England while William was absent, the Jacobites were busy plotting against his government. A leading Jacobite Lord Preston, had formerly served as Ambassador in Paris and was found willing to take over to France incriminating letters, particularly one from the Bishop of Ely to King James's Queen, in which he pledged his loyalty to her and zeal for the Prince of Wales. A servant of William's Queen, John Ashton, hired a vessel to take them over. It was unfortunate for the Jacobites that the owner of the vessel was a government agent, and Preston's and Ashton's letters were discovered. Preston, Ashton and a young man named Elliot were arrested. At their trial, Ashton behaved with more courage than Lord Preston, refusing to give away any secrets, and was condemned to death. According to Burnet, he was prepared to die, "and he suffered with great decency and seriousness". Preston was a weaker character. He had no wish to die, and his daughter urged Queen Mary to grant her father a reprieve, as did many others. After Preston had agreed to divulge the names of his fellow conspirators, the Earl of Clarendon, the Bishop of Ely, William Penn, Carmarthen and others, his own life was spared.

There is a letter, dated February 13, 1691, from Viscount Sidney to Lord Lucas, governor of the Tower of London:[2]

> The Queen being informed that the Earl of Clarendon, now a prisoner in your custody, is of late very much impaired in health, by reason of the close confinement he lies under, commands me to signify her pleasure to you that you permit him to have the liberty of walking about the Tower, provided it be at reasonable hours.

After some months King William, taking into consideration Clarendon's close relationship to his Queen, had him freed from prison, but confined to his house in the country.

For the most part William never behaved harshly to leading Jacobites, while Mary on one occasion was so charming to Thomas Bruce Earl of Ailesbury after he had been released from bail, inviting him to play bassett with her and seating him next her friend Lady Derby, that he expressed eternal gratitude to her.

Whilst at The Hague during 1691 William had a curious encounter with Olympe Mancini, Comtesse de Soissons, one of the celebrated Mancini sisters. She had lately been accused of poisoning the Queen of Spain and compelled to flee from Spain. However, invitations to her coffee parties at The Hague where she had fled, were much sought after. Among the potential guests she never invited was King William, so he invited himself. He told her to her face that he did not see why he should be treated as a son of a bitch *'en fils de putain'* and not asked to her coffee parties. Olympe once a favourite of King Louis, was much reluctant to invite him, saying, "You know what I am accused of, sire. If anything happened to you my life would not be worth an hour's purchase!"[3] William insisted and Madame de Soissons was also invited to one of his card parties, an intriguing occasion.

When a favourite young gentleman-in-waiting, Arnold Joost van Keppel, sustained a nasty fall in a hunting expedition, resulting in a broken leg, William visited him several times, reminding one of the constant visits his ancestor James I had made to Robert Carr when he fell from his horse. The French later accused William of being a homosexual. He certainly had homosexual tendencies, but there is little evidence that he was one.

During April the King paid a fortnight's visit to England. Mary was very excited, writing that "it seems like a dream that he had been here". On his return Mary came some of the way to Harwich.

In Ireland Ginckel prospered, gaining a victory over the Jacobites at Aughrim and succeeding in achieving the fall of Limerick.

On October 20, 1691, the King returned home from Margate, but the roads were so rough that his coach overturned. Bentinck Lord Portland fell heavily on William. Others travelling with him were Ouwerkerk, the Duke of Ormond and Lord Churchill. When the latter complained that his neck had been broken, the King told him "there was little danger of that by his speaking".[4] In the City of London William was welcomed home to the ringing of church bells and blazing bonfires. On arriving in Whitehall he eagerly asked: "Where is the Queen?" He hurried through the crowded ante-rooms to her apartments, kissed her several times and took her to Kensington House, where supper was awaiting them.

The King was very busily employed for the remainder of the year with meetings with his Privy Council, the opening of Parliament on November 2, the reception of the Bishop of London and many persons, and constant correspondence with the States. The Lord Mayor's Show that November 1691 was an elaborate water pageant, held on a sunny, mild, autumn day, "a most pleasing day" according to Evelyn. William's forty-first birthday was also celebrated by a resplendent ball at Kensington.

For some time William and Mary had been trying to persuade Dr. Tillotson, for whom they had a warm regard, to become Archbishop of Canterbury. He had no personal ambition, however, and put the arguments against his promotion as forcibly as possible to the King. Its only effect was to make William keener, for the soft and prudent counsels of this gentle prelate had impressed both King and Queen.[5] They succeeded in overcoming his opposition. Finally in 1691 Sancroft with six of his bishops continued to defy William by refusing to take the oaths and as already mentioned, about four hundred of the parochial clergy were also deprived of their sees and livings.

It might have been better for William if he had shown more understanding for Scotland and managed Scottish business himself, but this would have been difficult because he was so overworked in England. There was talk of him visiting Scotland, but he never did so. He left Scotland largely in the hands of the Reverend William Carstares, and to a lesser extent Bentinck conducted Scottish affairs. Since 1690 the Secretary of State for Scotland had been Sir John Dalrymple, Master of Stair, a clever man and a lawyer by profession, but possessing a fanatical hatred for Highlanders.

The Massacre of Glencoe (February 13, 1692) was the great blot on the reign of William and Mary. Since Killiecrankie the Highland clans had been lawless and restive, but those in authority had been patient with the Highlanders, seeking to win them over by peaceful means. During 1691, however, a proclamation was made ordering the Highland clans to swear allegiance to King William and Queen Mary by 1 January, 1692. All the chiefs swore the oaths of allegiance except MacDonald of Glencoe, the head of a small clan who inhabited a wild valley in Argyllshire. The Glencoe MacDonalds had a long history as cattle-thieves and troublesome raiders, being bitter enemies of the larger clan Campbell. Alasdair MacDonald of Glencoe, a man of a very proud nature, agreed to the oath of allegiance on January 6, 1692, five days late. By the middle of January the writer to the Signet and Sheriff-Clerk of Argyll had a certified list of those chiefs who had taken the oath at Inverary, including the name of Alasdair MacDonald of Glencoe.[6]

In London the Master of Stair did not at first know that the MacDonalds had surrendered and signed the oath, but he soon knew of it. It was Sir John Dalrymple, Master of Stair, who was mainly responsible for the hideous massacre,[7] but King William must share some of the blame for abetting him. King and Minister met during the evening of January 16 and by that date Dalrymple was well aware that MacDonald had signed the oath of allegiance. He told the cold and impassive King that the MacDonalds were thieves and murderers, whose removal would bring relief and satisfaction to all the people of Scotland.

Stair wrote to Sir Thomas Livingstone, Commander-in-Chief of Scotland, "For a just example of vengeance, I entreat that the thieving tribe in Glencoe may be rooted out in earnest." To Colonel Sir John Hill, Governor of Fort William, "Pray, when anything concerning Glencoe is resolved, let it be secret and sudden."

On February 13, 1692 Captain Robert Campbell of Glenlyon was ordered to fall upon the rebels, the MacDonalds of Glencoe, and to put all to the sword under seventy. So, on a bleak winter day of snow and ice, men of this tribe were treacherously and ruthlessly murdered. Some, however, escaped. According to a letter from Colonel Hill to the Earl of Portland, those men of Glencoe ... would submit to mercy if their lives may be granted them, upon giving security to live peacefully under the government, and not to rob, steal or receive stolen goods hereafter ... At the moment they lie dormant in caves and remote places.[8]

The Scottish Parliament were in recess from 1693-1695, but in that year William authorized a Parliamentary inquiry. Their Report first appeared in print in 1703. *The Massacre of Glencoe being a true narrative of the Barbarous Murther of the Glenco-men in the Highlands of Scotland, by way of military execution on Feb. 13, 1692.*[9]

John Hay, Marquis of Tweedale Lord High Chancellor of Scotland was Chief Commissioner, a nobleman involved in more than one Jacobite plot. He had made craven confessions. The Second Commissioner was William Earl of Annandale, whom few people trusted. He had supported the Revolution in 1689, but had hopes from King James. The Third Commissioner was Sir James Stewart, His Majesty's Solicitor and Lord Advocate. Adam Cockburn of Ormiston, Lord Justice Clerk, was a bigoted and zealous Presbyterian who believed that King William could do no wrong. There were two other Commissioners.

It is clear that the main blame for the Massacre lay with Dalrymple the Master of Stair:

We doe therefore beg that Your Majestie will give such orders about him for vindication of your government as you in Your Royall Wisdom shall think fitt.

The Commissioners also criticized military personnel.

Justice was never done, for the Master of Stair was merely dismissed from his offices of State. The Commission had concluded that there was nothing in the King's orders to warrant the massacre, but he should have at least ensured that Dalrymple was tried before a court of law. He again showed laxity in this case as he had done in the case of the barbarous murder of the de Witt brothers. William's fondness for the family influenced him not to take tougher action.

1692 was a year of crisis for William and Mary. They were furious when they heard that Anne had written an extremely contrite letter to her father at Saint-Germain asking for his forgiveness. Jacobite agents swarmed about the Court in England and many prominent men such as Marlborough, Godolphin and Russell corresponded with the Jacobite Court at Saint-Germain. It was a form of insurance policy in case anything should happen to William and Mary. William did not trust Marlborough, and it was essential for him to have absolute reliance on his Commander-in-Chief. Marlborough was jealous of Ginckel, who had been given the chief command in Ireland and thought that as the conqueror of Kinsale that he deserved promotion. He was discontented because he had expected to receive the Garter and one of his ambitions was to gain the cherished post of Master-General of the Ordnance. Both the King and Queen feared the bad influence on Princess Anne of Sarah Churchill.

On the morning of February 13, Marlborough as Lord-in-Waiting handed the taciturn King his shirt in his usual graceful way. A few hours later he was visited by Lord Nottingham, to be suddenly informed that he was dismissed from all his offices and told to keep away from Court. These were dangerous times. As a further French invasion was daily expected, the King may have feared that Marlborough was sending the French secret information. However, there was no proof. Most contemporaries were of the opinion that Marlborough was disgraced "for holding correspondence with King James". Among the letters of the Hatton family is one (February 1692):

> I thought I had given you a good account of it because it all came from Lord Carmarthen, Lord Nottingham and Lord Mar; and all agreed in this, that he had, besides other things of high misdemeanour, said he had held correspondence with King James.

John Evelyn wrote on February 28:

> Lord Marlborough having us'd words against the King, and been discharg'd from all his greate places, his wife was forbid the Court, and the Princesse of Denmark was desir'd by the Queene to dismiss her from her service, but she refusing to do so, goes away from the Court to Sion House.[10]

Sarah's temper on the dismissal of her husband may well be imagined, but Queen Mary disliked her and when her sister insisted on taking her to Court and stubbornly refused to be parted from her, she was very angry. Mary taxed Anne for giving Lady Marlborough an annuity of £1,000 from her parliamentary grant. Public sympathy in this affair was for Anne rather than Mary, because Anne was with child at the time and the Queen's attack was considered cruel in the circumstances. It was a spiteful gesture for her to order her sister to remove from the Cockpit because the Cockpit was her own property, having been settled on her by her uncle Charles II. Nor had the Queen the right to do so. Anne perforce was obliged to leave her home and asked her friend the Duchess of Somerset ('Carrots'), the daughter and heiress of the Earl of

136

Northumberland, for the loan of Syon House about eight miles from the Cockpit. This was granted her, though King William attempted to persuade the proud Duke of Somerset to withdraw his promise. Before removing to Syon House, Anne made one last attempt to propitiate the Queen at Kensington House. The King and Queen rather pettishly ordered that the Princess should be deprived of the Guards, who always attended her. This led to her coach being stopped in Brentford one evening in March when she was travelling from London to Syon, to be robbed by highwaymen.

Anne lay very ill and troubled at Syon House, having just given birth to an infant son, who immediately died. It was there that the Queen came to see her - the last time the sisters were ever to meet. Mary showed no sympathy, or understanding, merely saying, haughtily and curtly:

I have made the first step by coming to you, and now I expect that you should make the next by dismissing Lady Marlborough.

For Anne with her passionate attachment to Sarah had insisted on her presence at Syon. Anne answered her respectfully with a few words:

I have never in all my life disobeyed your Majesty, but in this one particular, and I hope at some time or other it will appear as unreasonable to Your Majesty as it does now to me.

The Queen swept from the room without another word, imparting her mind to Prince George as he attended her to her coach. Evelyn is one of the Prince of Denmark's contemporaries, who praises him: "he had the Danish countenance," he wrote:

blonde, of few words, spake French ill, seem'd somewhat heavy, but reported to be valiant, and indeede he had bravely rescu'd and brought off his brother the K. of Denmark in a battaile against the Swedes.[11]

John Churchill Earl of Marlborough, accused of high treason and for abetting and adhering to His Majesty's enemies, was consigned to the Tower on May 5. Among Churchill's supporters none were more vociferous than Admiral Russell, himself suspected of trafficking with Saint-Germain. He told William that he was wrong to strip Marlborough of his offices and to have him imprisoned. Sarah, devoted to her husband, wanted to share his imprisonment, but John advised her to remain with the princess. He spent five weeks in the Tower, and having been escorted to the

King's Bench on June 12, he found friends such as Lord Halifax and the Earl of Shrewsbury willing to act as sureties and to go bail for him. He was then released. Much of the evidence against Marlborough was fabricated by the Jacobites and cannot be relied on. That spring seethed with rumours that another French invasion was planned. "Surely, 'tis a very jealous time," wrote Sir Charles Lyttleton to Lord Hatton on May 10.

William had left England on March 14, leaving Mary as temporary Regent. He was in wretched health, for "he spit blood for a night and a day",[12] but it improved in Holland, although the weather remained very cold. In England in late April there had been cold and unseasonable weather, scarce a leaf on the trees. On March 31, William and Bentinck were both at Het Loo. Much to their dismay, however, there was no game in the coverts. William wanted to see the designs for murals for the great staircase and the upper rooms, and the frescoes on the staircase. While the King was at the Abbey of Bethlehem in May, there was a plot by a Frenchman named Grandval to murder him, but William did not take the matter seriously. Grandval confessed to the attempted assassination, saying he had proposed to follow the King and shoot him as he was riding about on his ordinary business. His confession probably saved him from being put to the torture.

May 1692 was a crucial time in the warfare between England and France, for under the command of Admiral Edward Russell the fleet of England and Holland won a glorious sea battle against the French Admiral Tourville - the Battle of La Hogue fought off the coast of Normandy. Queen Mary behaved superbly as Regent, acting calmly and deliberately, though deeply anxious that William would be defeated in Flanders. In her letter to Admiral Russell she declared her complete confidence in the English seamen under his command, arousing their enthusiasm. King Louis's tactics were mistaken ones, for both he and King James believed wrongly that Russell was a Jacobite ready to desert to them. He instructed the Comte de Tourville to attack the enemy fleet, underestimating their strength.

By May 15, 1692 the Allied fleet numbering 82 ships of the line, were assembled at Portsmouth, while Tourville commanded 44 warships. Russell, after a Council of War, decided to sail towards Cape Barfleur to meet the enemy there rather than to go down the Channel. The sea battle was hotly contested, for the red squadron under the command of Admiral Russell in the *Britannia* was attacked by Admiral Tourville's *Soleil Royal*, his flagship. The *Soleil Royal* came off worse in the encounter, "shot to pieces and left a burnt-out wreck".[13] Towards 2 o'clock in the afternoon Sir Cloudesley Shovell succeeded in breaking through the French fire; while Sir George Rooke destroyed twelve French ships and various transports.

Others were burnt at Cherbourg. The remainder of the French fleet were driven along the coast towards Cape La Hogue. We get a picture of the old King James at La Hogue, nostalgic for earlier times, watching the English seamen swarming up the high side of the French ships as he exclaimed: "Ah! None, but my brave English could do so brave an action." It was a decisive victory for the English fleet. However, Russell and Sir John Ashby of the Blue Squadron were accused of not taking proper measures to complete the destruction of the French.[14] The House of Commons maintained that Russell had behaved with courage and fidelity. He was temporarily removed from his command, but reinstated in November 1693 and appointed First Lord of the Admiralty.[15]

On land, however, King Louis continued to enjoy considerable success, capturing Namur after coming with a great army to besiege the city, a place of considerable importance. He also brought with him ladies and princes as was his custom. Continental victory continued to elude King William. He experienced another reverse at the Battle of Steenkerk (August 3, 1692) fighting against the great French Marshal Luxembourg, although the losses on both sides were enormous. It was a narrow victory for Luxembourg. There was fierce fighting by the British infantry under William's kinsman, Count Henry Solms leading the van against Louis XIV's Swiss regiments. The British blamed Solms subsequently for their defeat, saying that he had not provided support for them when hard pressed, and he was bitterly criticized in England. Among the 3,000 killed and wounded - the losses may have amounted to more - were Hugh MacKay, who had fought so gallantly at Killiecrankie. He was a man of the strictest principles, and Burnet wrote that he took great care of his soldiers' morals. He was much loved. A few days after Steenkerk, Grandval, accused of attempting to assassinate William III, was court-martialled, dying bravely on August 13. He declared that both King James and King Louis were consenting parties, and Queen Mary in her anxiety felt a new bitterness against her father.

After a stormy journey William returned to England towards the end of October. A few days later he wrote Heinsius:

This is a very fatiguing day for me. I opened Parliament this morning and have still to endure the celebrations of my birthday.

XVI WILLIAM IN ADVERSITY

Sir John Fortescue,[1] a recognized military authority, had no very high opinion of William III as a general. The King was Commander-in-Chief of the allied army and as the soul of the Alliance, was without doubt, best suited to the post. He had carefully studied the art of war and his phlegmatic temperament found genuine pleasure in the excitement of the battlefield, yet he cannot ever be described as a great general. He met with many reverses. He could devise good plans and up to a certain point execute them, but his physical health debarred him from steady and sustained effort. He never conducted a campaign with equal ability throughout. Yet he would manoeuvre admirably for weeks, and unfortunately forfeit all the advantages he had acquired by the carelessness of a single day. Of his conspicuous bravery in countless battles, there can be no question, and he never had any thought for his own safety, believing strongly in predestination and that everything was ordained by God. He lacked, however, the tactical instinct of a skilled strategist and the patience of a born commander, though as a negotiator he possessed this quality.

It is fair to add that William was pitted against the finest and strongest army in Europe. The French army was well equipped, and well trained. King Louis XIV was in supreme control of affairs, and General Luxembourg was one of the great generals of the seventeenth century. Marshal Boufflers was less consistent, but had flashes of genius.

In his choice of commanders, William sometimes erred, and he has been criticized for promoting Dutch soldiers over the heads of able English commanders. Such was Count Solms, who was much disliked by the English. Burnet relates, however, that Solms "was much disgusted with their heart and pride",[2] and he certainly was tactless in his relations with the English. Solms was eventually killed at the Battle of Landen, July 29, 1693, a few hours after his leg was shot off by a cannon ball. William's tactics at Landen, in Flanders, were criticized for not avoiding battle altogether, since his army was heavily outnumbered by Luxembourg's troops. In any event, his magnificent courage at Landen is a classic example of his bravery on active service.

Sir Winston Churchill claims that this battle was "unmatched in its slaughter except by Malplaquet and Borodino for two hundred years."[3] The casualties on both sides were in the region of fifteen thousand.

William seemed to bear a charmed life that day and fought like a man inspired. Burnet wrote of him: "he was all fire though without passion". Many times he led his troops to the charge. Men were falling all around him, threatened by the enemies' cannon. He was wounded in the side, but a musket-shot carried away part of his scarf, and another one went through his hat without harming him. His gallant behaviour earned the praise of the King of France and of his enemies.

There was an intense struggle for the village of Neerwinden held by the allied forces, and strongly fortified by the King. During the course of the action the young Duke of Berwick, natural son of James II, was captured by Brigadier Churchill, brother of the Earl of Marlborough, and brought before King William. Berwick had no reason to like William for having deprived his father of three crowns. The King, however, made him a very polite compliment, but Berwick merely answered by a low bow. To him he was merely the Prince of Orange and a usurper. William looked him steadily in the eye "and put on his hat, and I mine".[4]

Neerwinden was in French hands and reinforcements coming to their aid decided the battle. William managed to save his army from total destruction, ordering General Talmash to supervise the retreat and holding up the enemy as best he could. The French troops were as exhausted as the Allies and did not follow up their victory. William withdrew to Louvain where he wrote Mary immediately to reassure her he was safe. He also wrote to Bentinck, always a tremendous support, congratulating him on his escape, though wounded. His strong sense of religion comforted him and the necessity to submit to God's will.

Though defeated, William's prestige in France and indeed throughout Europe had never been higher. France was still triumphant, but there were ominous signs. Two bad harvests in succession had caused poverty and hardship in the provinces, resulting in King Louis making a liberal distribution for the relief of the poor. Efforts were now begun to make a general peace. Many French officers were demoralized, saying that another such battle would be their total ruin. They now talked respectfully of William as King of England.

William was in a querulous mood on returning to England that autumn. Mary said that he disapproved of everything the government had done since his absence overseas. Both William and Mary liked Nottingham better than any of his colleagues, but his enemies among the Whigs were determined to get rid of him, and William was forced to dismiss him as Secretary of State. The King tried hard to persuade Shrewsbury to accept the Seals, but the nobleman was unwilling. He then asked Elizabeth Villiers to visit Shrewsbury and to use her wiles to persuade him to change his mind. She had no better success. Elizabeth was an intimate friend of Miss Lundy, Shrewsbury's mistress, daughter of the former joint Governor of Londonderry. Of one interview with William, Elizabeth wrote: "I found the King in a temper, I wish you could have seen."

We hear very little of Elizabeth Villiers during the 1690s. It is very likely that she was no longer William's mistress, but the affair had always been conducted very discreetly. She took a lodging in Cheapside, and William, who still admired her for her brains and her wit, occasionally consulted her on political matters. Swift said later: "Her advice hath many years been asked and followed in the most important affairs of State."[5]

Whenever they were able, William and Mary stole away to Hampton Court. Daniel Defoe in his *Tour Through the Whole Island of Great Britain* writes that the plan of the garden was devised by William himself, especially the alterations that were made.[6] Mary collected a number of choice and other rare plants, supplied by gardeners, sent at considerable expense from Virginia, the Canary Islands and other places. Her collection was entrusted to the care of Dr. Plunkett, a distinguished herbalist. He helped her raise many foreign and tropical plants from seed in the hothouses in the Privy Gardens. William was always keen on water in his gardens, and loved fountains. He spent large sums of money on piping water at Hampton Court, but was disappointed never to get the pressure he wanted. At Het Loo - in a flat country - he was able to get jets as high as 30 feet. Adjoining Hampton Court is Molesey Heath, considered by the royal gardeners such as George London and Henry Wise as an excellent source of turf, as the grass was grazed by sheep.[7] William also brought over many orange trees from his gardens at Het Loo, and those still existing are of great age. There is an entry of a payment of £70.5s.6d made to Herman Jansen Valck for orange trees.

Sir John Dalrymple is critical of William in one respect, that he never felt sufficiently that the true grandeur of a prince, who was both Stadtholder of Holland and King of England, depended upon his acquiring and making use of the empire of the ocean.[8] He confessed that he did not understand sea affairs. In his reign, the Admiralty was first made a nursery for youth, and an asylum for old politicians, instead of a board of efficient men in sea business ... his ships were not fully manned, nor fully victualled, nor were the repairs thoroughly executed ... No care was taken to supply the seamen with fresh provisions, even in the Channel and the quality of their food was often poor, and their surgeons were unskilful ... The seamen were maltreated by their officers ... These unsatisfactory conditions made it impossible to obtain volunteers, and the pressed men deserted whenever they could ... According to Narcissus Luttrell, a great number of seamen's wives and widows protested shrilly on one occasion (September 2, 1693) that their men were owed arrears of pay. Four of them were admitted to the Council Chamber, where they were advised by the King to retire peaceably, for they would have their money to a farthing without any delay.

During the last year of her short life - Mary was to die during late December 1694 - the Queen conceived the idea of founding a hospital at Greenwich for the benefit of veteran seamen, and for the relief from want of their widows.[9] It was a noble project characteristic of Queen Mary's works of charity. Sir Christopher Wren had originally planned to demolish the Queen's House, but she was much opposed to this and would not sanction it. It was the work of Inigo Jones. The Queen's House was left intact between two domed pavilions. Delays occurred, for it was necessary for the Treasury and the Board of Works to provide estimates. The charter for its foundation was finally granted in October 1694, two months before Mary's death. However, the building work was held up because of a hard winter.

Another project dear to Mary's heart was the foundation in Virginia of William and Mary College. A New England clergyman, the Rev. James Blair, fired with enthusiasm, came over to England in 1693 and after an interview with the Queen obtained her full support. When William returned from abroad she readily received his consent. Burnet states that James Blair set on foot a voluntary subscription, which was very willingly found. The Queen for her part thought that it would be the means to propagate the gospel among the natives. When Blair returned to America bearing the charter of William and Mary College, Wren provided works for the building.

Among the Bentinck manuscripts in Nottingham University there is the copy of an address by the Governor of Massachusetts to King William:

> humbly supplicating your Majesties grace and favour for ye Continuance and Confirmation of our ancient charter Rights and Privileges.

For a man who never had any children, William was very fond of his namesake, the little Duke of Gloucester, Princess Anne's surviving son. The boy was military minded and his chief pleasure was in playing soldiers with a set he had acquired. Occasionally the King would review them. The young Bentincks, Lord Woodstock and his three younger sisters, were always welcome at Court. So was Lord Buckhurst, son of the Earl of Dorset, a special favourite of William's. Once at Kensington House Lord

Buckhurst banged on the King's study door as he had heard the Queen express a wish that William should come to tea. When the irritated King said, "Who is that?" "It's Lord Buck" answered the boy. "And what does Lord Buck want with me?" asked William. "The Queen says you're to come to tea now." It is said that the effort of putting Lord Buckhurst in a cart and running with him to Mary's drawing-room brought on a violent fit of coughing, for William had to sink into a chair. The story at least puts him in a very human light.

John Evelyn was much impressed when he visited Kensington House on July 13, 1693: "saw," he relates:

> the Queen's rare cabinets and collection of china, wch was wonderfully rich and plentifull, but especialy a large cabinet, looking-glasse frame and stands, all of amber, much of it white ... in her library were many bookes in English, French and Dutch, of all sorts, a cupboard of gold plate.

Always fair, Evelyn writes that he is of the opinion that a cabinet of silver filigree belonging to the exiled Queen Mary d'Este, he saw there, should have been sent to her.[10] That summer was very wet, "if one might call it summer," wrote Evelyn, "in wch there was no fruit, but corn was very plentifull."

Archbishop Sancroft was succeeded in his high office by John Tillotson, a man of a humble, saintly character, and much liked by William and Mary, to whom he was warmly attached. Bishop Burnet's reference to Sancroft is an example how biased he can be as a historian. He died in November 1693 from a stroke, in the same poor and dilapidated condition in which he had lived for some years; he died in a state of separation from the church. Burnet, however, cannot praise Tillotson too highly, preaching at his funeral service when he died in late 1694:

> he was the man of the truest judgement and best temper I had ever known: he had a clear head, with a most tender and compassionate heart.

William was again absent from England for six months, saying farewell to Mary at Gravesend on May 4, 1694 and travelling to Holland from Ostend. Where the previous summer had been eventful and dramatic, there was little activity on the war front that summer. On November 9 he returned and landed at Margate, to be greeted by Mary near London. The Queen was now thirty-two, troubled by poor health and failing eyesight. William, too, was far from well, suffering a bout of influenza after attending a ball given by his friend William Alvian of Nassau-Odijk. She was worried about her husband, who was working too hard and so late that he had to stay in Whitehall, instead of returning to Kensington. Then she was deeply upset when she lost a ruby from the ring which William had given her three days after their marriage.[11] It was soon recovered.

It was a sad time for both King and Queen. They were devastated by Archbishop Tillotson's death. The King described him as "the best man, that I ever knew, and the best friend that I ever had." A successor had to be found, and Mary probably would have preferred Dr. Stillingfleet, but he was too High Church for William's Calvinist taste, and Thomas Tenison, Bishop of Lincoln, was chosen. He had once preached Nell Gwyn's funeral sermon when Curate of St. Martins. Burnet is sycophantic in his praise of the Queen. She clearly had her faults, but for him she could do no wrong. He wrote:

> the Queen continued still to set a great example to the whole nation, which shined in all the parts of it ... She took ladies off from that idleness, which not only wasted their time, but exposed them to many temptations ... She wrought many hours a-day herself, with her ladies and her maids of honour working about her, while one read to them all.[12]

Her enemies charged her with having an affair with Shrewsbury, since early 1694 a Duke. She found him attractive, but it is extremely unlikely that there was ever anything improper in their relationship, for Mary was never unfaithful to William.

Shrewsbury was now back in power as Secretary of State. In his many letters to the King, Shrewsbury intercedes for the Earl of Marlborough:

> Some points remained, of a nature too tender for me to pretend to advise upon ... but if those could be accommodated to Your Majesty's satisfaction, I cannot but think he is capable of being very serviceable. It is so unquestionably his interest to be faithful that single argument makes me not doubt it.[13]

Admiral Russell constantly wrote to Shrewsbury complaining of William's parsimony and that he did not appreciate his services. In a letter of December 15, Shrewsbury wrote to the King regretting that "for want of legs (having the gout) I cannot visit you." The correspondence concerned Admiral Russell.

About December 18 the Queen became seriously ill. For some days she tried to conceal how ill she felt. Smallpox was raging that winter in London - a very cold one - and it was feared that she had caught smallpox for, unlike William, she had so far been immune from it. For a day or two she seemed better, but by December 21 spots appeared on her chest and it was evident that her life was endangered. She knew that she was dying. A night or two previously she had shut herself away in her closet. There she burnt many of her papers, including William's letters. It was now that she wrote her last requests to William, including a letter of strong remonstrance concerning some alleged irregularity. It has been assumed that it referred to Elizabeth Villiers, but there is no evidence that it did. The letter no longer exists. It may be that Mary was aware that William had lately been attracted to a younger woman than Elizabeth and wanted to warn him.

Mary lay back in bed attended by Dr. Radcliffe, though he was afterwards unfairly accused of negligence or unskilful treatment. As for William, he was absolutely grief-stricken to the astonishment of many people. He was thought by those who did not know him intimately, to be rigid and unemotional, but the truth was otherwise. Highly-strung and deeply reserved, he had always kept his emotions locked up within him, but he had long known her worth and deeply loved her. In his closet with Gilbert Burnet he gave vent to the most violent passion. Sobbing with great gasps, he cried out that there was no hope for the Queen. Both his mother and father had died from this loathsome disease, so it was natural for him to be pessimistic. He told Burnet that from being the happiest, he was going to be the most miserable creature on earth. He said that during the whole course of their marriage, he had never known one single fault in her.[14]

The King had a camp-bed arranged in the Queen's room, but seldom slept in it, agonized as he watched and tended her. The new archbishop, too, was in constant attendance and told William that he could not do his duty faithfully unless he told Mary of her desperate state. It seemed hardly necessary, for Mary was resigned to her fate. As was the custom on the death of a queen, the room was crowded with courtiers, lords and ladies and physicians. Bentinck (Portland) and other intimate friends begged the King to rest, but just before the Queen's death at 1 a.m. on December 28 he collapsed, being carried to his bed by Bentinck and Tenison. For some weeks he was incapable of attending to business, turning to the consolations of religion in his deep sorrow, though he had always been religious, instructed as he was in his youth by Jacob Trigland. During those terrible days William derived much help and comfort from his new favourite, Arnold Joust van Keppel, and he would refuse to see anybody except Bentinck, Burnet, and a favourite page, La Fontaine. The start of the bitter rivalry between Bentinck and Keppel for the King's affection now began, a development that would much embarrass and disturb William. He would become increasingly lonely after the death of his wife and would never marry again. Eight years of life remained for the forlorn widower.

XVII   A LONELY, SADDENED KING

David Ogg, a scholarly historian of considerable perception, thinks that Queen Mary was the most attractive of all the seventeenth century Stuarts,[1] but Mary's tragedy was that she was married to her father's chief enemy.

Burnet wrote that she was the most universally-lamented Princess, and deserved to be so, of any in our age, or in our history. Only a few Jacobites rejoiced. In her allusion to Mary's death, writing on October 12, 1695, Liselotte reveals her disgust that James II, the exiled King, was so petty as to order that no mourning should be worn by the French Court. She could not understand how any man could so completely forget his own child.[2]

Archbishop Tenison closeted with King William for long hours mentioned Elizabeth Villiers, boldly telling William that he had done his excellent wife great wrong by his adultery with Elizabeth Villiers. William took Tenison's reprimand in good part, promising to have nothing more to do with her. However, he treated her generously, settling estates on her worth £30,000 a year, in return for the various services she had done him. During November 1695 she married Lord George Hamilton, a distinguished soldier highly regarded by the King, who created him Earl of Orkney. She had several children by him.

In his *Journal to Stella* during September 1712, ten years after King William's death, Swift alludes to Lady Orkney, the late King's mistress, apparently still flourishing and living in a fine place near Taplow called Cliffden (Cliveden): "I am grown mighty acquaintance," he wrote, "she is perfectly kind, like a mother." Her brain still delighted him.

Queen Mary had expressed a written wish that her funeral should be simple and inexpensive, but it was not found until too late. Her bowels were deposited, according to custom, in King Henry VII's Chapel. Her funeral took place on March 5, 1695, a bitterly cold day. Evelyn wrote on February 27 that as much as £50,000 was spent "against her desire". He was present at the ceremony, writing: "Never was so universal a mourning, all the Parliament men had cloaks given them, and 400 poore women." There were all the nobility, Mayor, Aldermen, Judges, etc.[3] Archbishop Tenison preached a long sermon, while a boy's tender voice sang Purcell's

Elegy, *O Dive Custos Auricae Domus, Maria, Maria.* The Chief Mourner was Princess Anne, but she was again pregnant, and consequently represented by the Duchess of Somerset. In his great grief William was excused from attending the funeral.

Earlier, on December 31, 1694 both Houses of Parliament assembled with addresses of condolence, and the King made a suitable reply.

The repercussion from Mary's death was a reconciliation with Princess Anne, who visited her brother-in-law on January 12. Forgetting their former animosity, both wept copiously at their loss. Anne, despite their quarrels, had tried hard to see her sister during her last harrowing hours. William now restored to Anne her honours, including her guards. Friendship between them really never existed, but their relations henceforward were amicable enough.

Constant building work and hammering continued at Kensington House, having a harmful effect on the bereaved King. Bentinck (Portland) was so anxious about his friend that he insisted the King should go for a while to Richmond. There to distract his mind he did some shooting on horseback. The weather that winter was icy. The Thames froze over, and several hundred people continued to die every week. For the rest of his life, William wore a lock of Mary's hair next his heart and he would keep the twenty-eighth of December - the day of her death - as a day of meditation and constant prayer.

Mary had been equally beloved in Holland (the United Provinces) as in England. Matthew Prior, a poet, now a secretary at the English Embassy at The Hague, wrote to the Duke of Shrewsbury:

> The cruel news touches Holland to that degree that she may contend with England whose sorrow is greater ... We are all abundantly convinced that we have lost the best of Princesses."[4]

To the end of her short life Mary longed to see Holland again, a heartfelt longing never granted her. What bliss to see the fountains play in the gardens of Het Loo or to walk along those paths to the woods!

William never really fully recovered from her death. He turned more and more to his male friends, especially Keppel, an extremely handsome young man, as painted by Sir Godfrey Kneller, with enormous charm. He knew just how to handle the King.

By the spring (1695) the King was in better health, but he was spitting blood. He was impatient to embark again on his campaigns abroad. After proroguing Parliament on May 3, leaving a Council of Regency of seven men, Shrewsbury, Dorset, Pembroke, Somers now Lord Chancellor,

Devonshire, Godolphin, and Tenison Archbishop of Canterbury, William embarked for Flanders.

Marshal Luxembourg had died on January 4, 1695, King Louis's best general and a military genius. Saint-Simon had a low opinion of Marshal Villeroi, a man absolutely loyal and attached to Louis, but:

> one made for presiding over a ball, judging a tournament, or, if he had a voice, singing the part of a king or a hero at the opera, well suited also for setting fashions, and beyond that, for nothing.

Unwisely for sentimental motives the King of France gave Villeroi the command of Luxembourg's armies. Opposed to a far less formidable soldier, William acted with remarkable skill in concealing successfully from the enemy his plan to recapture Namur in the Spanish Netherlands. The French were over confident, thinking mistakenly that Namur was impregnable, for it had been recently repaired and fortified by the great engineer Vauban. Marshal Boufflers, a fine soldier, commanded a garrison of some 20,000 men, supported by Villeroi's army of 80,000 troops.

To undertake the siege William could rely on an army of 70,000 men, consisting of English, Dutch, Brandenburgers and Bavarians, and his ally Vandemont with a powerful force was in a well chosen strategic position ready to assist him. He succeeded in eluding the enemy, posting his troops under the walls of Ghent. Throughout July the siege continued with night attacks and heavy bombardment. William, as always impervious to danger, watched the proceedings under heavy cannon fire,[5] though men were killed at his feet.

Eventually Namur surrendered, though the French inflicted heavy losses on the allied army. Among those captured was Marshal Boufflers, but under Bentinck's guardianship he was ordered an easy detention and soon returned to Versailles, where he was graciously received by King Louis, who conferred on him a dukedom. This was one of King William's rare victories over the King of France, who always referred to him as the Prince of Orange up to the Treaty of Rijswijk (1697).

Liselotte, in her witty letters to her Aunt Sophie, mentions on October 12, 1695 the vast respect and admiration the French now had for William III. She wrote:

> Everywhere you hear remarks like, 'a great man, as great a king as he deserves to be', and so on. You are right when you say that the successful ones get all the admiration.[6]

Liselotte is referring to the success of William in storming the citadel of Namur during September. Everybody spoke of him now at Versailles as *le roi Guillaume*.

Soon 'Madame' cherished an ardent wish that her daughter Elizabeth Charlotte might marry the lonely widower king. She writes on August 8, 1697:

> All Paris, the army and the Court say that the King is considering my daughter, but I can't believe it. Even if it were true Mme Whore (Madame de Maintenon) would never permit it. I have never received anything but ill from that one.

Although she was very fond of her brother-in-law King Louis, she detested Madame de Maintenon, whom he had secretly married, blaming her for alienating the King from her. In reality William never seriously considered remarriage, although his name was coupled with various women. In any case there was one great obstacle to a remarriage with Elizabeth Charlotte, that of different religions.

One more eligible, potential bride was the German Louise Dorothea Sophia, daughter of William's older ally and cousin, Friedrich of Brandenburg. Matthew Prior reported to Shrewsbury very unfavourably on the lady:

> The princess is not ugly, but disagreeable, a tall miss at a boarding school, with a scraggy lean neck, very pale, and a great lover, I fancy, of chalk and tobacco pipes.[7]

Hardly a suitable bride to succeed William's Mary. William met her, but hurriedly escaped to Het Loo with its memories of Mary. There was no place more loved by William and he always left it reluctantly for England. There many English and Dutch were disappointed that the marriage overtures had come to nothing, an attitude that irritated the King. "What! Have the people then forgot the Queen so soon?! Well, if they have, I have not," he is alleged to have said.

William returned to England in October, to be given a splendid reception "fire and smoke, illuminations, and discharges of great guns."[8] That autumn after Parliament had been dissolved, the King made an unexpected progress in the countryside, visiting places he was unfamiliar with such as Leicester, Grantham and Lincoln. He had grown fond of Newmarket where his horse won the Town Plate. The weather was clement that autumn and William enjoyed himself. He hunted in Sherwood Forest and made a series of visits, including Castle Ashby,

Althorp and Welbeck, where he was entertained lavishly by the Duke of Newcastle. At Althorp he was entertained by Robert Spencer Lord Sunderland on October 26, who from 1693 onwards acted as a serious adviser. Robert Spencer had returned from exile, and by 1696 he was old for that age at fifty-four. He is a controversial character, hated and mistrusted by many of his contemporaries, including Princess Anne. His biographer Professor J.P. Kenyon, however, thinks that Sunderland by William III's reign had acquired "a certain political morality", and that he now wielded "his most beneficial and decisive influence".[9]

At Warwick William attended the service at St. Mary's. When he reached Oxford, however, the authorities were angered because the King had been ungracious enough to refuse to attend a banquet where much trouble had been taken to provide rarities. His ministers were urging him to return to London, where he arrived on November 9 after a fifty miles journey by coach from Woodstock.

William was anxious that progress should be made as soon as possible with the project, so dear to Mary's heart, in the building of a hospital at Greenwich to provide provision for disabled pensioner seamen. Work continued throughout 1696.

Two years earlier a most important event had transpired, the foundation of the Bank of England, inaugurated to finance William's war against Louis XIV. The Tories were afraid that it would be dominated by Whig financiers, and opposed it, arguing that they would grow wealthy at the public expense and use their gains to dominate the government. To guard against the monarchy becoming absolute, the Bank of England was prohibited from lending money to the Crown by Act of Parliament.[10] Two leading spirits behind the innovation were William Paterson and Charles Montague, Earl of Halifax, William's Chancellor of the Exchequer (not to be confused with George Savile Marquis of Halifax, the 'Trimmer'). The first home of the Bank was Powis House in Lincoln Fields.

Narcissus Luttrell's Diary contains many instances of the ferocious laws against criminals who debased the currency. These had little effect against coiners and clippers. By the autumn of 1695 the currency had become so debased that during January 1696 a new Act of Parliament was needed for the reform of the coinage. It was necessary that the new coin should be of standard weight and quality, with milled edges.[11] Isaac Newton was appointed Master of the Mint and devoted himself to the King's business, thinking that it should require his energy even more than higher mathematics. New mints were established at Exeter, York, Bristol, Norwich and Chester, to hasten the circulation of the new coinage.

During 1695-1696 and earlier, the Jacobites both in England and France were increasingly optimistic that William might be ousted, for he was far from popular. Means might be found when the King was overseas. This is reflected in Luttrell's writings.[12] On Tuesday June 11, he wrote:

> Yesterday being the birthday of the pretended Prince of Wales, several Jacobites mett in several places, and particularly at the Dogg Tavern in Drury Lane where with kettle drums, trumpets, etc. they caroused and having a bonfire near that place would have forced some of the spectators to have drunk the said Prince's health, which they refusing, occasioned a tumult, upon which the mob gathering, entred the Tavern, where they did much damage, and putt the Jacobites to flight, some of which are taken into custody. Captain Reynold Chivery was seized and examined and committed to Newgate by two Justices of the Peace.

According to Bishop Burnet the most active and determined of all King James II's agents after the Revolution was Nevill Payne,[13] an English Jacobite. While in prison in Stirling Castle, he was granted temporary freedom in 1699, to sally forth half a mile from the Castle daily to attend to his experiments on river navigation. These were most original. He provides a detailed account of the "vessels of my invention", powered by oars moved by men or horses and makes the extraordinary claim that a vessel of 1,000 tons could be moved at 60 m.p.h. by nine horses. Payne was thought to be the chief instigator of the Montgomery plot in 1690, and on its discovery was arrested. A special order was sent by King William on November 18 that torture must be applied. Sir William Lockhart was mistaken when he informed Lord Melville, then Secretary of State for Scotland, that if torture were applied to Payne, those that knew him best were of the opinion he would not be able to endure it, "for he is but a dastardly fellow". Payne endured his excruciating sufferings when torture was first applied to his thumbs and afterwards to one of his legs, with the utmost courage. Despite the torture, he failed to disclose any information.

A warrant against the accused man for an indictment for high treason before the Parliament was raised by the Lord Advocate. He was allowed the advantage of the open prison owing to his nephew Francis Payne's petitions and to be attended by his own physicians and surgeons. This order was overruled by King William (December 20, 1690) and Payne was put in close confinement.

According to the standards of the late seventeenth century, there was much cruelty in the appliance of torture, but William, though humane on the whole, may be blamed for exacerbating Payne's sufferings. He was still in prison as late as December 9, 1700 when the Duke of Queensbury, William's adviser on Scottish affairs, informed Carstares that it was not in their power to detain him longer and recommended that he should be set at liberty.[14]

1695 and the following year were renowned for Jacobite plots, involving the assassination of William. On February 19, 1695 an informer Captain Smythe wrote to the Duke of Shrewsbury:

> There is a resolution taken and formed and by authority from France, to seize upon the King and that at his diversion of shooting or hunting and if possible to carry him off.[15]

Sir George Barclay, a Scotsman recently created a Major-General, was to assassinate the King. On his way back from hunting at Richmond, with an escort of twenty-four men, William was to be ambushed and killed at Turnham Green. According to Bishop Burnet, one of the conspirators Captain Fisher betrayed the plot to the Earl of Portland (Bentinck), to be followed by an Irish officer named Pendergrass. He saw the King together with another conspirator La Ruea, a Frenchman. So William cancelled his plans for hunting. It is evident that a rising of the mob was planned in several parts of the City of London. "Upon this hurly-burly the French fleet will bring over the late King James," said Smythe. Both King James and his son the Duke of Berwick were involved in this plot, but Bentinck had no awareness of a plot to assassinate William.

Among the leading Jacobites was an ardent gentleman from Northumberland, Sir John Fenwick. During the days of crisis before the Battle of La Hogue (1692), Fenwick had made himself publicly rude to Queen Mary, and the King would never forgive him for that. Fenwick was one of the chief agents of insurrection until captured, concealed in a house somewhere between Great Bookham and Stoke in Surrey during June. After his arrest, Fenwick, to save his life, made dangerous accusations against Marlborough, Godolphin, Shrewsbury, William's Secretary of State, and Russell. Captain Floyd, a groom of the bedchamber to King James, was sent over to the exiled King by Marlborough and Russell, with assurances that the army and the fleet would be secured to act in his interest if he would grant them his pardon for what was passed. The answer to My Lord Marlborough was that he was the greatest of criminals where he had the greatest obligations, but if he did him extraordinary service he might hope for pardon.[16] King William was almost certainly aware that most of his advisers had been in contact with James, wanting to insure themselves against his possible return to power.

Actually, Fenwick's revelations against the Duke of Shrewsbury were more damaging than those against Marlborough, because Shrewsbury was William's trusted Secretary of State. James Vernon, Shrewsbury's secretary corresponded with Fenwick in his prison at Newgate on September 9, 1696:

> whether you are ready to give such further proofs to King William of such matters contained in your paper, as you desire to impart to the King himself. Secondly whether you were ready to reveal to the Lords Justices touching your whole knowledge of other things designed or cited against his Majesty or his government.

Sir John Fenwick replied from Newgate on September 21, "I have been very ill tonight, but James Vernon will certainly receive his reply by 10 o'clock tomorrow morning." When the Duke of Devonshire, Lord High Steward, on William's instructions examined Fenwick, he made various written accusations against Shrewsbury, maintaining that while he held office, he, together with Lord Godolphin, had secretly conspired with King James "by entering into a treaty with him through the medium of Lord Middleton, now James's Secretary of State in exile".[17]

Shrewsbury wrote to Portland on September 8, 1696:

> Sir John Fenwick's story is as wonderful to me as if he had accused me of coining; however, I shall always acknowledge the King's great goodness and generosity ... and Your Lordship's friendship in not permitting so foul a thought of your humble servant to receive credit one moment in your breast.

Deeply embarrassed, he wrote also to the King in Flanders, confessing that while out of office, he had held some communication with Lord Middleton, then in England, before he escaped to France to become King James's Secretary of State. Shrewsbury was related to Middleton through the Lady Catherine Bruce, his aunt. While Middleton was in the Tower, Shrewsbury had visited him several times. It was before the Battle of La Hogue. The two noblemen had sometimes supped together and Middleton admitted in confidence to Shrewsbury - he was fond of the bottle - that he was planning to go overseas. When Middleton asked him whether he could command him any service, Shrewsbury replied that if Middleton continued to pursue the course he had in mind, it would not lie in his power to do himself or any of his friends any service. Middleton was a far less extreme Jacobite than his predecessor Lord Melfort - a non-compounder, ready to bring James back under conditions, but he was to prove an able minister. (A non-compounder was an extreme Jacobite not prepared to restrict the King's prerogatives).

William was attached to Shrewsbury and behaved with intelligence and understanding, writing to him from Het Loo:

> You may judge of my astonishment at Fenwick's effrontery in accusing you. You are, I trust, too fully convinced of the entire confidence which I place in you, to imagine that such an accusation has made any impression on me, or that if it had, I should have sent you this paper. You will observe *the sincerity of this honest man*, who only accuses those in my service, and not one of his own party.

William was well aware that most of his ministers had corresponded with St. Germain. The King was kindly, writing a sympathetic letter when Shrewsbury was injured in a hunting accident, hoping that he would be soon able to bear the motion of a carriage. Shrewsbury, as was his wont, begged the King to let him resign, but the King would not hear of it. There are frequent mentions of Fenwick in contemporary documents. A Bill of Attainder for high treason was brought against him in Parliament and he was executed on Tower Hill on January 27, 1697.

Princess Anne was William's heir to succeed him if he should die, and her surviving son William Duke of Gloucester came next in the succession. He was by no means strong in health. Luttrell relates on Saturday May 25, 1695:

> Yesterday the duke of Gloucester had 5 physitians with him being taken ill with an intermittent feavor and it was feared it would have proved to be the smallpox, but this day he is much better.

Like many small boys, Gloucester's chief diversion was to play at soldiers. Now aged seven, a godson of the King, William greatly admired the King, following his career in Flanders with avid interest. His devoted Welsh servant Lewis Jenkin wrote a memoir about the young Prince:[18] "Nothing pleased him but drums and arms, and stories of war," he related. "I used frequently to tell him the stories of Alexander and Caesar and such renowned heroes of old." When Gloucester was aged nine, the King pondered hard who should be appointed to the office of his governor. He himself favoured Shrewsbury, but he declined the honour because of alleged ill health. Princess Anne naturally enough wanted Marlborough, though opposed by Portland, who disliked him. Keppel, however, supported Marlborough and also Lord Sunderland. Marlborough was finally chosen by the King, who, using more gracious words than usual, urged him to "Teach him but to know (be? what you are), and my nephew cannot want for accomplishments." By this time William knew Marlborough's worth.

At one time William even considered inviting over from France the Prince of Wales to be brought up as a Protestant and designated his successor, but his father would never have countenanced it.

William admired men of principle and honesty whatever their political opinions. Such a man was Sir Charles Littleton, a distinguished soldier and Brigadier General under James II. When William offered Littleton a regiment and to send him as Major General to Flanders after the Revolution - he had often expressed sentiments against the growth of French power - Sir Charles declined. When William asked him his reason, Littleton remarked:

> Because I received great obligations from my old master. I fear he will be in the French camp; and if he should be there, I cannot answer for myself that I should not desert to him.

The King impressed, answered, "You are a man of honour, I will not desire you to act against your principles." "Disturb not the government and we shall be very good friends."

Lord Portland continued to receive lavish grants from the King. It was a mistake, however, to favour his foreign favourites to such an extent. Lord Galway wrote to Lord Lexington (February 18, 1696) that William had granted to Portland the lordships of Denbigh, Bronfield and Yale and other lands in Wales, but was compelled to revoke the grant because of a spirited remonstrance from the gentlemen of the Principality,[19] highly incensed at the proposed transfer to a foreigner of the ancient domains of the Prince of Wales.

Jealousy gnawed at Portland's heart because of William's increasing favours to Keppel, now aged twenty-six. He was nineteen years younger than the King, having been born in 1669. When on February 10, 1697 Keppel was created Earl of Albemarle, despite a protest from the Earl of Bath to whom this title with a dukedom had been promised by Charles II if the male line of George Monck, Duke of Albemarle should fail, all Europe gasped. Keppel was the King's favourite companion. A complete contrast to Portland, Keppel wanted to please where Bentinck was increasingly dour and surly. His conversation amused the King, and they would spend hours together. Though the English disliked William's Dutch favourites, he was much more popular than Portland. Burnet wrote that Keppel was so engrossed in his own pleasures that he could scarce submit to the restraints of a Court. He had a mistress - a brunette in Chelsea and did not marry until 1701, Geertruid Johaina Quirina van der Duyn, daughter of the King's Master of the Buckhounds. She gave him one son and a daughter.

Keppel admired Marlborough and used his influence with the King to favour him. When Keppel brought a message from William to Sunderland he said: "This young man brings and carries a message well, but Portland is so dull an animal that he can neither fetch or carry."[20] When a new Venetian ambassador arrived in London in 1696 he wrote of Keppel:

> His Majesty regards him with pleasure as if he is a tender plant that he himself wanted to cultivate in the hope that it will bear fruit ... Until now, the love of the King alone offers him a marvellous prospect for success.

In France and elsewhere in Europe it was openly rumoured that William's relationship with the newly honoured Albemarle was homosexual. The King was reputed to have been in love with Albemarle as if with a woman and they say he used to kiss his hands before the whole Court. The German-born Duchess of Orléans could never forget her early fondness for Prince William of Orange, but in her witty allusions to Albemarle in her letters, she cannot be relied on. In a conversation with a Monsieur de Wassenaer on April 24, 1698, her son the future Regent had asked an Englishman if Keppel was a man of any merit. "Yes," he replied, "he has the merit of being seventeen years of age and very handsome. That is why the King of England has use for him." Actually in 1698 Keppel would have been twenty-nine years of age. He was a man of some intelligence, and military ability and William entrusted him with a good deal of confidential business. It may well be that William, starved of affection in his last eight years since Mary's death, saw in Albemarle the substitute son he had never had. On his part Albemarle was sincerely attached to the King, and being by nature kindly and thoughtful rendered him service.

As if to compensate Portland for creating Keppel Earl of Albemarle, William made him Knight of the Garter. He was now immensely rich. His love of money was strong, but not odious. Macaulay states that he "took without scruple whatever he could honestly take, but he was incapable of stooping to an act of baseness."[21]

What Portland keenly resented - and it was natural for him to feel in such a way - was that he was no longer first among the friends and confidants of the King. His jealousy of Albemarle knew no bounds. He threatened during March 1697 to resign all his Court appointments.

XVIII PORTLAND AND ALBEMARLE

Deeply shocked by Portland's letter, William wrote to him immediately, imploring him to change his mind. Memories of long ago came back to him of Bentinck saving his life when at the age of twenty-five he lay on his sick bed suffering from smallpox, of Bentinck always so brave and selfless, his faithful servant and friend alike, in adversity and good times.

> Nothing is left me but to beg you, by all the ties that should be dearest to you, to change this pernicious decision and I feel sure that if you retain the least affection for me you will not refuse this prayer, however hard it may seem to you.[1]

Portland yielded to William's entreaties reluctantly, perhaps because of the King's precarious health - he was suffering from a quartan ague. He had served him thirty-three years.

The best remedy was to leave for Het Loo where William enjoyed hunting the hare, and his health improved.[2] When Portland realized that the King and Albemarle were spending long hours in each other's company, he was smitten by violent jealousy. He again told the King that he was determined to leave his service. From his army headquarters at Iseringen, William wrote Portland another long letter begging him to change his mind.

It was the King's reputation, particularly his honour that troubled Portland. "Sire, it is your honour which I have at heart," he wrote the King.

> The kindness which your Majesty has for a young man, and the way in which you seem to authorize his liberties and impertinences make the world say things that I am ashamed to hear.

Portland is implying that people were openly saying that there was a homosexual relationship between William and Albemarle. Portland hastened to assure the King that he believed him as far removed as any man in the world from "these things", but he had been thunderstruck when he had realized that the malicious talk prevalent in England was also heard at The Hague and in the army, "tarnishing a reputation which has never hitherto been subject to such accusations." Nothing would content Bentinck unless Keppel was dismissed and this William refused to do. The King must act now to protect his reputation which had always been so dear to him. Finally Portland begged the King to pardon his freedom of speech, "which if it is unfitting from anyone is fitting for a man, who loves you as I do."[3] Relations remained strained.

Perhaps Portland, who had known William most of his life, was not absolutely convinced that William's relations with Albemarle were not homosexual. He desperately wanted the King to assure him of his innocence. Portland had been married twice, was popular with women, and it would be absurd to think there had been anything improper in his own relationship with William.

The King promised Bentinck that he would do his utmost to stop "these horrible calumnies". He told him:

It seems to be very extraordinary that it should be impossible to have esteem and regard for a young man without it being criminal.

Both William and Portland were intimate friends of Charles Henri, the Prince de Vaudemont, the illegitimate son of Duke Charles IV of Lorraine. William had much helped his military career, especially when he was serving with the Spanish forces in Holland. He now persuaded Vaudemont to act as mediator and to dissuade Bentinck from resigning, and in this he succeeded, changing Portland's strong inclination to leave William's service. He was soon to serve as William's first ambassador to be appointed after the Treaty of Rijswijk (May 1697). Bentinck, owing to his prestige, his fluent knowledge of French and of European affairs, enjoyed much more popularity in France than in England, where he was maligned as a hated foreigner. There in France he was more affable, being an experienced diplomat.

By 1697 people in England, Holland and France were clamouring for peace. On May 9 King William arrived in Rijswijk, a small, pretty place on the road between The Hague and Delft, where William's grandfather had once owned a house. Sweden acted as mediator between the contesting powers at the talks. There were great difficulties since two main questions existed. William was anxious that James and his Queen should be removed from Saint-Germain and that he himself should be recognized as King of England by Louis XIV, but the King of France was extremely reluctant that James and Maria Beatrice should leave Saint-Germain. William was also adamant that his Protestant principality of Orange should be restored to him. Louis agreed to return Orange to the King, but remained reluctant to commit himself over James.

According to Matthew Prior, poet and diplomat, who acted as Secretary to Portland's delegation, Portland was on excellent terms with Marshal Boufflers and raised the matter of the exiled King James's presence at Saint-Germain when the two met at Halle not far from Brussels. He received the mistaken impression that it was proposed to remove James to Avignon in Provence. In that case Portland assured him, William would have no objection to conceding to a French claim that Maria Beatrice should be paid £50,000. In his additional instructions that William gave Portland, he says:

> We cannot think it reasonable to furnish such sums while we have ground to suspect that they may be employed for carrying on designs against our person and government and therefore as occasion may serve, you shall make it understood that the way to the punctual payment of the said pension is by removing the just reason we may have for distrusts and jealousies while we find the late King and Queen affect to continue their residence so near the Court of France.

The Queen was now badly off. However, it was not to be. James and Maria Beatrice stayed on at Saint-Germain. Matthew Prior's letters are witty and entertaining,[4] but he had no respect for fallen greatness and refers to James thus:

> the old bully is lean, worn, and riv'led, not unlike Neal the projector; the Queen looks very melancholy well enough, their equipages are all very ragged and contemptible.

He is critical, however, of the English government for withholding the Queen's pension. For him "the Jacobites are rare fellows". William told Bentinck to tell the French government that James's Queen's pension would be paid so soon as they moved from Saint-Germain.

There is an account in the form of a diary of Portland's magnificent embassy entering Paris in the British Library.[5] It was Sunday March 18, 1698. An enormous procession of noblemen took part in it, six carriages, twelve led horses, fifty outriders and twelve pages. The embassy of five month's duration cost as much as £80,000. Portland was well suited to his post. A man of distinguished appearance, he was a model of courtesy and good breeding. All the French nobility vied with one another to do him honour. With King Louis XIV, Portland established excellent relations, sometimes meeting three times in one day and discussing all kinds of matters. He was shown great favour, even given the royal candlestick at the King's *couchée* one evening. Portland gained the impression as he wrote to

King William that the French had the greatest admiration for the King of England. Matthew Prior wrote to the Earl of Pembroke:

> It is incredible what true respect and veneration they bear to King William. *Le plus beau prince du monde* are the least things they say of him.[6]

Liselotte Duchess of Orléans, eager to meet the Earl of Portland, talked to him about King William. On September 15, 1697 only a few months before, she had written to the Electress of Hanover, eulogizing the Prince of Wales:

> I am extremely fond of this prince (James Francis Edward). It is impossible to see him without falling in love with him. He has such a charming disposition I think that in time he will become a great king, although he is only nine years old. I am sure that already he would rule better than his father.

His mother Queen Maria of Modena was on very friendly terms with Madame de Maintenon, privately married to King Louis, and because of this she remained aloof and hostile, unwilling to meet Portland. As Maria Beatrice had given birth in 1692 to a daughter Louise Mary,* the warming-pan story is absurd. Portland enjoyed himself enormously, the guest of Liselotte's husband Philippe, 'Monsieur' at a lavish dinner at Saint-Cloud. Bentinck wrote King William:

> Your Majesty would be pleased with the situation, the beautiful natural waters, the fine views and the great variety there is in the place.

However, he was not at all impressed with the lack of flowers at Versailles, though springtime was magnificent. William wanted Bentinck to scour the Paris shops for Gobelins tapestries and rare French furniture for Het Loo, but the result was disappointing.

About this time Sir William Trumbull wrote to Lord Lexington about an alleged attempt to assassinate the King by a certain Count Buselli, who wore a bushy black beard and lived in a castle near Mantua.[7] William made light of the affair, but his advisers were much troubled by rumours of attempted assassination until his death.

---

* A most attractive girl resembling her aunt Henriette-Anne (Minette).

One important, confidential matter in which King William was much interested was the Spanish succession, and he instructed Bentinck to discuss this difficult affair with King Louis. Carlos II King of Spain - Carlos the Bewitched (El Hechizado) as he was known by his subjects - was the sovereign of vast dominions, the son of Philip IV. A man of feeble health and character, he still survived in 1698 against the expectations of all the Chancelleries of Europe. He was without an heir to the throne, so the moment he died it was certain that the vast territories he ruled over would be disputed by avaricious claimants and it was likely there would be a general European war, particularly if one of the claimants succeeded to the whole Spanish Empire. As always in Europe, William's policy was dictated by his insistence on the balance of power.

The rival claimants were mainly three. The Bourbon candidate was Louis XIV's younger grandson Philippe Duke of Anjou, a mere boy of nine years old in 1696. Maria Theresa, Louis's former Queen, Philip IV's older daughter, had been made to renounce all her rights both for herself and her descendants, on her marriage. However, the French had made one condition that Maria Theresa's dowry should be paid, but it had never been paid. So, the King could claim that the renunciation was invalid.[8] The Archduke Charles, another claimant, was aged thirteen, the son of the Emperor Leopold by his second wife. He was directly descended from Charles V. The third claimant was Bavarian; a child of six, José Fernando.

All the countries concerned were war weary in 1698 and wanted a peace settlement, and after tedious negotiations, a partition treaty was signed secretly between England, France and the States General in Holland. France was to receive Naples, Sicily and some Spanish border territory, José Fernando of Bavaria was to get Spain and the Low Countries, while the Archduke Charles's share was Milan. The secret treaty was soon known by everybody, including Carlos himself and his ambassador in London. William was deeply weary of war and as he wrote Bentinck, knowing that his indifferent health would not prolong his life much longer, was determined "to do anything I can in honour and conscience to prevent a new war."

A fascinating encounter between William and the towering giant, Peter the Czar of Russia - he was six foot seven inches - took place in 1697. They first met in Utrecht during Peter's tour of Europe and formed a strange contrast, the slight William with his bent back and asthmatic wheeze and the genial Peter - known to us today as Peter the Great. Ever since adolescence William, persistent, self-dedicated, and brave, had been his hero.[9] With his insatiable curiosity and interest in ships, and his eager interest in Dutch shipwrights, wanting to ascertain their secrets, Peter tried to persuade William to join him in a Christian alliance against the Turks, but William rejected his overtures. Peter liked Holland with its meadows filled with grazing cows, its windmills, and its canals full of boats and barges. The Dutch politician Nicholas Witsen escorted the Czar to Texel on the North Sea coast and on his visits. Intending to visit England during January 1698, Peter sailed in *The Yorke*, a warship lent him by the King, together with *The Romney* and three smaller ships to escort him there. The vessels were commanded by Vice-Admiral Mitchell.

London in 1698 was a city of contrasts, one of violence where murders were frequent and also public floggings and executions. However, there was much grace and beauty in the fifty-two churches being built by Sir Christopher Wren and the magnificent St. Paul's, where on the eve of the Czar's arrival the choir had been opened for public worship, the first time since the Great Fire of 1666. The numerous coffee houses were a feature of the capital where witty, intelligent conversation was indulged in on literary matters, on politics, on shipping and agriculture.

On January 23, accompanied by Admiral Mitchell and two Russians, Peter drove to Kensington House to pay King William a visit. It was now that the King persuaded Peter to sit for a portrait by Sir Godfrey Kneller, a portrait still hanging in the King's Gallery in Kensington Palace.

Bishop Burnet's impressions of the Czar are of considerable interest:[10]

> He is a man of a very hot temper, soon inflamed, and very brutal in his passion, he raises his natural heat by drinking much brandy ... he wants not capacity, and has a larger measure of knowledge than might be expected from his education, which was very indifferent, a want of judgement, with an instability of temper, appear too often and too evidently.

Burnet remarked that he was mechanically-minded, liked working with his hands and "seems designed by nature rather to be a ship carpenter than a great prince." He told the historian that he intended to build a great fleet at Azuph, so as to attack the Ottoman Empire. His greatness was certainly not as evident to his contemporaries as it is today, but he is a controversial character and had a reputation for cruelty.

Czar Peter preferred informal visits to ceremonial occasions, and became very friendly with Peregrine Osborne, Marquis of Carmarthen, a son of Lord Danby, created by William, Marquis of Carmarthen, and subsequently Duke of Leeds. The two, fond of drinking, would frequent a tavern in Great Tower Street to imbibe Peter's favourite drink, a cup of brandy laced with peppers. It was renamed the Czar of Muscovy.[11]

Peter first stayed in a simple house at 21 Norfolk Street, looking out on a river bank. There, William came by carriage to visit the Czar, but he had closed the window in his room as was the custom in Russia in winter, and William, suffering from asthma, was unable to breathe and implored him to open the window. Thankfully he deeply inhaled the cold air that flooded the room. Peter insisted on being incognito during his time in England. What fascinated him most were the many ships moored in the Pool of London. 1698 was a particularly cold winter - as late as April 21 John Evelyn was writing in his *Diary* "An exceeding sharp and cold season".

The diarist was not too happy when the Czar of Muscovy hired his celebrated home, Sayes Court at Deptford, which was his joy and pride. Sayes Court swarmed with Russians, who in their dirty habits took no trouble to keep Evelyn's house clean, nor his much loved gardens. His steward prepared him for the worst:

> There is a house full of people, and right nasty. The Czar lies next your library, and dines in the parlour next your study ... The King is expected here this day, the best parlour is pretty clear for him to be entertained in. The King pays for all he has.

Later, after the Czar had left the kingdom, Evelyn saw for himself on June 9 in what a wretched state Peter had left his house. Sir Christopher Wren and Mr. London, the King's gardener, had to visit Sayes Court and estimated that £150 was needed for repairs, a large sum in those days.

The Czar was a great ladies man and was very fond of going to the theatre and flirting with the pretty actresses. When the Czar returned home on April 21, his parting gift to William was a ruby valued at £10,000.

XIX   AFTER RIJSWIJK

Now there was an uneasy peace, an ambassador from France had been appointed to the Court of St. James. He was Count Tallard, a man enjoying a favourable reputation as a soldier and a diplomat. Louis XIV could not have given the post to anybody more suited, for he was to establish excellent relations with William III, the enemy of France, gaining a high impression of the King's character and qualities. Matthew Prior mentions Tallard when corresponding on March 16, 1698 with Shrewsbury's Under-Secretary of State, James Vernon, who did much of his administrative work. Tallard was delayed in his embassy by contrary winds at Calais. When he finally arrived in London he introduced an innovation not hitherto practised by other ambassadors. When the King attended St. James's Chapel it was usual for his coach alone to enter the inner court, but Count Tallard did the same "twice or thrice" with his coach, so that the Swedish ambassador and the Emperor Leopold's envoy claimed the same privilege. Prior, a little maliciously, would write to Portland on December 10, 1698:

> Count Tallard arrived here on Saturday, and went immediately to Versailles, where he would have the world think he is locked up several hours together with the King (of France) every day, which is so true to the French vanity that I see English air could not cure it.[1]

When King William visited Holland about the end of July (1698), Prior wrote to Portland that the King's intention was to confirm an alliance with the Duke of Zell, the Electors of Brandenburg and Hanover, and other German princes, in case France should commit any act upon the death of Carlos II King of Spain to which they were averse. William was too much a realist to rely altogether on French promises. Tallard reported in the spring that "people murmur here at the journey to Holland".[2]

He was a very shrewd observer. He soon realized that Albemarle the high favour of William, "considerably increased of late"; he took cognizance of all affairs, while the influence of the Earl of Portland was on the decline. He soon grew aware that the King of England was very far from being master here; he was generally hated by all the great men and the whole of the nobility. Tallard thought that the people were still favourably inclined towards him, though less so than at the beginning.

Tallard was especially impressed by William's infinite patience with which he handled turbulent parliaments and his ministers. He was a man of his word; always abiding by it. "He is honourable in all he does, his conduct is sincere," he wrote Louis. When he suggested to the King of France that he should put in a plea for Portland, Louis told him not to meddle in domestic affairs, meaning the quarrel between Portland and Albemarle.

William was sometimes disgusted with England, complaining of the insularity of the English and their apparent inability to realize the danger they stood in from foreign aggression. In one of his frequent bad moods he called England "*Le vilain pays*", but he had a strong sense of kingly responsibility. Towards the end of his life many of his contemporaries realized that he was a far-sighted statesman, a European determined to resist France or, for that matter, any other State terrorizing or dominating the rest.

The destruction of Whitehall Palace - the seat of government - by an accidental fire due to the carelessness of a Dutch maid, occurred on Tuesday, January 4, 1698. Nearly all the buildings were destroyed except for Inigo Jones's beautiful Banqueting House, which still delights us today. William, who had avoided living in Whitehall, was perceptive enough to appreciate the sentiments of the English, who would feel the loss far more than himself. He wrote to Heinsius in such a way and after a visit to the blackened ruins he swore that "if God would give him leave he would rebuild it, and much finer than before".[3] The indefatigable Sir Christopher Wren was summoned and soon conceived a plan for a grand rebuilding of Whitehall. By 1698 Windsor Castle was William's favourite dwelling, for Hampton Court had too many memories of Mary and he hardly ever went there except towards the end.

James Vernon, who handled much of Shrewsbury's business, wrote to his patron in late 1698:[4] "The King is not very right in health. He neither eats nor sleeps so well as he used to do." William complained that "he was hardly used", misunderstood by the people whom he ruled.

Tallard kept the alert Louis XIV fully informed of affairs. William never bothered to conceal his satisfaction when leaving England for Holland. Tallard wrote on July 30:

his countenance was expressive of the joy which he felt at going to Holland; he took no pains whatever to conceal it from the English, to say the truth they speak very openly about it.[5]

It was unwise of the King not to conceal his feelings.

When he returned to England in late November, William found a new and hostile House of Commons, fiercely xenophobic in its hatred of all foreigners, Dutchmen and Frenchmen. Tallard wrote to King Louis: "The House of Commons has acted as in a fury." They wanted to cut down the army to the ridiculous level of 7,000, all native-born English in England, 12,000 in Ireland, either Irish or Scotch, and 6,000 in Scotland. William thought it was madness and ruinous, for it was essential to maintain the defences of the country against aggressors.

What upset William even more was the decision of the Commons to banish from the kingdom his beloved Blue Dutch Foot Guards, his pride and his joy. They had played a distinguished part in all his campaigns. As Macaulay wrote:[6]

> That brigade had been the first in the army to enter the capital, being entrusted with the vital task of occupying Whitehall in December 1688 and guarding James II.

What Macaulay omits to mention is that many Englishmen resented the Dutch assuming these duties when they themselves were absolutely capable of performing them. However, Parliament was ungrateful in their insistence that the Dutch Blue Guards must go. They had also been the first to plunge into the waters of the Boyne in June 1690.

William was so cruelly mortified and incensed by Parliament that he even seriously considered abdication at this juncture. He thought longingly of Het Loo where he could retire to in peace. He wrote to Heinsius: "Affairs in Parliament are so desperate that I shall soon have to take a step that will cause a great sensation in the world." The Commons had disregarded his advice. They must now reap the consequences. He wrote what he thought his last speech from the throne:

> I came into this kingdom, at the desire of the nation, to save it from ruin, and to preserve your religion, your laws, and liberties. And, for that end, I have been obliged to maintain a long and burdensome war for this kingdom, which, by the grace of God, and the bravery of this nation, is at present ended in a good peace, under which you may live happily and in quiet, provided you will contribute towards your own security in the manner I had recommended to you, at the opening of the sessions.[7]

This speech, in the event, was never delivered.

When William showed the contents to his extremely able Lord Chancellor, Lord Somers, a Whig, Somers was aghast at the very idea of the King's abdication. He pleaded with him to alter his mind.

This is extravagance, Sir, this is madness. I implore Your Majesty for the sake of your own honour, not to say to anybody else what you have said to me.

William listened patiently, but refused for some time to continue as King of England. Very reluctantly he agreed to stay, because of his strong sense of duty. The insistence of Lord Somers almost certainly influenced him.

During late January 1699 the young Electoral Prince of Bavaria, the favoured candidate for the throne of Carlos II of Spain, died in mysterious circumstances. The protracted negotiations resumed between Portland and Tallard. When the Second Partition Treaty was eventually signed on February 21, 1700 it was proposed that the Archduke Charles should be created King of Spain in the event of Carlos II's death.

It is likely that William in his earlier days as King would never have accepted the decision of the Commons to cut down the army to 7,000 men or to banish his Blue Dutch Guards abroad. The Earl of Portland when conferring with Tallard was of this opinion, telling the ambassador that:

now the King was old (he was forty-eight in November 1698) he preferred calmness and mildness to what appeared to be the best for his interest.[8]

It was a bitter, unhappy period for William. When the Earl of Portland insisted on retiring towards the end of April 1699, William ascribed his motive as "blind jealousy". The King wrote to the Pensionary Heinsius in Holland: "I regret to be obliged to inform you that the Earl of Portland has at length retired and that nothing was able to prevent him." William, however, after much persuasion managed to get him to continue the vital negotiations with Tallard. The King had done everything possible to give satisfaction to Portland. To Heinsius, William complained of the mass of impertinences the Commons had inflicted on him.

William occasionally quarrelled with Albemarle, and once at Het Loo, Albemarle retired to the country to nurse his resentment. His place in the Dutch Secretariat was filled by d'Allonne, a former secretary of the Queen's and as he was a partisan of the Earl of Portland it was considered a victory for him over his rival, but Albemarle was only briefly out of favour. He was created Knight of the Most Noble Order of the Garter in 1700, an honour already held by Portland. It was unwise, however, of the

King to appoint Albemarle over the Second Duke of Ormonde's head, as the first commander of the Guards. Such a storm of protest followed that the King was obliged to countermand the appointment.

When the Dutch Guards started their march to the coast on April 7 (1699), the people viewed their departure rather with sorrow than with triumph. Many of them had married English wives, who had borne them children. A Dutch soldier said: "a pretty figure you would have made, if we had not come."[9] Now they were going, the English showed their favour. Strong xenophobia still gripped the country. When the House of Commons made a petition to William that he should dismiss all foreigners except Prince George of Denmark from his service, he prorogued Parliament until the autumn and sighing with relief, returned to Holland. In the Gelderland his health always improved.

In Scotland William was even more unpopular than in England. Her colonial venture in the Isthmus of Darien in Panama had resulted in dismal failure. It had been badly planned, for Darien was ridden with disease and yellow fever. When the Scotch colonists died of fever William showed some sympathy, but did nothing to support them. He was blamed for inaction. It is unfortunate that he never visited Scotland, although he had intended to stay in Holyrood House. He certainly wanted a closer union of England and Scotland.

William was also in trouble for the many grants of land he had made to those who had given him devoted service in Ireland, like Godart van Ginckel Earl of Athlone, Portland, Albemarle and Henry Sidney Earl of Romney. A Parliamentary Commission was appointed to examine these grants, consisting of seven Members of Parliament. The King had rewarded Elizabeth Villiers, his former mistress, with 90,000 acres of Irish land. During February 1700 the Commission voted that these grants should be revoked, to be used by Trustees to pay off the national debt. The King, meanwhile, became more and more exasperated by the enmity of many of the members.

On July 24, 1700, the eleventh birthday of the Duke of Gloucester was celebrated at Windsor when he took part in the elaborate rejoicings. There was a splendid banquet at Windsor, followed by fireworks. Unfortunately the young duke, never strong, was exhausted by the celebration. He retired to bed, the victim of a malignant fever, and within a few days was dead, to the universal sorrow of the nation. According to Bishop Burnet, the boy duke had a wonderful memory and very good judgement. If he had succeeded his mother Princess Anne, he might have proved a remarkable king. It was the Earl of Marlborough's duty as Governor to inform the King of the sad news. William was in Holland and replied from Het Loo on August 4 in French: "It is so great a loss to me, as well as to all England, that it pierces my heart with affliction."

Princess Anne never really recovered from the tragic death of her only surviving son, and henceforward she would always sign her letters to Sarah Marlborough 'Your poor, unfortunate Morley'. The coffin containing the body of the prince was borne in a coach among several others through Windsor Park, thence to Staines and via Hounslow to Westminster Abbey where he was buried in Henry VII's Chapel.

Liselotte wrote to her beloved Aunt Sophie Electress of Hanover on August 12 from St. Cloud:

> I expect you know that the Duke of Gloucester is dead. If the English decided not to allow our Prince of Wales to succeed King William, you would be the person closest to the Crown. It would be nice if you became a Queen. I wish it more for you than for myself.

Sophie, youngest daughter of Elizabeth of Bohemia, was a grand-daughter of James I. In another letter about eight months later, Liselotte refers to Princess Anne:

> The Princess of Denmark is said to drink so heavily that her body is quite burnt up. She will never have any living children, and King William's health is so delicate that he can't live long. So you will soon sit on your grandfather's throne, and I shall be overjoyed.

Owing to her Stuart blood Sophie always retained sympathy for James Francis Edward, Prince of Wales. Liselotte, a highly intelligent woman, had even more sympathy for this unfortunate prince. Writing four years after King William's death to a correspondent, she says:

> How can you possibly think that our young King of England (James III, known as the Old Pretender in England) is a changeling and not the Queen's (Maria of Modena's son)? I would stake my head on his being the rightful child. For one thing, he and his mother resemble each other like two drops of water. For another, a lady not at all partial to the Queen was present at the birth and told me, for the sake of simple truth, that she saw this child still attached to the umbilical cord. She has no doubt at all that he is the Queen's son. The English treat their monarchs so curiously that it's not surprising there is no rush to become their ruler. Ma Tante is quite right when she regards this child as the true heir.

There were other Stuart descendants having a claim to William's throne, but they were all Catholics.

William himself pondered the matter hard and favoured the Protestant succession through the Electress Sophie. In 1700, however, she was an old lady of seventy. His influence was decisive in making Parliament pass the Act of Settlement (1701) in which the Crown was to devolve on the Protestant Electress Sophie and her successors on the death of Queen Anne. It is probable today that this Act should be repealed or at least changed, for its usefulness no longer applies.

On November 1, 1700 there occurred an event of historic importance, the long expected death of the pathetic, superstitious, diseased Carlos II of Spain in Madrid. Prior to his death he had made a new will under the influence of Portocarrero, Cardinal-Archbishop of Toledo, bequeathing his vast dominions to Philippe Duke of Anjou, second son of the Dauphin and grandson of Le Roi Soleil. It was one of the grandest occasions in the life of Louis XIV, at once magnificent and theatrical, as he commanded the doors of his study to be opened, and the courtiers to enter. With a dramatic gesture he said: "Gentlemen, here is the King of Spain", as he showed them the Duke of Anjou, a young prince aged nineteen. "Be a good Spaniard, that is your first duty now", he admonished him, "but remember you were born a Frenchman, and so maintain union between the two nations." The Spanish Ambassador fell on his knees and clasped the Duke's hand. "The Pyrenees have ceased to exist," he said. Liselotte wrote that Anjou seldom laughed and was very serious. She had accosted him about this time. At a hunt she said, "Pass, Great King! May your Majesty pass."[10]

It was indeed embarrassing for King Louis. He was faced with two alternatives. He either had to accept the will of Carlos II and perjure himself in the eyes of his co-signatories to the Treaties of Partition or agree to the enormous Spanish dominions going to his rival the Austrian Archduke Charles.

William, on hearing of King Louis's action in breaking the agreement was much mortified. Momentarily at least it seemed to him that his life's work in forging the Grand Alliance had been all in vain. He bitterly blamed himself for trusting to French promises. He wrote to Heinsius:

> I never relied much on engagements with France: but must confess that I did not think they would, in the face of the whole world, break a solemn treaty before it was well accomplished.[11]

He had worked passionately for a balance of power in Europe. Now a new danger loomed, the establishment of a Franco-Spanish world empire, resulting in the possible defeat of England and Holland. Meanwhile Parliament with typical complacency hastened to recognize Philip V as King of Spain. William wondered at the insularity of the English, unwilling to see to the defences of the country with an inadequate army. It was vital to William, despite feeling ill, to start rebuilding the Grand Alliance. Then came the ominous news in February 1701 that Louis XIV had occupied the Spanish Netherlands.

Nobody had worked harder than Tallard in his negotiations with Portland for the Partition Treaties. When he returned to France, however, he was furious that his labours lay in tatters. Saint-Simon the French historian brilliantly conveys his feelings.

At home Parliament clamoured for the impeachment of the Whig peers, Somers, Portland, Charles Montagu Baron Halifax (a founder of the Bank of England) and Edward Russell Earl of Orford, all concerned with the Partition Treaties. William was deeply perplexed, but waited, hoping that the mood of Parliament might change.

There remained some patriotic Englishmen conscious of the dire perils confronting the country. William had drawn closer to the Earl of Marlborough from 1700 onwards, sensing his great ability both as a soldier and as a diplomat, and instinctively realizing that he was the man of the future, ready to carry out the King's policies when he was dead. The Lords behaved more realistically than the Commons, acquitting the accused ministers of impeachment, much to the fury of the Commons.

One Englishman who did not share the insular prejudices of his fellow countrymen was Daniel Defoe, satirical writer and journalist, a man from a humble background. He formed a tremendous admiration for King William. When a writer named Tutchin wrote hostile verses, *The Foreigners*, against William and Dutchmen, Defoe was very angry and retorted in his celebrated satire *The True-born Englishman* (January 1701). He explains in his Preface his reasons for writing his work:

> But when I see the Town full of lampoons and invectives against Dutchmen, *only* because they are foreigners; and the King (William III) reproached and insulted by insolent pedants and ballad-making poets, for employing foreigners, and for being a foreigner himself: I confess myself moved by it to remind our nation of their own original; thereby to let them see what a banter is put upon themselves in it; since speaking of Englishmen *ab origine* we are really *all foreigners ourselves*.[12]

We blame the King that he relies too much on strangers, Germans, Huguenots, and Dutch; and seldom would his great affairs of State to

173

English Councillors communicate. The fact might very well be answered thus. He has so often been betrayed by us, he must have been a madman to rely on English gentlemen's fidelity.

His poem led to an introduction to the King, and both William and Defoe struck up a good understanding. In his *The Legion Memorial* he was not afraid to attack the House of Commons. Five gentlemen of Kent, fearing that their county lay most exposed to foreign invasion, drew up the celebrated Kentish petition in which they implored Parliament to provide adequate defence for the safety of the country and to raise supplies to aid their allies. They were immediately arrested and sent to the Gatehouse. Then on May 14, 1701 Defoe, guarded by sixteen gentlemen of quality (he may have been disguised as a woman), strode into the Commons and handed his *Legion's Memorial* to the Speaker. The Commons in this pamphlet was attacked on several grounds: for illegally detaining the Kentish petitioners, for failing to vote supplies, for removing ministers serving the King on unproven charges, and for deserting the Dutch, exposed to attack by the French. They were criticized for their "saucy indecent reproaches" respecting His Majesty and reminded that they were elected servants of the people and not above the law. The nation demanded that if the King of France would not listen to reason, King William must be asked to declare war on him. It was bold and courageous of Defoe, for he might have been arrested and imprisoned. The Lords, aware of the danger, differed from the Commons, imploring the King, in an address, to abide by all existing treaties between England, Holland and the Emperor Leopold. During late June, despite violent protests from the Commons, the accused Whig ministers, Somers, Halifax and Orford were acquitted.

XX WILLIAM'S FAILING HEALTH

There was a grandeur about King William's and Marlborough's journey to The Hague in the middle of July 1701. Now that the King had a partial mandate from Parliament for war against France, he was eager to involve Marlborough, whom he had formerly distrusted in European affairs, and introduce him to the numerous foreign ambassadors at The Hague and, above all, to train him as the future leader of the allied coalition against France. William was an old, sick man suffering agonies from his swollen legs and other ailments. He knew that he had only a short lease of life ahead of him. When Marlborough began his vital discussions with Heinsius, a firm friendship sprang up between them. Whilst at The Hague he was lodged at the Mauritshuis (House of Prince Maurice) where Charles II had once feasted before the Restoration, and where the Earl of Marlborough had been William's guest.[1] There Marlborough, handsome and urbane, had stood at the top of the elegant staircase, exercising his charm on the statesmen of Europe, as Professor Trevelyan wrote: "Seeming to understand all and sympathize with everyone." It was certainly a remarkable achievement to keep that great warrior King Charles XII of Sweden out of Western and Central Europe, for the Swedes were Francophile and partial to bribes.

The negotiations preceding the vital Treaty of Grand Alliance were the work of King William, Heinsius and Marlborough, and the Treaty was signed by England, the United Provinces and Austria on September 7, 1701. Later most of the German princes adhered to the Treaty, except for Bavaria, which was for a time on the French side. By the Treaty, William committed the allies to fighting for the partition of the Spanish Empire, though negotiations were not ruled out. The United Provinces promised to raise an army of 120,000, while England's share would be 40,000 and that of the Emperor Leopold, 90,000. The Treaty was later ratified by Parliament in England.

It is curious to consider that William and Marlborough were exactly of the same age, for they had both been born in 1650 and were now fifty-one. They presented a complete contrast, William slight in appearance and looking ill and emaciated, to beholders, a sick man suffering from asthma and a constant cough, while Marlborough was at the height of his powers, brimful of health.

On August 1 the King left for Het Loo and it was there in September that he heard from Lord Manchester, his Ambassador in France, that his father-in-law, King James had died at Saint-Germain.

James, during the last year of his life was a pathetic character. When Liselotte visited him and Queen Maria in late 1700 he talked incessantly about Sophie Electress of Hanover. She wrote Sophie that James's stammer was worse than ever. With tears of love welling in his eyes he had stuttered: *"O O O pour cela eh-eh-eh-eh me - m'a toujours aimé."*

There was a dramatic scene at his bedside as he lay dying on September 16, attended by his devoted wife, and his son the Prince of Wales, aged thirteen, and enchanting little daughter Princess Louise Marie aged nine. It was now that King Louis, when he came to say farewell to the dying king, made his grand gesture of acknowledging the Prince of Wales as King James III. James II, his beard grown long "like a Capuchin friar", murmured his thanks for all that Louis had done for him, while many Jacobites and Frenchmen present sank to their knees at the King of France's feet to show their gratitude. Most were in tears.

Louis's recognition of the Prince of Wales as King of England was given against the advice of his Foreign Minister Torcy and other councillors. There were mixed feelings on Louis's part, but his natural chivalry and generosity, his genuine friendship with Maria of Modena and his close association with the Stuarts persuaded him to support their claim. Louis believed in God-given authority,[2] that kings were originally chosen by God and possessed powers and gifts transmitted from father to son. It marked his repugnance of the ascent to the throne of William III and Queen Mary II in 1689. He was mindful that the English Parliament had passed the Act of Settlement in February 1701 in which it was stated that Sophie the Protestant Electress was designated the Princess of Denmark's successor after her death as Queen. William had used every endeavour to enact this legislation.

By his action, however, the King of France violated the Treaty of Rijswijk and he was much criticized. He had recognized William as *de facto* King of England, though a French historian Monsieur Pierre Gaxotte, denies this, arguing in his work that the King's action was no violation.[3]

On hearing of the death of the exiled King at Het Loo, William said not a word, but his pale cheek flushed. He pulled his hat over his eyes to conceal the change in his face. He immediately ordered Lord Manchester to leave France and ordered the Lord Justices to see that the French representative, Poussin, should depart from England. Poussin was supping, when he heard of the King's decision, at the *Blue Posts*, a tavern much frequented by Jacobites, and was in the company of three of the most virulent Members of Parliament. It was highly embarrassing for Members of Parliament to be seen in such society.

Neither Parliament nor the people of England could accept a King being foisted upon them by the King of France. For the majority of Englishmen, James Francis Edward was the Pretender, and nothing was more influential in making the people unite behind William and clamour for war against France. No longer was Parliament opposed to raising the vast amount of money needed to sustain a war.

William, during August 1701, sent Lord Macclesfield on a mission to Sophie Electress of Hanover to present her with the Act of Settlement. He and his large entourage were royally entertained in Hanover and he received a lavish gift of a ewer and basin of solid gold, according to seventeenth century custom. Earlier the King had entertained Sophie at Het Loo, with whom he enjoyed excellent relations. She took care to admire the gardens and beautiful lawns, which were ironed smooth by an enormous roller drawn by horse.[4]

Did William really say of Sophie's eldest son George Louis, destined to be King of England (1714), according to Defoe, that he knew no Prince in Europe so fit to be King of England as the Elector of Hanover? George took little interest in England when he became King and never bothered to learn its language. Defoe later wrote: "God grant the King George to have more comfort of his crown than we suffered KING WILLIAM to have."[5]

During 1701 the King remained long in Holland, advised by his doctors owing to his feeble health. In October he paid a brief visit to Honselaersdijck, a home dear to him where he had twenty-four years ago brought Mary as his young wife. Perhaps as he went driving in the Lange Voorhout in The Hague on a breezy autumn October day, watching the yellow leaves of the lime trees slowly drift to earth, he knew that his own life was almost over.

In early November his doctors considered that he was fit enough to travel to England. During the afternoon of November 4 he landed early at Margate. It was the thirteenth anniversary of his landing in Brixham. London was making great preparations to welcome their King, but a journey along Cornhill, Cheapside, Fleet Street and the Strand was considered by his doctors too much strain for a sick man. William stayed one night in Greenwich. While London celebrated his homecoming with the thunder of the cannon of the Tower, with bonfires and the peal of church bells, William rode along quiet country roads. On reaching Hampton Court he went immediately to bed. There he was obliged to receive countless delegations with their speeches.

William's health no doubt deteriorated from 1700 onwards. From his infancy he had always been troubled with a weakness in his lungs, an incessant cough and asthmatical weakness.[6] His German doctor Liebergen considered that the King suffered from anaemia, but none of his doctors mentions tuberculosis of the lungs - a disease from which William of Orange probably suffered. The King's favourite doctor was undoubtedly Bidloo, his fellow-countryman, who became a real friend and deeply attached to him. Gorvaert Bidloo was very skilled and knowledgeable, and wrote an expert book on human anatomy. Born a year before William, he had been Superintendent of Military Hospitals in Holland and Professor of Anatomy at Leiden.[7] Bidloo treated the King for his swollen legs, which gave him agonizing pain. He prescribed bandaging and friction. Possibly William was affected by psychological factors, for when he escaped to Het Loo he always made an amazing recovery and seemed in much better health than in England. Although he often suffered from bad health towards the end, he never neglected his work. William's English doctors included Dr. Radcliffe who had attended Mary in her last illness, Dr. Lawrence and Dr. Millington. William's legs were swollen with dropsy. Dr. Radcliffe was tactless enough to say to the King on one occasion, "I would not have your two legs for your two kingdoms." According to accounts in the British Library his doctors certainly prescribed queer remedies.

On June 2, 1700, for instance, Dr. Radcliffe prescribed the powder of crab claws compound with a pearl julep, while eight days later Dr. Radcliffe and Dr. Lawrence prescribed the use of ale impregnated with the leaves of wild carrot-seeds, ground ivy, fire-tops, etc.[8] In many ways William was his own best doctor - he once said to Bidloo, every man should be his own doctor after the age of 30 - for William had sensible tastes, eating a great deal of fresh fruit though never, or very seldom, between meals. He liked green vegetables. His breakfast was only a dish of chocolate without any water in it. He sometimes drank beer or wine, which for five or six months during the year was cooled in ice and the beer was always bottled. He was a moderate drinker until towards the end of his life when he tended to drink too much, probably to ease his pain.

Bidloo, who was constantly in attendance on the King at Hampton Court, kept a diary of his last months.[9] William spent as much time as possible in the gardens, buying some Italian statues for them. Bidloo was eager to serve William for he sensed his greatness. The King continued to hold councils and grant audiences.

For the last time, the King opened Parliament, containing a majority of Whig members. He told them: "The eyes of all Europe are upon this Parliament; all matters are at a standstill till your resolutions are known". He stressed once more:

If you do in good earnest wish to see England hold the balance of Europe, and to be indeed at the head of the Protestant interest, it will appear by your right improving the present opportunity.[10]

Awake at last to the urgent danger, parliament and people did not hesitate to vote for the essential supplies to save Europe from the domination of a single power. William was never to see the mighty battles of the War of the Spanish Succession, Blenheim (1704), Ramillies (1706), Oudenaarde (1708), and Malplaquet, the bloodiest battle of the four, nor the crowning peace of the Treaty of Utrecht (1713).

During the last few months of his life, William resumed his intimacy with William Bentinck Earl of Portland, who was now living retired at the Ranger's lodge in Windsor Great Park with his second wife, a niece of Sir William Temple. One day when they were walking in Hampton Court gardens, William said to his friend "that he found himself so weak that he did not expect to live another summer".[11] Portland and Albemarle now ended their intrigues and quarrels against one another.

Shortly before his death William, who had often blundered in his relations with Scotland, sent a message to the House of Commons urging them to make a union between England and Scotland. It was to materialize in 1707 during the reign of his successor Queen Anne.

On February 24, 1702 as he was riding a horse that he had never ridden before, near Hampton Court[12] (one British Library account says near Hounslow Heath), his horse stumbled on a rabbit-warren or molehill. The King sustained a nasty fall, breaking his collar-bone. Vernon is the only contemporary who mentions the molehill, though popular imagination prefers this story to any other. William himself declared that he was riding on level ground. The King was brought back to the Palace where the bone was set by Ronjet, his Huguenot surgeon. The King, as was his wont, made light of the accident, dining at Hampton Court, and sleeping most of the journey back to Kensington House. The jolting of the coach, however, had displaced the bone, and Dr. Bidloo was obliged to reset it before the King could go to bed.[13] However, many people remained over confident, probably wishful thinking:

H.M. slept very well the night following and has been so well ever since that there is all the reason in the world to hope this accident will have no ill consequence and that His Majesty will be perfectly recovered of it in a few days.

On March 6 a Whitehall correspondent reported:

The King was taken last Wednesday with a fitt of an ague, which was pretty violent for several hours. Yesterday it returned. He was taken with a painful cough and vomiting and could keep nothing in his stomach.[14]

It was now evident that the King was dying. "One lung was inflamed to the point of mortification, and he could hardly eat anything." In the early hours, the Earl of Albemarle arrived from Holland, where he had been sent on a political mission, and William gave orders that he should rest before coming to make his report. It was to Keppel that William was to give the keys of his desk and cabinet, while he gently murmured: "*Je tire vers ma fin.*" The favourite was deeply distressed.

In his lucid moments William was able to give a commission of lords the power to act for him, including the Abjuration Bill excluding the so-called Pretender Prince of Wales from the succession. During his last days he depended much on the faithful Bidloo, and when he had been unable to sleep, leaned against his shoulder saying, faintly: "I could sleep in this posture, sit nearer me, and hold me so for a little while."

It was March 10. The doctors, after consulting together thought it was high time to summon Tenison, the Archbishop of Canterbury, to administer the Sacraments. He arrived together with Bishop Burnet. At 5 a.m. the King received the Sacraments, thanking Bidloo especially and his personal servants for their many services.

Just before the end, at 8 a.m., Bentinck was admitted to the bedchamber. The message summoning him had somehow gone astray. "For the last time", murmured the dying man, and taking Bentinck's hand pressed it against his heart. Perhaps William would have preferred to live on for a little while, though not in the agony he was now enduring. He was ready for death.

* * *

The Council assembled immediately at St. James's, giving the necessary orders for proclaiming the new Queen Anne.

William was mourned deeply by his intimate friends, Lord Albemarle, Bentinck Earl of Portland, William Carstares, the King's Scottish chaplain, the Duke of Shrewsbury now married to an Italian wife and much grieved. In Holland his loss was keenly felt and the church bells chimed three times daily for six weeks. France learnt of William's death from a banker in Paris, Samuel Bernard. Liselotte refers to it on April 22 from Versailles: "I was not surprised that King William died with such *fermeté*." A friend of hers wrote that Lord Albemarle was on the point of following his master,* he was ill to death with grief. She admitted that his death had made her sad and that an almanack for March 20, 1702 had predicted his death.[15] The Jacobites were naturally overjoyed, drinking a toast to "The little gentleman in black velvet" - the mole on whose hill his horse may have stumbled. Like all men touched with greatness, he had many enemies and these rejoiced at his death, especially some of the Loevesteiners in Holland.

Mary of Modena, much more charitable than her late husband, never spoke of William III with venom. She told the exiled English at Saint-Germain to refrain from expressing joy. She was known for her charity, never saying anything harmful about anybody.

King Louis had through the years developed a healthy respect for William, but as his lifelong opponent, had little reason to like him. He forbade mourning, but had the good taste not to openly rejoice at his enemy's death.

William had never been popular in England, and few people felt his loss. He had the reputation of being a cold, remote man, inaccessible and inclined to be morose and sullen. This is to some extent a false impression. He was capable of great warmth to his friends, both English and foreign, and no trouble was too much for somebody he loved. Little mention has been made of his emotional and highly-strung nature. He could even be affable and gay if it suited him. William mellowed towards the end of his life. The attractive Countess of Rutland tells a delightful story of the King's graciousness on one occasion at Kensington House in 1701:

> After his playing a litel at the gold tabel he rise and went to goe to the orther tabels, as he allways dus, so I came back to mack the King's way, and pressed the ladys behind to do so to, which the King seeing said it was 'No mater, my Lady Rutland, for I can come over the stool', so strid over it and when (he) came just by me stopped and told me I looked mighty well ... and told me I was so grat a stranger he hopeed I would not leve then.[16]

As King, William did much more for the British Navy than he is given credit for by Dalrymple. He was a pioneer in British naval strategy, advising his ministers to acquire Gibraltar. He was also responsible for the building of Plymouth naval dockyard, and keen to pursue the beginnings of Greenwich Hospital, a project of his Queen's. Naval pensions were also first introduced during his reign.

---

* Albemarle lived on to fight bravely in the ensuing war.

He had no love of war for its own sake, and unlike Louis XIV did not appreciate *la gloire*. True, he was excessively fond of campaigning, not least because it took him away from the weary grind of government at home. He gloried in the excitement of battle among men, but he was probably happier in the open air, engaged on long hunting expeditions. He thought of war, however, as "this great evil", but he worked hard for the Partition Treaties in his declining years, thus trying to prevent the War of the Spanish Succession. When he failed, he renewed his efforts to form the Grand Alliance, probably his greatest achievement. His behaviour was full of contradiction: he was humane on the one hand, but did not oppose the torturing of prisoners.

William is a deeply controversial character, loved by the few and condemned and criticized by the many. He is, however, better understood in our own age than by his contemporaries.

He was of an autocratic temper, sometimes in conflict with his Parliaments, obliging him to accept a diminution of the Royal prerogative and other prerogatives of the Crown.

The freedom of the press (1695) and the judiciary were features in his reign of thirteen years. An absolute king was a creation of England's past. William could be criticized for being too careless and contemptuous of English traditions. He was never willing to conceal his dislike of ceremonial occasions.

Thomas Lediard, the historian, described William as "moderate in prosperity, unshaken in adversity, wise in his councils, bold at the head of his armies, faithful to his allies, and dreadful to his enemies."[17] Not the least of his achievements was to unite England and Holland, two inveterate rivals in trade and commerce. He did not like contradiction, nor to have his actions censured, but his knowledge of men made him wary of flatterers. He maintained good relations with the Church of England, and refrained from oppressing the Dissenters.

I would question Lediard's assertion that "his genius lay chiefly in war", for the King's talents in composing the Grand Alliances against France, cannot be sufficiently stressed. He himself bore no personal rancour against the French, admiring that great nation for her art and having many Frenchmen among his friends. If he had lived longer, he might well have shortened the War of the Spanish Succession by his political sagacity. He was for the most part too lavish of money in his generosity to Portland and Albemarle, and other favourites, but too niggardly in rewarding services to those who brought him valuable intelligence. It is hard to criticize him for spending too much in the building of Het Loo, Hampton Court or Kensington House. William never sought popularity, but his mind had been soured by the perverseness of the English and he made little attempt to understand them.

It is surprising that in the long notice[18] devoted to William III, it is stated that he disliked learning and art. It is not true. He was indeed keenly interested in art and collected pictures. A favourite picture was the so-called 'Zoological Garden of William III' by M. d'Hondecoeter, which used to hang in his private cabinet at Het Loo. Even when stationed at Salisbury during the invasion, he found time to visit Wilton, the Earl of Pembroke's historic house, to see its treasures and wonderful pictures. Though no intellectual, he was interested in learning, education and social reform. And it was he who encouraged men of erudition such as Edmund Halley and Isaac Newton.

In his private life William was a very different character than that depicted by many historians. He was kindly, often thoughtful of others, tolerant, reticent and secretive. It is hardly likely that his wife Mary would have loved him if he had been as cold and remote a personality as many supposed. In reality he was in his later life, a kindly husband, caring, affectionate and even domesticated at times. His morality was typical of his age, but he was on the whole a better man than many of his contemporaries. However, he was sometimes thoughtless in his behaviour towards Mary, neglecting her often out of necessity, to fight in the Dutch wars. He learnt to love her after his fashion. He left the whole of his Orange estates to his cousin Jan Willem Friso of Nassau-Dietz, whilst he became Stadtholder of Friesland, Groningen and other parts of the United Provinces.

He was given a simple burial as he had desired. His body was borne to the Great Abbey Church of Westminster on April 12, 1702, to be buried by Mary's side in Henry VII's Chapel.

William remained a passionate Dutchman to the end, largely a stranger to the island race he reigned over, but he had paved the way for England's greatness in the eighteenth century.

To sum up this portrait of William, what is more appropriate than the measured words of a contemporary, albeit an enemy, the Duke of Berwick, a fine soldier:

Although I have no cause to bless the memory of this Prince, I cannot deny him the faculties of a great man, and, if he had not been a usurper, of a great King. He had extraordinary intelligence, was an astute politician, and no matter the obstacles in the way, never turned aside from his object.

To attest his ambition to dethrone a prince at once his uncle and father "by means revolting to the conscience of an honest man and contrary to the dictates of Christianity", was an act Berwick could neither forget nor forgive. William's motives are enigmatic and are likely to remain so.

NOTES

Chapter I
1.   *Les Mémoires du Burgrave and Comte Fréderic de Dohna, 1621-85.*
2.   *William of Orange,* Nesca Robb, Vol. I.
3.   *Lives of the Princesses of England,* M.A. Everett Green, Vol. VI.
4.   *William of Orange,* Nesca Robb, Vol. I.
5.   *Letters of Queen Elizabeth of Bohemia,* ed. Baker.
6.   Ibid., p. 181.
7.   Birch Mss. 4460. British Library.
8.   *William of Orange,* Nesca Robb, Vol. I.
9.   *Letters of Queen Elizabeth of Bohemia,* ed. Baker.

Chapter II
1.   *State Papers,* Thurloe, Vol. I, p. 664.
2.   Ormonde Mss. H.H. Commission New Series, Vol. I, p. 303.
3.   *State Papers,* Thurloe.
4.   *Letters of Queen Elizabeth of Bohemia,* ed. Baker.
5.   Mss. Koninklijke Bibliotheck, The Hague.
6.   Ibid.
7.   *Letters of Queen Elizabeth of Bohemia,* ed. Baker.
8.   *State Papers,* Thurloe.
9.   *William and Mary,* van der Zee, p.31.
10. *Letters of Queen Elizabeth of Bohemia,* ed. Baker, p. 334.
11. *William of Orange,* Nesca Robb.
12. *Diary and Correspondence of Samuel Pepys* with Notes by Lord Braybrooke, Vol. I, p. 61.
13. *William of Orange,* Nesca Robb.
14. Ibid.
15. *Letters of Queen Elizabeth of Bohemia,* ed. Baker.
16. *William of Orange,* Nesca Robb.
17. *Letters of Queen Elizabeth of Bohemia,* ed. Baker.

Chapter III
1.   *William Bentinck and William III,* Marion Grew (1924).
2.   *William and Mary,* van der Zee, p. 35.

3.   Abstinez-vous autant que vous pouvez du boisson et principalement des femmes et de tout autre debauche.

4.   *James II*, F.C. Turner.

5.   *Le Fevre Portalis, John de Witt* (1885), Vol. I, p. 477.

6.   Ibid.

7.   *Life of Sir William Temple*, T.P. Courtenay, Vol. I, pp. 285-286.

8.   There is also an account in Marion Grew's *William Bentinck and William III*.

9.   Baker Mss. Cambridge University Library.

10.   Ibid.

11.   *William and Mary*, van der Zee, p. 35.

Chapter IV

1.   *Louis XIV*, Vincent Cronin (1964), pp. 190-91.

2.   *William III and the Defence of Holland, 1672-74*, Mary Trevelyan (1930).

3.   *William and Mary*, van der Zee.

4.   *Diary*, John Evelyn, Vol. II, pp. 371-2.

5.   *William and Mary*, van der Zee.

6.   *William of Orange*, Nesca Robb, Vol. I, p. 214.

7.   Ibid., Vol. I.

8.   *William III and the Defence of Holland*, Mary Trevelyan.

9.   Ibid.

10.   *A Character of the Trimmer*, being a short life of the First Marquis of Halifax, H.C. Foxcroft (1946).

11.   Ibid.

12.   *William and Mary*, van der Zee.

13.   Ibid., p. 73.

14.   K.H.A. Mss. 16.IXb, The Hague.

15.   *William III and the Defence of Holland*, Mary Trevelyan.

16.   *Correspondentie*, N. Japikse.

Chapter V

1.   *William III and the Defence of Holland*, Mary Trevelyan.

2.   *William's Mary*, Elizabeth Hamilton.

3.   *Journalen*, C. Huygens.

4.   *Correspondentie*, N. Japikse.

5.   See *William of Orange and the English Opposition* (1672-4), K.H.D. Haley (Oxford, 1953).

6.   Ibid.

7.   William to Ossory, March 1675.

8.   *Life of Sir William Temple*, T.P. Courtnay, Vol. IV, p. 80.

9.   *Life of Sir William Temple*, T.P. Courtnay, Vol. IV, p. 84.
10. Ibid., Vol. II, p. 310.
11. *Life of William Carstares*, prefaced to McCormick, State Papers Edinburgh
     (1774).
12. *William of Orange*, Nesca Robb.
13. *Life of Sir William Temple*, T.P. Courtnay, Vol. II.
14. Ibid., Vol. IV, p. 132.
15. Ibid., Vol. II, p. 368.
16. *Life of James, Duke of Ormonde*, Thomas Carte, Vol. IV, 589-606.
17. *Life of Sir William Temple*, T.P. Courtnay, Vol. II, p. 44.

Chapter VI
1.   *Diary of Samuel Pepys*, ed. Braybrooke, Vol. IV, p. 147.
2.   *William's Mary*, Elizabeth Hamilton.
3.   *Letters of Two Queens*, B. Bathurst, pp. 46. 48. This letter is not dated but, perhaps, written in 1676. Frances Apsley's letters to Mary were probably destroyed before Mary came to England.
4.   *Life of Sir William Temple*, T.P. Courtnay, Vol. II.
5.   First published in 1673. The son of a clergyman of Exeter. Edited by George Percy Elliott (Camden Society).
6.   Ibid.
7.   *Letters from Liselotte*. Translated and edited by Maria Kroll (1970).
8.   *Diary of Dr. Edward Lake*.
9.   Ibid., p. 70.
10. See *Life of Tillotson*, Thomas Birch, (1753), pp. 50-55.

Chapter VII
1.   Lettres et Mémoires de Marie Reine d'Angleterre epouse de Guillaume III.
2.   *William's Mary*, Elizabeth Hamilton.
3.   *The Life and Times of William the Third and Stadtholder of Holland*, Vols. I and II (London, 1835)
4.   *William and Mary*, van der Zee, p. 369; *History of England during the Reign of William III (1744-6)*, James Ralph.
5.   *William and Mary*, van der Zee.
6.   *Letters of Two Queens*, B. Bathurst (1924).
7.   *Reign of Charles II*, David Ogg.
8.   *The Stuart Age* (England 1603--1714), Barry Coward.
9.   *Life of Sir William Temple*, Vol. II, p. 484.

Chapter VIII

1. *James II*, Jock Haswell (1972).
2. *Memoirs of Great Britain and Ireland*, J. Dalrymple, Vol. I, 1790.
3. Ibid.
4. *Diary of Times of Charles II*, H. Sidney, Vols. I and II, edited by Blencowe.
5. *Memoirs of Great Britain and Ireland*, J. Dalrymple, Vol. I, 1790.
6. *Diary of Times of Charles II*, H. Sidney, Vol. I, pp. 154-156.
7. Ibid., pp. 161-163.
8. Ibid., Vol. II, pp. 15f.
9. Ibid., Vol. III, pp. 28-29.
10. *Diary*, John Evelyn.
11. *Robert Spencer Earl of Sunderland 1641-1702*, J.P. Kenyon.
12. Ibid.
13. *Diary of Times of Charles II*, H. Sidney, Vol. II.
14. *Memoirs of Great Britain and Ireland*, J. Dalrymple.

Chapter IX

1. *Négociations en Hollande depuis 1679-1684*, Comte d'Avaux.
2. *William of Orange*, Nesca Robb.
3. *Négotiations en Hollande depuis 1679-1684*, Comte d'Avaux, Vol. I.
4. *Memoirs and Reflections* (London 1721), Sir Richard Bulstrode; *History of His Own Time*, G. Burnet.
5. *Négotiations en Hollande depuis 1679-1684*, Comte d'Avaux, Vol. I, 169-170.
6. Ibid., Vol. I, p. 179 (Oct. 13, 1681).
7. *William of Orange*, Nesca Robb.
8. *Négotiations en Hollande depuis 1679-1684*, Comte d'Avaux, Vol. I, 284-285.
9. *James Duke of Monmouth*, Bryan Bevan, p. 156.
10, *Memoirs*, Sir John Reresby (Yorkshire Squire).
11. *Memoirs*, Earl of Ailesbury, Vol. I.
12. *Memoirs of Great Britain and Ireland*, J. Dalrymple, Vol. I, 1790.
13. Prince William to King Charles II, 2 October 1684.
14. *William of Orange*, Nesca Robb, p. 208.
15. *Négotiations en Hollande depuis 1679-1684*, Vol. IV, p. 210.
16. Ibid., Vol. IV, p. 241.
17. By mistake d'Avaux refers to him as James I.

Chapter X

1. *Hyde Correspondence*, Vol. I, 124f. Laurence Hyde was created Earl of Rochester after 1680.

2.	See *The Jacobite Movement*, Sir Charles Petrie, pp. 64 and 65.
3.	Burnet was born in 1643 and died in 1715. Add. Mss. British Library 6584.
4.	*William's Mary*, Elizabeth Hamilton.
5.	*Journal to Stella*, Jonathan Swift, Vol. II, Oxford.
6.	See the account in Daniel de Bourbon's book, but most of William of Orange's biographies mention the incident.
7.	H.C. Foxcroft supplement to Burnet, p. 191; *The Stuarts in Love*, Maurice Ashley in his chapter 'The Strange Love of William and Mary".
8.	*The Stuarts in Love*, Maurice Ashley.
9.	*History of His Own Time*, G. Burnet.
10.	*The Stuarts in Love*, Maurice Ashley.

Chapter XI
1.	*The Stuart Age* (England 1603-1714), Barry Coward.
2.	*The Jacobite Movement*, Sir Charles Petrie.
3.	*The Stuart Age*, Barry Coward.
4.	*History of His Own Time*, G. Burnet, Vol. 3.
5.	*English Historical Review* XLV, p. 397.
6.	*James II*, Jack Haswell.
7.	*William's Mary*, Elizabeth Hamilton.
8.	*Letters and Diplomatic Instructions of Queen Anne* edited by Beatrice Curtis Brown (1935).
9.	*Memoirs of Great Britain and Ireland*, J. Dalrymple (Appendix 1773); also *Queen over the Water*, Mary Hopkirk.
10.	*Letters and Diplomatic Instructions of Queen Anne*, ed. Curtis Brown.
11.	*Queen over the Water*, Mary Hopkirk.
12.	*Letters and Diplomatic Instructions of Queen Anne*, ed. Curtis Brown.
13.	*The Descent on England*, John Carswell.
14.	*The Stuart Age* , Barry Coward.
15.	*Der Fall des Hauses Stuart,* O. Klopp, Vienna; also *William of Orange*, Nesca Robb, Vol. II.
16.	The Portland Mss. 2087-2178 are in the University Library, Nottingham; *The Descent on England*, John Carswell.

Chapter XII
1.	*William of Orange*, Nesca Robb, Vol. II.
2.	H.M.C. Dartmouth Mss. V, p. 171.
3.	Ibid., V, p. 138; *The Descent on England*, John Carswell.
4.	*History of His Own Time*, G. Burnet, Vol. III, p. 127.

5.   Dartmouth Mss., October 26, 1688; *Marlborough the Man*, Bryan Bevan.

6.   *Diary of Henry Earl of Clarendon* 1687-1690, Vol. II.

7.   *History of His Own Time*, G. Burnet, Vol. III, p. 320.

8.   *The Descent on England*, John Carswell.

9.   *The Marshal Duke of Berwick*, Charles Petrie.

10.   *William of Orange*, Nesca Robb, Vol. II.

11.   Original papers containing the secret history of Great Britain, etc. in two   vols. (London 1775).

12.   *Diary of Henry Earl of Clarendon*, Vol. II, p. 229, edited from the original mss.

13.   Ibid., Vol. II.

14.   Ibid., Vol. II.

Chapter XIII

1.   *William of Orange*, Nesca Robb, Vol. II, p. 277.

2.   *Diary*, John Evelyn, Vol. III, p. 263.

3.   *Memoirs of Mary Queen of England and those of James II and William III to the Electress Sophie of Hanover*, ed. Dr. Doebner.

4.   *Diary*, John Evelyn.

5.   *Memoirs of the Duke of Berwick*, Vol. I, 95.

6.   *William and Mary*, van der Zee, p. 279.

7.   *History of His Own Time*, G. Burnet, Vol. 3, p. 2.

8.   *Private and Original Correspondence of Charles Talbot Earl of Shrewsbury* (created Duke 1694), edited by W. Coxe.

9.   *History of His Own Time*, G. Burnet, Vol. 3, p. 2.

10.   *William of Orange*, Nesca Robb, Vol. II.

11.   *Dictionary of National Biography* edited by Sidney Lee (1895).

Chapter XIV

1.   *History of the Siege of Londonderry*, Cecil D. Milligan (1951).

2.   *History of England*, Thomas Babington Macaulay, Vol. III, p. 233.

3.   Ibid., Vol. III.

4.   *History of His Own Time*, G. Burnet, Vol. III, p. 17.

5.   *The Stuart Age* (England 1603-1714), Barry Coward.

6.   *Diary of Thomas Bellingham*, complete transcript and notes edited by Anthony Hewitson (1908).

7.   *William of Orange*, Nesca Robb, Vol. II. This story of William is probably authentic. Rene Bulmer's forge was Crome Hill near Drumble where Rene Bulmer had a forge.

8.   *The Jacobite Movement*, Sir Charles Petrie (1959).

9.   *Diary of Thomas Bellingham*, ed. Hewitson.

10.   *Memoirs of Great and Ireland,* J. Dalrymple, Vol. 3.
11.   Ibid. It is also mentioned in L.C. Davidson's *Catherine of Braganza* (1908).
12.   *The Navy in the War of William III* (1689-1697), J. Eyrmann (1953).
13.   *Diary,* Narcissus Luttrell, Vol. II, p. 125.
14.   *Dictionary of National Biography,* ed. Stephen.
15.   For a more detailed description of Hampton Court at the time of William and Mary see Bryan Little's *Christopher Wren.*

Chapter XV
1.   *Henry Purcell Glory of His Age* (1995).
2.   *Calendar of State Papers Domestic.*
3.   *Jancourt d'Ausson Mémoires.*
4.   *Calendar of State Papers Domestic,* October 20, 1691.
5.   *History of His Own Time,* G. Burnet, Vol. III, p. 83.
6.   See King William's Chest State Papers 8/12/46. The original documents such as the Report of the Commission of Inquiry in the Public Record Office.
7.   The story of Glencoe has been well told by John Prebble in his book *Glencoe.* (Penguin Books, 1968).
8.   King William's Chest State Papers 8/12/46. Public Record Office.
9.   Ibid.
10.   *Diary,* John Evelyn, Vol. III, p. 314.
11.   Ibid., Vol. III, p. 92.
12.   *Mary of Orange, Memoirs,* Dr. Doebner. Also *William of Orange,* Nesca Robb.
13.   *Louis XIV,* Philippe Erlanger.
14.   *D.N.B.* Russell, ed. Leslie Stephen. There is an interesting picture of 'The Battle of La Hogue' by C. Bouwmeester after R. de Hooght. Huis Lambert
        van Meertem Museum, Delft.
15.   *William of Orange,* Nesca Robb.

Chapter XVI
1.   See his *History of the Army,* Vol. I, 356.
2.   *History of His Own Time,* G. Burnet, Vol. III.
3.   *Marlborough, His Life and Times,* Sir Winston Churchill, Vol. I, p. 416.
4.   *The Marshal Duke of Berwick,* Sir Charles Petrie. *Mémoire du Marechale Duc le Berwick,* Berwick.
5.   H.M.C. Bath Mss. (1904), p. 226.
6.   *History of Hampton Court,* Ernest Law, Vol. III.
7.   *Times Magazine,* Saturday, May 6, 1995.

8.   *Memoirs of Great Britain and Ireland,* J. Dalrymple, Vol. III, p. 237.
9.   Diary of Narcissus Luttrell. April 1693. "On Thursday the Queen goes to view the new hospital at Greenwich for sick and wounded seamen and will go to Portsmouth to see the fleet."
10. *Diary,* John Evelyn, edited by William Bray, p. 326.
11. *William's Mary,* Elizabeth Hamilton.
12. *History of the Reign of William and Mary,* Vol. 3, p. 147.
13. See *Private and Original Correspondence of Charles Talbot Duke of Shrewsbury,* edited by Coxe, London 1821.
14. Harleian Mss. 6584. British Library. H.C. Foxcroft's Supplement to Burnet's *History of His Own Time.*

Chapter XVII

1.   See his *England in the Reign of James II and William III,* 1955.
2.   *Letters from Liselotte,* ed. Maria Kroll, p. 71.
3.   *Diary,* John Evelyn, Vol. III, p. 339.
4.   H.M.C. Bath (Prior Papers). *William and Mary,* van der Zee.
5.   *William of Orange,* Nesca Robb, Vol. II.
6.   *Letters from Liselotte,* ed. Maria Kroll, p. 70.
7.   *William and Mary,* van der Zee, p. 411.
8.   *The Lexington Papers.*
9.   *Robert Spencer Earl of Sunderland (1641-1702),* J.P. Kenyon (1958).
10. See *William and Mary,* Leslie John Miller (1974).
11. *William and Mary,* Nesca Robb, Vol. II, p. 384.
12. *A Brief Historical Relation of State Affairs,* Narcissus Luttrell.
13. He lived from 1672-1710. There is much interesting material in the National Library Edinburgh, Acc. 10383.
14. Leven and Melville Papers. Bannatyn Club. See also Mark Napier's *Memorials of Graham of Claverhouse Viscount Dundee* - a Jacobite. Macaulay could never find any reason to censure William III.
15. Historical Mss. Commission Duke of Buccleuch, Part II, p. 304.
16. Ibid.
17. *Marlborough the Man,* Bryan Bevan.
18. *Memoirs of the Duke of Gloucester,* ed. Loftie (1881).
19. *The Lexington Papers* or some account of the Courts of London and Vienna at the conclusion of the seventeenth century. Extracted from the Correspondence of Robert Sutton, Lord Lexington.
20. Dartmouth footnote to Burnet *History,* Vol. 4, p. 412.
21. *D.N.B.* Portland, ed. Stephen.

Chapter XVIII
1. *William and Mary*, van der Zee, pp. 417 and 418.
2. *Correspondentie*, N. Japikje, vol. I, p. 198.
3. Ibid., vol. I, p. 199.
4. See his Correspondence H.M.C. Marquis of Bath, Vol. III.
5. Harleian Mss. 6584. There is also a very rare printed copy in the London Library.
6. H.M.C. Bath (Prior Papers), Vol. III, p. 279.
7. *William of Orange*, Nesca Robb, Part II.
8. *Carlos the Bewitched*, The Last Spanish Habsburg (1962).
9. *Peter the Great : His Life and Work*, Robert Massie, 1981.
10. See Vol. III, p. 245.
11. *Peter the Great*, Robert Massie.

Chapter XIX
1. H.M.C. Bath (Prior Papers).
2. *Letters of William and Louis XIV*, Paul Grimblot (2 vols.).
3. *A Brief Historical Relation of State Affairs*, Luttrell, Vol. 4, p. 335. *William and Mary*, van der Zee.
4. *Letters of William and Louis XIV*, Paul Grimblot, Vol. 2 (1848).
5. Ibid.
6. See his *History of England*, Vol. V, p. 151 (1861 edition).
7. This speech is in the British Library.
8. *Letters of William III and Louis XIV*, Paul Grimblot, Vol. II.
9. *History of England*, Macaulay, Vol. IV, P. 180.
10. *Letters from Liselotte*. Madame thought the Duc d'Anjou had fine qualities, but he was not as intelligent as his younger brother the Duc de Berri.
11. William to Heinsius. November 16, 1700. *William of Orange*, Nesca Robb, Vol. II, p. 460.
12. *An English Garner* : Later Stuart tracts with an introduction by George A. Aitken, E. Arber.

Chapter XX
1. *Marlborough the Man*, Bryan Bevan.
2. *Louis XIV*, Vincent Cronin.
3. *La France de Louis XIV; The Jacobite Movement*, Charles Petrie.
4. *Sophie Electress of Hanover* (1903).
5. *An English Garner*, E. Arber.
6. *Biographical Adversaries* 1603-1708. British Library.
7. *William of Orange*, Nesca Robb, Vol. 2.
8. *Biographical Adversaries* 1603-1708. British Library 15724.

9. *William and Mary*, van der Zee. Verhael der Laaste Ziekte en de het overlijden van Willem de III.

10. *History of England during the reign of King William* (published 1744-6), Ralph, Vol. II.

11. *William and Mary*, van der Zee.

12. Add. Mss. 7074 fol. 192, British Library.

13. Ibid.

14. Ibid., fol. 195.

15. *Letters from Liselotte*, p. 207.

16. H.M.C. Rutland Mss. II, p. 166f.

17. *The Naval History of England in all its Branches from the Norman Conquest*, etc.

18. *D.N.B.* edited by Sidney Lee.

BIBLIOGRAPHY

Ailesbury, Thomas Bruce, 2nd Earl of, *Memoirs* (Roxburghe Club, 1890).

Arber, E., *An English Garner* : Later Stuart Tracts with an Introduction by George A. Aitken.

Ashley, Maurice, *The Stuarts in Love* (1963).

Avaux, Jean-Antoine de Mesmes, Comte d', *Negociations en Hollande depuis 1679 jusqu'en 1684* (6 vols., Paris 1752).

Baker, L.M., compiler *The Letters of Elizabeth Queen of Bohemia* (1953).

Bellingham, B., *Diary of Thomas Bellingham*. An officer under William III. Complete transcript and notes by Anthony Hewitson (1908).

Berwick, *Mémoires du Marechale Duc de Berwick*, écrits par lui-même (2 vols., Paris 1778).

Bevan, Bryan, *Marlborough the Man (1975)*.
         James Duke of Monmouth (1973).

Birch, Thomas, *Life of John Tillotson*, Dean of Canterbury and Archbishop (1753).

Bohemia. Letters of Elizabeth Queen of Bohemia, compiled by L.M. Baker, edited by C.V. Wedgewood (1953).

Burford, E.J. *Royal St. James's* (1988).

Burnet, Bishop Gilbert, *History of His Own Time*, 4 vols. (London 1838).

Burnet, *Supplement*. A Supplement to Burnet's *History of His Own Time*, ed. H.C. Foxcroft.

Calendar of State Papers Domestic. 1869 and following years.

Campbell, Margaret, *Henry Purcell*. Glory of His Age (1995).

Carswell, John, *The Descent on England* (1969).

Carte, Thomas, *The Life of James, Duke of Ormonde*. Life of Queen Mary Ii.

Chapman, Hester, *The Tragedy of Charles II* (1964).

Churchill, Sir Winston, *Marlborough, His Life and Times* (Vol. I, 1933).

Clarendon, Diary of, Henry Earl of, 1687-1691.

Courtenay, T.P., *Life of Sir William Temple*, complete in 4 vols. (1814).

Coward, Barry, *The Stuart Age*. England 1603-1714 (second edition).

Coxe, W. (ed.), *Private and Original Correspondence of Charles Talbot, Earl of Shrewsbury, with King William. The leaders of the Whig Party, etc.* (London 1821).

Cronin, Vincent, *Louis XIV* (1964).

Dalrymple, Sir John, *Memoirs of Great Britain and Ireland* (3 vols., 1771-88).

Dartmouth, H.M.C., V.

Davidson, Lilian Campbell, *Catherine of Braganza.*

Defoe, Daniel, *The True-Born Englishman. The Legion Memorial.*
　　　　A Tour through the Whole Island of Great Britain.

Dictionary of National Biography, edited by Sir Sidney Lee.

Discours sur la nourriture de Monseigneur son Altesse le Prince d'Orange, Sir
　　　　Constantine Huygens.

Ellis, Henry, *Original Letters Illustrative of English History,* Vol. IV.

Erlanger, Philippe, *Louis XIV* (translated from the French by Stephen Cox).

Evelyn, John, *Diary* (edited from original Mss. by William Bray). 4 vols.
　　　　Memoirs and Correspondence, Vols. 3 & 5.

Everett Green, M. A. *Lives of the Princesses of England.*
　　　　　　　　　　Life of Mary Henrietta Princess of Orange (edited by
　　　　　　　　　　William Bray).

Eyrmann, J., *The Navy in the War of William III* (1689-1697), published 1953.

Fleming, Robert, *Discourse on the death of King William* (London 1703).

Ford, Charles, *Blue Guide to Holland.*

Fortescue, Sir John, *History of the Army,* Vol. I.

Foxcroft, Helen C., *The Life and Letters of Sir George Savile, Bart., First Marquis
　　　　of Halifax (2 vols., London 1898).*

Gaxotte, Pierre, *La France de Louis XIV.*

Grew, Marion, *William Bentinck and William III* (London 1924).

Grimblot, Paul, *Letters of William III and Louis XIV* (2 vols., London 1848).

Hallam, Henry, *Constitutional History of England from accession of Henry VII to
　　　　death of George II.* 4 vols.

Hamilton, Elizabeth, *William's Mary* (London 1972).

Haswell, Jock, *James II* (1972).

Het Loo Palace and Gardens. A booket.

Hill, Christopher, *The Century of Revolution* 1663-1714.

Hopkins, M.R., *Anne of England* (1934).

Hopkirk, Mary, *Queen over the Water* (1954).

Kenyon, J.P., *Robert Spencer Earl of Sunderland* (1641-1702).

Japikse, N., *Correspondentie.*

Kroll, Maria, *Sophie Electress of Hanover.* A personal portrait (1973).

Lake, E., *Camden Miscellany,* vol. I. Diary of Dr. Edward Lake (Camden
　　　　Society, 1846).

Law, Ernest, *History of Hampton Court,* vol. III, p. 226 (1904).

Lediard, Thomas, *The Naval History of England in all its Branches from the
　　　　Norman Conquest, etc.*

Letters and Diplomatic Instructions of Queen Anne edited by Beatrice Curtis
　　　　Brown (1935).

Letters from Liselotte (Elizabeth Charlotte and Duchess of Orleans) 1652-1722,
    translated and edited by Maria Kroll (1970).

Lettres et Mémoires de Marie Reine d'Angleterre épouse de Guillaume III.

The Lexington Papers or some account of the Courts of London and Vienna,
    at the conclusion of the seventeenth century. Extracted from the
    official and private correspondence of Robert Sutton, Lord
    Lexington, British Minister at Vienna, 1694-1698.

Little, Bryan, *Christopher Wren.*

Luttrell, Narcissus, *A Brief Historical Relation of State Affairs* from Sept. 1678
    to April 1714, in six volumes (Oxford 1857).

Massie, Robert, *Peter the Great* (1980).

Nada, John, *Carlos the Bewitched* (1962).

Petrie, Sir Charles, *The Marshal Duke of Berwick* (London 1953).
                    The Jacobite Movement (1959).

Plowden, Alison, *The Stuart Princesses* (1996).

Pontalis, Le Fevre, *John de Witt,* Vol. I (1885).

Prebble, John, *Glencoe.* The Story of the Massacre (London 1968).

Ralph, James, *History of England during the reign of William III*, I, p. 369.

Reresby, Sir John, *Memoirs*

Robb, Nesca, *William of Orange*, Vols. I and II (1962 and 1966).

Sidney, Henry, *Diary of Time of Charles II*, vols. 1 and 2 (1843 edited with
    notes by R.W. Blencowe.

Swift, Jonathan, *Journal to Stella*, Vol. II.
                Works, London 1883.

Temple, Sir William, *Works : Observations upon the United Provinces*, 4 vols.
    (London 1814).

Thurloe, John, *State Papers*, Vol. I and Vol. II, edited by T. Birch (7 volumes,
    1742).

Trevelyan, George Macaulay, *England under the Stuarts.*

Trevelyan, M., *William III and the Defence of Holland* (1930).

Turner, F.C., *James II* (1948).

Van der Zee, Henri and Barbara, *William and Mary* (1973).

Vernon, James, *Letters illustrative of the reign of William III from 1696-1708.*

Mss. Research   Baker Mss. University Library, Cambridge.
                Birch Mss. 4466. British Library.
                Koninklijke Bibliotheek (National Library), The Hage
                    Mss.
                Portland Mss. Nottingham University Library.
                Public Record Office. King William's Chest S.P.
                    8/12/46.

The original documents concerning *The Massacre of Glencoe* (1702) can be seen in the Public Record Office, including the Report of the Commission of Inquiry (1695).

Bath Mss. H.M.C.I (1904).

Harleian Mss. 6584. British Library.

Bath H.M.C. (Prior Papers).

Duke of Buccleuch Mss. H.M.C. II.

Biographical Adversaries 1603-1708. British Library 15724.

Add. Mss. 7074. British Library.

Public Record Office. Scottish Parliamentary.

INDEX

Abjuration Bill, 180

Ailesbury, Earl of, Lord Thomas
Bruce, 78, 132

Albemarle, 1st Earl of, *see* Keppel,
Arnold Joost van

d'Albeville, Ignatius White, Marquis
of, 93-94, 100

Allonne, 169

Amalia, *see Solms*-Braunfeldt,
Princess Amalia von

Anglo-Dutch Wars, first, 7, second,
19

d'Anjou, Philippe, *see* Philip V of
Spain, 163, 172, as Philip V, 173

Annandale, William, Earl of, 135

Anne, Princess and Queen of
England, 40-41, 48-49, 51-53, 60,
81-82, 92, 95; prejudices her sister's mind against her stepmother,
96-97, 104, 106; deserts her father
James II, 111, 114, 116; dislike of
William, 117, 135-137, 143, 149,
156, 170-171; becomes Queen,
180

Apsley, Frances (later Lady Bathurst)
48-49, 56-57, 59

Argyll, Archibald Campbell, 9th
Earl, 84-85

Arlington, Earl of, Henry Bennett,
22, 27, 34-35, 38, 43-45, 49

d'Avaux, Jean Antoine de Mesmes,
Comte, 62, 73-75, 77, 80-81, 87,
98, 114

Baker, Colonel Henry, co-Governor
of Londonderry, 121

van Banchem, 37

Bank of England, its foundation,
152

Barclay, Sir George, 154

Barillon, Paul, French Ambassador,
51, 97

Bathurst, Sir Benjamin, 49

Beachy Head, Battle of, 125-126

Bellingham, Colonel, 124-125

Bentinck, Anne (née Villiers), 58, 66

Bentinck, Hans Willem, 1st Earl of
Portland, 18, 21; his friendship
with William, 26, 37, 45-46, 55,
58, 63; William's devotion, 66, 80,
84, 88, 98-99, 106, 109; created
Earl of Portland, 115, 124, 134,
146-147; rivalry with Keppel, 149-
150, 154, 156-158; jealousy of
Albemarle, 159-161; appointed
Ambassador in France, 162-163,
166, 169-170, 179-180, 182

Berkeley, Sir Charles, created Lord
Falmouth, 14, 19

Berwick, James Fitzjames, Duke of,
James II's illegitimate son, 105,
108, 113, 141, 154, 184

Beverninck, Conrad van, 32

Beverwaert, Emilia, van, 12, 69

Bidloo, Gorvaert, William's Dutch
doctor, 178-180

Bill of Rights, 118-119

Binnenhof, the birthplace of Prince
William, 5, 19, 63

Blair, Rev. James, New England
Clergyman, 143

Blake, Admiral, 7

Blenheim, Battle of, 183

Boers, William, 6

Boufflers, Marshal, 140, 150, 161

Boyne, Battle of the (1690), 123-124,
128

Brandenburg, Elector of, 6, 16,
William's uncle, 69

Brandon, Lord, 79
Breda, Peace of, 20
Browning, Michael Capt, 121
Buckhurst, Lord, 143-44
Buckingham, second Duke of,
  George Villiers, 25, 35, 115
Bulstrode, Sir Richard, 79
Burnet, Bishop Gilbert, historian,
  22-23, 65; his estimate of the
  Duke of York, 85-86; his love for
  Princess Mary, 89, 92, 94, 97,100,
  103-104, 113-114, 122-123, 129,
  132, 139-141, 144-145, 147, 180
Bushey Park, 130

Caermarthen, Marquis of, see
  Osborne, Sir Thomas and Earl of
  Danby
Cairnes, Counsellor, 120
Campbell of Glenlyon, Captain
  Robert, 134
Campsie, Henry, 120
Carstares, Rev. William, 45, 103,
  134, 180
Castanaga, Marquis de, 79, 131
Catherine of Braganza, Queen of
  Charles II, 17, 19, 24, 53-54, 64,
  68, 126
Chamberlain, Dr. Hugh, 97
Chapuzeau, Samuel, William's
  French tutor, 11, 15, 20,
Charles I, King of England, 2-4, 15,
  27
Charles II, Prince of Wales in exile
  and King of England, William's
  uncle, 4-5, 7-10, 12-14; restored
  to kingdom, 16, 19, 24-30, 35, 37-
  38, 40-45, 47, 49-54, 59-72, 74-
  80, 83; death of king, 88, 136
Charles II, King of Spain, 21;Carlos
  the Bewitched,163; death of,
  169,172
Charles Louis, Elector Palantine, 11,
  15-16
Charles XII of Sweden, 175
Charles, Archduke, 163
Charlotte Philiberta of Nassau-
  Beverwaert (Lotte), 43-44
Chudleigh, Thomas, 76, 80, 84

Churchill, John, later Earl and Duke
  of Marlborough, 46, 53, 84, 94,
  105, 115, 122, 128, 133, 135-36;
  disgraced, 137-138, 145, 154,
  158, 170, 173, 175-176
Churchill, Sarah, Countess of
  Marlborough, 106, 112, 117, 128,
  136-37
Clarendon, Edward Hyde, 1st Earl
  of, 13-16
Clarendon, Henry Hyde, 2nd Earl
  of, 91, 97, 104, 108-109, 113, 132
Coleman, Edward, 60
Compton, Bishop Henry, 53, 97,
  106, 114
Convention Parliament, 111
Cornbury, Lord, 104-5
Cosimo, heir to Duke of Tuscany,
  22
Covell, Dr., 88
Craven, Lord, 108
Crewe, Dr.., Bishop of Durham, 53
Croissy, Charles Colbert, Marquis
  de, 25-26
Cromwell, Oliver, Lord Protector, 7

Dalrymple, Sir John, Master of
  Stair, Secretary of State fo Scotland,
  134-35
Dalrymple, Sir John of Cranstoun
  (descendant of above), 142, 181
Danby, first Earl of, see Sir Thomas
  Osborne (his descendant)
Dartmouth, George Legge, Earl of,
  102-3, 106
Declaration of Indulgence (second),
  96
Defoe, Daniel, 142, 173-4, 177
Delamere, George Booth, 2nd
  Baron, 104, 108, created Earl of
  Warrington, 116
Den Briel, The, 102-103
Devonshire, William Cavendish,
  third Earl of, 98, 150; as Duke,
  155
Dijkvelt, Everard van Weede van,
  93-94, 102, 110
Discours sur la Nourriture de Monseigneur
  son altesse le Prince d'Orange, 10

Dohna, Count Frederick von, 4, 24
Dorset, Earl of, 106, 116, 143
Dover, Treaty of, 25-26
Downing, Sir George, 16
Drelincourt, Monsieur, one of
    William's doctors, 57
Dryden, John, poet and author, 71
Dundee, John Graham of
    Claverhouse, Viscount, 109, 117-
    118
Dutch Blue Guards, 123, 168-170

Elizabeth of Bohemia (Winter
    Queen), 2, 4, 7, 10-11, 13, 15-17
Ellis, William, 27
d'Estrades, Godefroi, Comte, 18, 21
Essex, Arthur Capel, Earl of, 70, 77,
    84
Evelyn, John, Diarist, 11, 24, 31-32,
    68-69, 110, 112, 144, 148, 165
Evertzen, Admiral, 99, 127
Exclusion Bills, first (1679), 69-71

Fagel, Caspar, Grand Pensionary,
    38, 42-43; death, 106
Fenwick, Sir John, 154-156
Ferguson, Robert, 77, 84
Feversham, Louis de Duras, Earl of,
    85, 105, 107, 126
Fortescue, Sir John, 140
Frederick Henry, Prince of Orange,
    William's grandfather, 1-3, 7, 45,
    56

Gaxotte, Pierre, French historian,
    176
George of Denmark, Prince, 81-82,
    105, 117, 137, 170
George Louis, Prince of Hanover,
    George I of England, 69, 76, 82,
    177
Geraerts. Balthasar, 1
Ghent, van, Baron, 19-20, 33
Ginckel, Godart, van, Earl of
    Athlone, 128, 170
Glencoe, Massacre of, 37, 134-135
Gloucester, Harry, duke of, 13-15,
    24

Gloucester, William Henry, duke of,
    117, 143, 156, 170-71
Godfrey, Sir Edmondbury, 60, 84
Godolphin, Sidney, first Earl of, 135
Gourville, de, 20, 37
Governor of Massachusetts, Boston,
    143
Grafton, Duke of, 105, 128
Grand Alliance, Treaty of, 175
Grandval, Monsieur, 138
Greenwich Hospital, 143, 181
Gwyn, Nell, 65, 145

Halifax, Sir George Savile, first
    Marquis of, 27, 34-35, 53, 65-66,
    70-71, 78, 106, 108, 115-116, 152
Hampton Court Palace, 24, 114,
    128, 130, 142, 167, 177-80, 182
Hamilton, Lord George, 148
Hanover, Ernest Augustus, Duke of,
    69
Hanover, Sophie, Electress of, 11-
    12, 21, 69, 82, 124, 150, 162,
    172, 176-177
Heinsius, Anthony, Pensionary of
    Delft and Holland, 76-77, 117,
    172, 175
Henrietta Maria, Queen Charles I,
    2-4, 14
Henriette Catherine of Orange,
    Princess, 12
Henriette, Duchesse de Orléans, 9,
    25
Herbert, Admiral, Arthur, Earl of
    Torrington, 98-99, 116, 125-29
Het Loo, William's Palace near
    Apeldoorn, 55, 86, 94, 151, 159,
    169, 171, 176-177
Hill, Colonel Sir John, 134
Hondecoeter, artist, 183
Honselaersdijk Palace, 54-6, 62, 102
Hooper, Dr. Richard, Princess
    Mary's chaplain, 58, 68
Huis ten Bosch, 10, 45, 55
Hunter, John of Maghera, 122
Huygens, Sir Constantine, 10, 26-
    27, 55

Huygens, Constantine, Jr., 41, 46, 56, 69, 106, 116
Hyde, Anne, first Duchess of York, 13-15, 24, 40, 48, 65
Hyde, Lawrence, *see* Earl of Rochester

Jacobites, The, 113, 118-120, 124-125, 127, 131, 135, 138, 152,155, 161, 177, 181
James I, King of England, 3, 87
James, Duke of York, King of England, 5, 13-15, 19, 26, 28, 31, 40-41; his second marriage, 43, 47-52, 54, 60, 64-72, 74-75, 77-79; becomes King, 83-85, 87-89, 91; character, 92-102, 104-108; King flees to France, 109-110, 113, 118-120, 122-125, 132, 135-136, 138-139, 141, 148, 157, 160-161, 176; dies at St. Germain, 181
James Francis Edward, Prince of Wales, birth in St. James's Palace, 97, 99, 106, 153, 157, 163, 176-177, 180
Jermyn, Harry, 12,
Jenkin, Lewis, 156
Jenkins, Sir Leoline, 72-73
Jennings, Sarah, see Countess of Marlborough
John Maurice of Nassau-Siegen, 2, 32-33
Jones, Inigo, 143
Journal to Stella, Swift's book, 148

Ken, Dr. Thomas, Princess Mary's chaplain, 68, 74, 96, 113
Kensington House, 116, 128, 137, 149, 164, 179, 182
Keppel, Arnold Joost van, first Earl of Albemarle, 87, 107, 146-147, 156-160, 166, 169-170, 179-181
Kerouaille, Louise de, Duchess of Portsmouth, 124
Killiecrankie, Battle of (1689), 118, 134
Kirke, Percy, Major-General, 121
Kneller, Sir Godfrey, 87

La Hogue, battle of, 138-139
Lake, Dr., Bishop of Chichester, 97-98
Landen, Battle of, 140-141
Langford, Mrs., 40, 58, 74, 88
Lawrence, Dr. William's doctor, 178
Lely, Sir Peter, 87
Leopold, the Emperor, 39, 174-175
Lexington, Lord, 157, 162
Liebergen, Dr., William III's German doctor, 44, 178
'Liselotte', see d'Orléans, Charlotte Elizabeth, 11-12, 21
Littleton, Sir Charles, 157
Lloyd, Bishop of St. Asaph, 97-98
London, George, royal gardener, 142
Louis XIV, King of France, 2, 18, 20-22, 26, 29-31; invades Holland, 33, 35, 41-42, 50-51, 56; mentioned as 'Sun King', 58, 60-61, 73, 75-76, 85, 91, 99-100, 109-110, 129, 131-132, 138-141, 151-152, 160-163, 166-167, 172-174, 176-177, 181
Louise Mary, Princess, 162, 176
Lumley, Richard, Earl of Scarborough, 98
Luttrell's, Narcissus, 129, 143, 152-153, 156
Luxembourg, Marshal, Francois-Henri de Montmorency-Bouteville, 31, 140, 150

Mackay, General Hugh, 118, 139, 158
Macaulay, Thomas Babington, 121, 168
Macclesfield, Lord, 177
Maintenon, Madame de, 151, 162
Malplaquet, Battle of, 141, 179
Mancini, Olympe, Comtesse de Soissons, 132
Manchester, Charles Montagu, first first Duke of, 177
Maria Beatrice d'Este of Modena, 41; marries Duke of York, 51-53, 59-60, 63,89, 95-97, 106-107,

110; Queen in exile, 112, 132, 144, 160-62, 176, 181
Maria Theresa, Queen of France, 18, 21, 39, 163
Maria de Medici, widowed Queen of Henri IV, 3
Marot, Daniel, 86
Mary, Princess of Orange, the Princess Royal, 3-6, 9, 12-15, 23-24, 55
Mary II, Princess of Orange, Queen of England (1689),47-60, 62-63, 66, 68-69, 72-74, 79-81, 83-90, 92-97, 101-102, 106, 111-112; Mary and her husband proclaimed joint King and Queen of England, 113-114, 116-117, 121-122; appointed Regent, 123, 125; her letters to William, 126-130, 132-133, 135-138, 141-146; death, 148, 151,154, 158, 183
Maurice, Prince of Orange, 1
Mauritshuis, Palace, The Hague, 13, 175
Mazarin, Jules, Cardinal, 18-20
Middleton, Lord, 155
Millington, Dr., William's doctor, 178
Minette, see Henriette, Duchesse de Orléans
Monmouth, Anne Scott, Duchess of 60
Monmouth, James Scott, Duke of, 64, 67, 70-73, 78-81, 83-86
Montagu, Ralph, 60-61
Montague, Charles, Earl of Halifax, Founder of the Bank of England, (1694), 152, 173-174
Moulin, Peter du, 42-43

Nantes, Edict of, 91
Nassau-Zuylestein, William Frederick, 10
Nicholas, Sir Edward, Secretary of State, 7
Nijmegen, peace treaty of, 61, 75-76, 99
Nottingham, Daniel Finch, second Earl of, 106-107, 114; Secretary of State, 115-116, 122, 126-127, 136, 141

Oates, Titus, 59-60, 72, 119
Odijk, William Adrian of Nassau, 44,54-55
Orange, a small principality in south of France, 1, 18, 76
Orford, Earl of, see Edward Russell
d'Orivel, Sieur, William of Orange's riding instructor, 21
Orkney, Earl of, Lord George Hamilton, 148
Orleans Charlotte Elizabeth, second Duchess of, 11-12, 21, 52, 124, 150-151, 158, 162, 171-172, 176, 180-181
Orleans, Philippe, Duke of, 'Monsieur', 46, 162
Ormonde, Duke of, 24, 105
Osborne, Sir Thomas, first Earl of Danby, Marquis of Carmarthen, 27, 49, 54, 60-61, 94-95, 115, 121, 136, 164
Ossory, Thomas Butler, Earl of, 24, William's fondness for, 26, 30-31, 43-44, 58, 68-69, death of, William's sorrow, 125
Oudenaarde, Battle of, 179
Ouwerkerk, Henry of Nassau, 44, 55, 58, 69

Paterson, William, 152
Payne, Neville, 119, 153-154
Penn, William, the Quaker, 92-93
Pepys, Samuel, 13; quoted, 48, 102, 129
Peter, Czar of Russia, the Great, 163-165
Peter, Father, 105
Peterborough, Henry Mordaunt, 41
Philip IV, King of Spain, 4, 18
Philippe, Duke of Orleans, 12
Plunkett, Dr., 142
Portocarrero, Cardinal-Archbishop of Toledo, 172
Poussin, Monsieur, French representative London, 176-177

Powell, Justice, 98
Prior, Matthew, poet and diplomat, 149, 161-162, 166
Purcell, Henry, 132; his elegy, 149

Queen's House, The, Greenwich, 143

Radcliffe, Dr. John, 146, 178
Ragineau, Abraham, 8
Ramillies, Battle of, 179
Reresby, Sir John, quoted, 65, 79
Rights, Bill of, 118
Rijswijk, Treaty of, 150, 160
Rochester, Earl of, John Wilmot, 53
Rochester, Earl of, Laurence Hyde, created Earl after 1680, 46, 56, 59, 71, 83
Roman, Jacob, 86
Royal Charles, The 13, 19
Rumbold, Colonel, 77
Russell, Edward, Admiral, Earl of Orford, 122, 126, 129, 137-139, 145, 154, 173-174
Russell, Lord William, 70, 75, 77
Rutland, Countess of, 181
Ruyter, Admiral Michiel de, 31, 36, 39-40, 46
Rye House plot, 75-76, 78

Saint-Denis, battle of, 58
Saint-Evrémonde, Seigneur de, 20, 22
Saint-Simon, 150
Sancroft, William, Archbishop of Canterbury, 62-63, 96-97, 110, 112, 144
Sarsfield, Patrick, 124, 128
Sarotti, Venetian ambassador, 119
Savile, Henry, 53
Schomberg, Armand, Marshal, 102, 105, 123-124
Sedgemoor, Battle of, 85
Settlement, Act of, 172, 176
Shaftesbury, Anthony Ashley Cooper, first Earl of, 60-62, 64-65, 70, 77

Shrewsbury, Charles Talbot, 12th Earl of, later duke of, 98, 114-115, 121-122, 141-143, 145, 154-155 157
Sidney, Algernon, 76-77
Sidney, Henry, Earl of Romney, 57, 65-66, 68, 76, 87-88, 98, 115, 132
Siege of Londonderry, 120-121
Skelton, Sir Bevil, 84, 88, 93
Solmes, Count, 103, 139-140
Somers, Lord, 149, 173-174
Somerset, Duchess of, 136, 149
Somerset, Duke of, 137
Solms-Braunfeldt, Princess Amalia von, 2; marries Frederick Henry, 3-6; entertains her grandson William, 10-12, 16; relations with grandson, 20, 35; death of, 45
Sophie, *see* Electress of Hanover
Stafford, Earl of, 72
Steenkerk, Battle of, 139
Strafford, Earl of, 4
Sunderland, Robert Spencer, second Earl of, 65, 68, 70-72, 92, 94, 98, 152
Sunderland, Lady, 70, 95
Swift, Jonathan, 87, 142, 148
Sylvius, Sir Gabriel, 38, 45

Tallard, Camile d'Hostum, comte, French diplomat, 166-169
Talman, William, 130
Talmash, General, 141
Temple, John, 113
Temple, Sir William, English diplomat, 22, 38, 44-47, 50, 59, 61, 113, 179
Tenison, Archbishop Thomas, 145-146, 148, 180
Test Act, the (1672), 91-92
Thurloe Papers, The, 12
Tichelaar, Willem (William), 36-37
Tienen, van, 11
Tijou, Jean, 130
Tillotson, John, Dr. 54, 144; Archbishop of Canterbury dies, (1694), 145

Torcy, de, Foreign Minister of
France, 176
Torrington, Earl of, *see* Admiral
Herbert
Tourville, Admiral, 126, 138
Trigland, Reverend Cornelius,
William's tutor, 8, 11, 20, 36
Triple Alliance, 22, 29-30
Tromp, van, Admiral, 7
Turenne, Vicomte de, 31
Turner, Bishop of Ely, 97-98
Tweedale, John Hay, Marquis of,
135
Tyrconnel, Richard Talbot, Earl of,
91, 113, 120

Utrecht, Treaty of, 179

Valen, van, Lieutenant, 37
Vauban, Sebastien de, 39
Vaudemont, Charles Henri, Prince
de, 160
Vernon, James, 154-155, 166, 179
Villiers, Anne, 44, 58
Villiers, Elizabeth, William's mis-
tress, 56, 58, 86-88, 90,143,147;
marries Lord George Hamilton,
created Earl of Orkney, 148, 170
Villiers, Lady Frances, 40, 53

Waldeck, Count von, 46, 76, 128
Walker, Reverend George, 121, 124
Walters, Lucy, 12
Wentworth, Lady Henrietta, 78-79,
81, 84
Wentworth, Lady Isabella, 97
Werffm Pieter van der, 11
Westminster Abbey, 15, 114, 148,
171, 183
Westminster Hall, 3, 72
Westphalia, Treaty of, 5, 15
White, Bishop of Peterborough, 96-
97
William II, William's father, 2-6
William, Prince of Orange and
King William III of England: his
birth, 3; forebears, 5-20; 'a child
of State', 21-23; character, 24;
visits uncle Charles in England,
25-26; visits Cambridge, 26; visits
Oxford, 27; first experience of
war, 32; declared Stadtholder, 35-
37; his behaviour on murder of de
Witt brothers, 38; marries
Princess Mary, 53-54; advises
Duke of Monmouth, 84-87; relations with Elizabeth Villiers, 88-
90; William's expedition sails,
101-102; lands in Torbay, 103;
William and Mary reign jointly,
112-114; his interest in Ireland,
120-122; battle of the Boyne, 123;
plots against him, 133-134;
William and the massacre of
Glencoe, 135; William's grief at
Mary's death, 147-150; plot to
assassinate king, 155; jealousy of
favourites, Portland and
Albemarle, 159-160; was William
homosexual, 160-163; William's
encounter with Czar Peter, 164-
165; his accident on horseback,
179; death, 180; further analysis
of his character, 182-183
William the Silent, William's ances-
tor, 3, 11
William, Prince of Anhalt, 12
William and Mary College,
America, 143
Wise, Henry, royal gardener, 142
Witsen, Nicholas, 110, 114, 164
Witt, Cornelius de, 33, 36, 37
Witt, Johan de, Grand Pensionary,
5-6. 14, 19-20, 22, 29-30, 33-34,
36-37-38, 135
Woodstock, Lord, 143
Wren, Sir Christopher, 116-117,
130, 164-165, 167
Wright, Chief Justice, 98

Zell, Duke of, 74
Zuylestein, Frederick van Nassau,
10, 16
Zuylestein, his son, 74, 97